TRACES OF THE HOLOCAUST

Traces of the Holocaust

Journeying in and out of the Ghettos

Tim Cole

continuum

Published by the Continuum International Publishing Group

The Tower Building	80 Maiden Lane
11 York Road	Suite 704
London	New York
SE1 7NX	NY 1003

www.continuumbooks.com

First published 2011

British Library Cataloguing-in-Publication Data
A catalogue record for this book is available from the British Library.

ISBN: HB: 978-1-4411-7559-5
PB: 978-1-4411-6996-9

Typeset by Fakenham Photosetting Ltd, Fakenham, Norfolk
Printed and bound in India

For Alisha and Lauren

Contents

Acknowledgements

I've been working on this book for a while, and so the list of people to thank feels dauntingly long. Intellectually, I owe a considerable debt to those whose written work has inspired me. In particular, Randy Braham's many volumes have been a constant presence by my desk as I've researched and written, but reading through the notes you will see the very tip of the iceberg of other careful scholarship that I owe so much to. As well as that more distanced relationship that we have as academics reading and responding to each others' work through writing, I am also thankful for the insightful comments of academics who I've discussed parts of the book with, or who have asked probing questions when I have presented some of the ideas here in conference or research seminar papers in a wide variety of places. Similarly probing, and useful, were the comments of anonymous reviewers of an early draft of several chapters and a number of journal articles based on parts of this book (I reference these earlier developments of some of the ideas here in the notes). Of particular importance have been colleagues in Bristol who have read versions of various chapters, provided encouragement to keep on writing, and in the case of Jamie Carstairs offered his photographic expertise. I am fortunate to be surrounded by a supportive and stimulating group of historians in my home department.

During the research for this project, I am thankful for the help of a large number of archivists and librarians, but particular mention should go to Ferenc Katona at the United States Holocaust Memorial Museum archives who has helped time and time again with both insight and humour, and to Judy Cohen at the United States Holocaust Memorial Museum photo archives. I am very grateful to both Judit Brody and Kitty Balint-Kurti for their generosity in sharing both documents and their memories with me. Archival research and extended writing has been made possible through the generosity of a number of institutions. I first started collecting materials while the Pearl Resnick Postdoctoral Fellow in the Center for Advanced Holocaust Studies at the United States Holocaust Memorial Museum, working on my previous book. Further research and writing was made possible by a Research Fellowship granted by the Leverhulme Trust. The final stage of research and writing was undertaken under the auspices of a University Research Fellowship funded by the University of Bristol. I am grateful to all three institutions for their support.

During research trips to Hungary, Ádám and Dóra Szabados and family, and Laci and Hajnalka Sümegi and family have provided generous hospitality. In

Washington, DC, I enjoyed the hospitality of Brad and Abi Byrd, and John and Kat Casson. At home, my wife Julie has put up with numerous absences as I have researched, presented on and written this book. Finally I am very grateful to Robin Baird Smith at Continuum for believing in this book, and me. I have been pleased to work on a book with Robin that is on a topic that has a personal resonance for him.

Writing this book I have been interrupted by a number of wonderful distractions. Academically, I have been involved in two stimulating collaborative research projects. At Bristol, I have been part of an Arts & Humanities Research Council-funded Landscape and Environment research project into 'Militarized Landscapes in Britain, France and the United States'. That has taken me from thinking about Hungary in 1944, to writing about the hills of upland Wales in the second half of the twentieth century. My colleagues on that project – Peter Coates, Chris Pearson and Marianne Dudley – have been great company over the last few years as we have explored together military landscapes across the south-west of Britain. Beyond Bristol, I have been very fortunate to find another inspiring group of research collaborators brought together through a shared interest in Holocaust Geographies. From initially working together in a two-week Summer Research Workshop hosted by the Center for Advanced Holocaust Studies at the United States Holocaust Memorial Museum in Washington, DC, we have continued research collaboration under the auspices of an NSF research grant. My colleagues on the Holocaust Geographies project – Alberto Giordano, Anne Kelly Knowles, Waitman Beorn, Anna Holian, Simone Gigliotti, Paul Jaskot, Marc Masurovsky and Erik Steiner – have provided a fruitful arena for collaborative intellectual discovery. I am very grateful to them all. Thinking about other things – militarized landscapes and historical GIS and the Holocaust – has, no doubt, helped me to think differently about this book.

But these academic distractions pale into insignificance besides the best distractions of these last few years: the birth of two daughters. Our first daughter – Alisha – was born literally just a few hours after I completed the index of my previous book. A couple of years ago she was joined by her little sister, Lauren. This book is dedicated to both of them. I promised Alisha that I would dedicate my next book to her and as every parent knows, it is very important to keep your promises to your kids! Writing this book I have often thought of parents living in Hungary in the first half of the 1940s whose ability to meet their promises to their children was so terribly restricted and curtailed. Having children myself has made me think about the history that I research and write about in a rather different way. Something of the focus of this book no doubt owes much to the presence of Alisha and Lauren in my day-to-day life over the last few years of thinking about how to write social histories of the Holocaust in Hungary.

Tim Cole
Bristol, September 2010

Prologue

PROLOGUE: TRACES OF THE HOLOCAUST

There is a scene in Claude Lanzmann's acclaimed documentary film *Shoah* that shows the late Raul Hilberg sitting in his study in a wintry Vermont holding a piece of paper in his hand. As he explains to Lanzmann, this 'is the *Fahrplananordnung 587* (timetable order 587), which is typical for special trains', detailing a transport to the death camp at Treblinka in September 1942. Hilberg translates the document for Lanzmann who is obviously captivated by it:

> Lanzmann: But why is this document so fascinating, as a matter of fact? Because I was at Treblinka, and to have the two things together ...
> Hilberg: Well, you see, when I hold a document in my hand, particularly if it's an original document, then I hold something which is actually something that the original bureaucrat held in his hand. It's an artefact. It's a leftover. It's the only leftover there is. The dead are not around.[1]

For both of them this document links the present and the past, the living and the dead.[2] *Fahrplananordnung 587* forms a bridge between two very different worlds: for Hilberg the worlds of Vermont and Berlin, for Lanzmann the worlds of Vermont and Treblinka.

But watching Lanzmann you have a sense that these worlds are both metaphorically and literally thousands of miles apart. He struggles to connect *Fahrplananordnung 587* and what it outlines and enacts. There is something terrifyingly banal about a single sheet of paper being part of the process of transporting people to their deaths. *Fahrplananordnung 587* does not simply record that 10,000 'Jews'[3] were taken to Treblinka in September 1942, but initiated this action. In the very act of choosing the words, constructing the paragraphs and typing this document out, the bureaucrat who so fascinated Hilberg enacted a critical element – deportation – of the event that we know as the Holocaust. It is an example of the destructive potential of paperwork within state bureaucracies. The typewriter was the weapon of the desk killer.[4] Lists were drawn up, memoranda and orders issued, receipts and transport chits completed. If the Holocaust was enacted by 'ordinary men',[5] it was also, in part at least, enacted through ordinary paperwork: thousands upon thousands of sheets of paper carefully typed out like *Fahrplananordnung 587*.[6] This paperwork that Hilberg dissects and Lanzmann stabs at with his finger, is one trace among so many of the implementation of a policy of mass murder enacted against European Jews and other victims under the cover of the Second World War. Some of this paperwork was destroyed. But much survives, found now in archives across Europe, or on microfilm reels in Yad Vashem in west Jerusalem or the archives of the United States Holocaust Memorial Museum in Washington, DC.

My use of the term 'trace' to describe *Fahrplananordnung 587* – and the millions of other surviving texts that were generated during the early 1940s – draws on the work of Peter Burke, who self-consciously chooses to use 'traces' rather than the more commonly used word 'sources' to talk about the stuff that we historians draw upon as we narrate the past. He does this to, 'draw attention to the fact that history is not a deductive science, but an activity and a craft'.[7] His thinking owes much to Gustaf Reiner who, more than half a century ago, reminded us that, 'the historian cannot have a direct knowledge of past events. But he [sic] may assume that they have had some effect, that they have left "relics" behind them, as Collingwood says, or "traces".'[8] The task of the historian, Burke suggests, is to work with the wide variety of relics and traces (or to use Hilberg's language to Lanzmann, 'artifacts' or 'leftovers') of the past – 'manuscripts, printed books, buildings, furniture, the landscape ... paintings, statues, engravings, photographs'[9] – because 'to be acquainted with a trace brings us nearer to the event by which it was left'.[10] After all, as Burke notes, 'surely, a trace is nothing but the still perceptible termination or culmination of a sequence of events or of several sequences of events'.[11]

For Burke, there are two possible ways to work with the traces of the past. One – and the more normal mode of operation of the historian – is to start from the historical event and then look for the traces that remain of this event in the present. The other is to work from the surviving traces back to the events that generated them.[12] In many ways, *Traces of the Holocaust* has emerged through a process of bouncing between these two approaches. In part it is a study of some of the events, places and people that made up the Holocaust. The focus is on the country of Hungary, a nation unusual for the lateness and speed of implementation of ghettoization and deportation. Although this ally of Nazi Germany had implemented anti-Jewish legislation in the late 1930s and early 1940s, there had been a consistent refusal of German demands for deportations.[13] In the early 1940s Hungary was something of an island of safety for Jews amidst a sea of destruction. All of this changed in the aftermath of the German occupation of Hungary in March 1944. A pro-Nazi Hungarian government was instituted and during the spring and early summer of 1944 a series of anti-Jewish measures were rapidly introduced. Jews were marked with a yellow star, placed into ghettos in the larger towns and cities, and ultimately – the Jews in the capital aside – deported out of the country with the vast majority being taken by train to Auschwitz-Birkenau. What is striking about the unrolling of these Holocaust elements – marking with a yellow star, ghettoization, deportation – in Hungary is not only how late on in the war they came, but also how rapidly they took place. There were only fifty-six days between the occupation and the first mass deportations taking place, and then another fifty-six days between this and the last deportation trains leaving Hungary. In the early summer of 1944, a total of more than 430,000 Hungarian Jews were deported in eight weeks, the vast majority to Auschwitz-Birkenau.[14]

But my aim here is not to offer a comprehensive history of the Holocaust in Hungary. That has been done in two important books – Randolph Braham's pioneering work that drew in the main on national level Hungarian state archives, and Christian Gerlach and Götz Aly's more recent study that draws primarily on German documents.[15] These works differ in important ways in their understanding of why the Holocaust was implemented in Hungary. In what approaches the playing out of the so-called intentionalist v. functionalist debate that dominated Holocaust studies in the 1970s and 1980s in miniature, these authors differ over whether a Nazi master plan for deportations was implemented in Hungary, or greater importance should be assigned to the local dynamic in the radicalization of measures. Rather than focusing on the big question of causation – as Braham and Gerlach and Aly do – this book has a narrower focus on social histories of ghettoization and deportation.

I have long been struck by Elie Wiesel's description of his own experience of the Holocaust in wartime Hungary as one of increasing concentration in less and less physical space. 'The universe began shrinking,' wrote Wiesel, '[F]irst we were supposed to leave our towns and concentrate in the larger cities. Then the towns shrank to the ghetto, and the ghetto to a house, the house to a room, the room to a cattle car ...'[16] His words point to the Holocaust being experienced as a profoundly spatial event.[17] But alongside this story of increasing physical concentration (segregation and control), is a spatio-temporal story of the Holocaust experienced as movement (to and from ghettos and camps) and stasis (in ghettos and cattle cars) that Wiesel hints at. After the relative quiet of the first years of the war, 1944 was, for most Hungarian Jews, a year characterized by a series of dislocating Holocaust journeys. Those living in small villages were transported to urban ghettos in nearby towns and cities. Those Jews who already lived in towns and cities where ghettos were placed in some cases stayed put, or moved to the ghetto set up a few streets away or over on the other side of town. Here Jews lived in ghettos for just a matter of weeks, prior to being taken to the railway station and on to the closest entrainment point. From there, most were taken on the several-day journey to Auschwitz-Birkenau, which was either terminus or staging post on another series of journeys into a dispersed network of concentration camps.

In the first part of this book, I adopt a place-based approach and follow a number of journeys into and out of a handful of Hungarian ghettos: Veszprém, Nyíregyháza, Szeged, the ghettos in Tolna county, and Körmend. In Chapter 1, I examine who ended up in the ghetto in Veszprém, who didn't, and who was removed from the ghetto, honing in on the marked gendering of the Hungarian Holocaust. In Chapter 2, I turn to rural carters who transported Jews into and out of ghettos around Nyíregyháza, raising questions over the motivations behind the mass participation of men and women in facilitating Holocaust journeys. In Chapter 3, I am interested in debates in Szeged over where to put urban ghettos and the ways in which 'ordinary' Hungarians took an active role in those discussions. In Chapter 4, I explore the ways in which sensitivities over the concerns of non-Jews shaped the ghettos planned and implemented in Tolna county and the implications of this for ordinary Jewish families. In Chapter 5, I look at the daily journeys in and out of the ghetto in Körmend as some limited semblance of 'normal' life continued in spite of segregation.

In Part II of this book I am interested in how journeys into and out of ghettos were narrated by those we tend to dub perpetrators, victims and bystanders.[18] In Chapter 6, I examine non-Jews who watched (and photographed) the (final) journeys of Jews from ghettos to railway stations. In Chapters 7 and 8, I examine two contrasting narratives of the processes of ghettoization and deportation found in the reports penned by one of the perpetrators of the Holocaust in Hungary, and in a diary, memoir and letters written by three members of one Jewish family. In the epilogue, the strands that run through the book – place and space, movement and stasis, people and their stories, similarities and differences – come together in brief reflections on what are perhaps best described as 'counter journeys', seen in comings and goings between the countryside and the capital in 1944.

Focusing on the journeys that Hungarian Jews made into and out of ghettos, and the ways in which those journeys were narrated, allows me to explore who took, initiated, aided and watched Holocaust journeys. Ultimately this is a social history of the complex ways in which Hungarians – both Jews and non-Jews, state officials at a variety of scales and ordinary men and women – interacted as Jews were concentrated and deported within a hectic few weeks and months. Throughout a number of overlapping themes emerge. First, far from being hidden away, ghettoization and deportation were highly visible processes. Not only did ordinary Hungarians witness these events, but also they participated in a variety of ways. Second, far from being gender-neutral, the Holocaust as it was enacted in Hungary was a gendered event, with Jewish men and Jewish women in their twenties, thirties and forties experiencing markedly different processes and places. Third, one striking element of the implementation of ghettoization and deportation in Hungary is the centrality of asset-stripping or, to use a less euphemistic phrase, 'robbing the Jews'.[19] Key to the events of 1944 was an economic attack on Jews by the different organs of the Hungarian state, and populace. Fourth, while a number of overarching stories (visibility, gendering and economics) can be identified, there are also multiple stories. Things looked different from place to place, and person to person. This is a theme that I return to in the epilogue, but throughout, I highlight difference as well as commonality, and indeed have sought to write difference self-consciously into this book by adopting an intentionally fragmentary narrative strategy. It is here that I have worked with the second – and more novel – approach suggested by Burke, which is moving from the surviving traces of the past back to events.

While Wiesel's words provided me with the story that I wanted to tell, the question of how to narrate spatio-temporal journeys within and out of Hungary was more difficult. A chronological approach that works well for a single city or region does not lend itself to the nation as a whole.[20] Although ghettoization and deportation were implemented extremely rapidly in Hungary, the fact that this was done on a zonal basis meant that deportations were already taking place from some ghettos in the east of the country, before Jews further west had even been placed into ghettos. This zonal implementation suggests a regional structure, which was adopted in Braham's nation-wide study of the Holocaust in Hungary, as well as a recent massive place-based encyclopaedia edited by Braham.[21] However, while this approach lends itself well to providing basic coverage of each town and city where ghettos were set up within comprehensive reference works, it would be rather repetitive in a book that is more conceptual and thematic in approach. Rather than adopting a chronological or regional approach, I have worked with a broadly thematic structure that is intentionally fragmentary and partial, rather than making claims for representative comprehensiveness. If it was Wiesel who gave me my central focus on spatial-temporal processes, it was the small town of Körmend in western Hungary that suggested my narrative approach.

Working through reel after reel of microfilmed documents in the archives of the United States Holocaust Memorial Museum, one set of documents jumped out at me.[22] They were a series of passes permitting Jews to leave the ghetto, and a smaller number of non-Jews to enter the ghetto set up in Körmend.[23] Reading through the rest of the microfilm reels I very much hoped that I might find ghetto passes from other Hungarian ghettos, but I didn't. From the secondary literature, my own knowledge of the archives in Hungary and conversations with historians with a knowledge of individual county archives, it seems that nothing like this full set of ghetto passes from Körmend survives from anywhere else in Hungary. It is clear that this was not the only Hungarian ghetto that Jews were permitted to leave, for example to undertake shopping or work.[24] But it does appear to be the only Hungarian ghetto where a seemingly complete trace of those journeys out of (and into) the ghetto survives.

This got me thinking. Those daily journeys into and out of Hungarian ghettos were one story that I obviously wanted to tell. However, my fear was that if I cited these passes within a chapter examining, say, daily life in Hungarian ghettos, I would end up erasing the place-specific uniqueness of this particular trace. In the end, I decided to work with their uniqueness in a more intentional and explicit way. The more I thought about it, the more I felt that the strategy I was considering adopting with this particular archival trace might work as a way of structuring the entire book. After all, the unevenness of the survival of particular traces of the Holocaust in Hungary is not limited solely to ghetto passes being found in such a complete form only from Körmend. Ghetto maps only appear to have survived from a few of the close to 150 towns and cities where they were set up. Photographs of Jews being deported from these ghettos likewise come from only a small number of places. Only a handful of wartime diaries written by Hungarian Jews survive. In the end I decided to work with this unevenness in the survival of particular traces of the Holocaust past in an explicit way.

The end result is a book that tells a series of stories about journeys into and out of Hungarian ghettos, each framed around different and particularly (and in some cases, uniquely) rich material traces of this past: name lists (Chapter 1), orders and receipts (Chapter 2), newspapers (Chapter 3), maps (Chapter 4), passes (Chapter 5), photographs (Chapter 6), reports (Chapter 7), diaries, memoirs and letters (Chapter 8). My decision to work with distinct traces in each chapter means that the book is perhaps best seen as a series of sightings drawn from particular texts. I do not attempt to tell a – let alone *the* – national story of the implementation of a series of anti-Jewish measures in Hungary in 1944 culminating in the mass deportation of the majority of the Jewish population of the country to Auschwitz-Birkenau.[25] Instead, I tell a series of what Hayden Lorimer dubs 'small stories',[26] each of which reflects the possibilities and limitations of a particular material trace of this past. Rather than homogenizing different material traces as sources to be drawn on in narrating a single story, I tell stories along the way that emerge from distinct traces (demanding a different reading). These small stories are worth exploring because, as John Roth, points out, '[S]ound Holocaust teaching and research must concentrate on the particularity of the Holocaust, for the evil – and the good – exists in the details.'[27] This is a book about details given that the devil is in the detail.

But my decision to adopt a fragmentary narrative approach also reflects broader methodological concerns. Whatever your view of postmodern critiques of historical writing inspired by 'the literary turn', it seems that flagging the fact that histories are written, adopting narrative structures and tropes, is a useful reminder that history is mediated through the historian. Not only do we make choices about what and who to include and exclude (and we always exclude far more than we include), but also about how to frame the histories we write and the narrative voice we adopt. As Hayden White pointed out, the tendency has been for historians to adopt the narrative style of nineteenth-century literature in writing history, given that history as an academic discipline was largely formed in that context.[28] However, within the last few decades a number of writers have chosen more experimental narrative forms in their constructions of the past.[29] To give just one example, Richard Price's groundbreaking study *Alabi's World* told the story of Maroon society in the eighteenth century in an intentionally multi-perspectival manner, utilizing four distinct voices throughout.[30] In this book I have also sought to develop a multi-perspectival narrative, although this comes less from distinct voices than distinct traces. My experience in writing this book has mirrored that of Richard Price who suggested that, '[D]ifferent historical or ethnographic situations lend themselves to different literary forms (and vice-versa), and that the ethnographer or historian should … face each society or period – or for that matter each potential book – in a form that does not come pre-selected or ready-made, in order to effectively evoke that particular society, or that particular historical moment.'[31] I do not offer multi-perspectival narratives framed around distinct material traces of the past as *the* way to write history, but rather *one* way that seems to fit with both the nature of the traces and the subject matter that I work with here.

Reflecting on trends in Holocaust historiography, Dan Stone calls for historians to generate 'new narratives' given 'the obviously chaotic nature' of an event that 'questions that very reliance on coherence, traditionally the *obbligato* of narrative'. Yet, there remains, as Stone points out, an overwhelming tendency to narrate the Holocaust, 'in such a way as to render it coherent'.[32] This can be seen in both scholarly and popular tellings of the Holocaust in Hungary. Randolph Braham's groundbreaking study offered a chronologically linear narrative that traced the 'prelude to destruction', 'the road to destruction', 'the processes of ... destruction' through a number of 'phases' before ending with 'liberation, restitution, retribution' and postwar 'Hungarian reactions to the Holocaust'.[33] The result is a tendency to smooth out differences both in time and space within a narrative that laid out the unrolling of a Nazi German master plan in Hungary. You might expect differences in place to emerge more fully in the recently published *Geographical Encyclopedia of the Hungarian Holocaust*. Drawing on national, regional and local archives, this massive multi-authored three-volume work provides a place inventory of Jewish communities throughout Hungary. However, differences are submerged in a common chronological and thematic structuring of entries that follow a set pattern of detailing prewar life, ghettoization, deportation and the small trickle of survivors who returned.[34]

The adoption of a linear narrative (the beginning of prewar life, the middle of ghettoization and deportation, and the end of postwar life stretching to the present) is perhaps most clearly seen in James Moll's popular documentary filmic telling of the Hungarian Holocaust as *The Last Days*. As the title suggests, the larger story contained in this film is that the Hungarian Holocaust was the culmination and final chapter in the bigger pan-European story of an essentially common process of Nazi antisemitism. The film, in the words of executive producer Steven Spielberg, 'follows five Hungarians who fell victim to Adolf Hitler's final genocidal push at the end of the Second World War',[35] skilfully editing their separate voices together minus the questions so that they effectively tell a single, coherent and linear story. There are times when differences in experiences are hinted at – for example, male survivors talking about labour service and their fear of being subjected to a 'trouser test' to see if they were circumcised – but these ideas are never really explored.[36] In contrast, I seek here to bring difference to the fore through my focus upon particular places and people.

'How representative are the places and people that I work with?' is a question that has often been raised when I have discussed this project with colleagues.[37] As I have already noted, my entire narrative strategy is born from a realization of the unrepresentativeness of the traces that I frame the book around: an unrepresentativeness that I foreground rather than erase. Returning once more to those ghetto passes that so fascinated me when I first came across them, I make no claims about them being broadly representative of the porousness of all Hungarian ghettos, nor of ghettos across Europe. Place matters. Ghettos were different. Some ghetto fences were, as was the case in Körmend, relatively permeable, others were almost impenetrable.[38] But it is not only the case that Körmend appears exceptional in being a place where there was so much two-way traffic through the ghetto gate. There is another layer of exceptionality when looking at just who it was who could come and go in the summer of 1944. Not all Jews could leave the ghetto. Not all non-Jews could enter the ghetto. In short, the passes point to the exceptional journeys of exceptional people in an exceptional place, which begs the question: 'Why could these people exit and enter this ghetto (and others both here and elsewhere could not)?'

Here the approach adopted by micro history is perhaps insightful. Historians of Europe in the early modern period have seized upon exceptional, rather than representative, stories precisely because of their potential for uncovering broader assumptions, values, meanings and experiences. [39] Carlo Ginzburg's study of a sixteenth-century miller, Menocchio,[40] or Natalie Zemon Davis' *The Return of Martin Guerre*, come to mind as examples of the potential value of a deep reading of exceptional stories. It is their very exceptionality which is their attraction, with Natalie Zemon Davis arguing that the fact that Martin Guerre's story, 'is an unusual case serves me well, for a remarkable dispute can sometimes uncover motivations and values that are lost in the welter of the everyday'.[41]

In part, micro history is an attractive approach given its goal of developing, what Carlo Ginzburg called, 'a prosopography from below'.[42] There is a place for writing prosopographies from below of the Holocaust given, as Ruth Wisse suggests, that 'individualizing the Holocaust undoes the levelling work of the Nazi regime'.[43] This was clearly in the mind of the Warsaw *Oneg Shabbat* member, Israel Lichtenstein, who left a 'last will and testament' that not only 'expressed his pride for his work in the *Oneg Shabbat* and his desire to be remembered for it',[44] but also named and described his wife and young daughter. As Zoe Waxman argues, he did this because of a desire that his wife 'be be remembered as a talented artist' and his twenty-month old daughter 'as a gifted child. It was important for him that they did not become nameless victims.'[45]

Yet, within the historiography of the Holocaust the names of the perpetrators tend to be more visible than the names of 'ordinary victims' or 'ordinary bystanders' (ironic given the Jewish tradition of silencing the name of Haman during Purim.) This is particularly true of the Nazi Party and State elite, but it extends down to lower levels both within and outside Germany. Christopher Browning introduced us to Major 'Papa' Trapp and the men of Police Battalion 101 in his groundbreaking micro history of one group of perpetrators which he positioned within the German social history tradition of *Alltagsgeschichte* (the history of everyday life).[46] The naming of national and local collaborators can be seen within Hungarian Holocaust historiography.[47] However, named victims (and bystanders) tend to remain peripheral to historical writing, if not to memorial practices.[48] In part this is a result of the tendency to privilege paperwork from the higher echelons of the perpetrators. As Raul Hilberg noted in his own reflections on the variety of sources available to historians of the Holocaust, 'in transmissions to higher echelons, names are turned into numbers ...',[49] words echoed in Peter Haidu's conclusion that 'German sources reveal the bureaucratic complexity of the process of extermination, but they deal with people only in the aggregate'.[50] But it also reflects a tendency to privilege causation in Holocaust historiography over social history approaches.

In this book I write the obscure(d) into history. In Chapter 1, I am interested in the chief rabbi – Lajos Kun – who drew up name lists in Veszprém, but also those who did or did not end up on those lists: Mrs Lázár S., Dr and Mrs Aladár B., and the families of Dénes S. and Oszkár F.[51] In Chapter 2, I work with the paperwork created by a local official in Nyíregyháza – Dr Gönczy – as well as farmers like János M., Mrs József H. and Mrs János K. Chapter 3 focuses on the writers and readers of the local press in Szeged, and Chapter 4 on mapmakers in Tolna county as well as the experiences of the D family and the small number of other Jews who joined them in their home turned into micro ghetto in Tolna in June 1944. Chapter 5 tells the stories of Jews and non-Jews leaving and entering the ghetto in Körmend: two Jewish doctors Dr Ignác P. and Dr Gyula Sz., teenagers like Ernő H. and Zoltán M., the tinsmith Sándor F. and the barber János G., workers at the Frim steam saw mill and the two journeys out of the ghetto taken by Matyás R. The second of those two journeys was photographed by an unknown photographer, whose images I examine in Chapter 6. In Chapter 7, I use the reports written by gendarmerie Lieutenant-Colonel László Ferenczy to explore his thinking as the ghettoization and deportation process he oversaw was enacted. Other ways of telling this story emerge in Chapter 8 where I look at the narrating of ghettoization, deportation and escape from Nagyvárad by three members of the same family. In the epilogue, I focus on three eleven-year-old children – György András M., György Konrád and Judit Brody – who made counter-journeys in the spring and summer of 1944.

But writing unknowns into Holocaust historiography is more than simply an opportunity to name those who Edward Muir and Guido Ruggiero have memorably described as 'the lost peoples of Europe'.[52] Micro history not only writes the subaltern into the historical narrative, but also seeks to reveal complexity,[53] and point to power lying not only at the centre.[54] As Giovanni Levi notes, micro history, 'takes the particular as its starting point (a particular which is often highly specific and individual, and would be impossible to describe as a typical case) and proceeds to identify its meaning in the light of its own specific context'.[55] While not explicitly seeing his own work as micro history, Mark Roseman's *A Past in Hiding* can be read in just such terms. Telling what he sees as the unique story of Marianne Ellenbogen's experiences of hiding in Nazi Germany, and her memories of her past, Roseman confesses,

> I initially decided to write this book ... to preserve an extraordinary survival story, not because I expected to gain major insights into the Third Reich and the Holocaust. Marianne's life seemed too singular to offer more than peripheral insights into the nightmare from which she had so unusually managed to escape. Survival was so much against the normal run of things for a Jew caught in Germany or German-occupied Europe after 1939 that in telling Marianne's story I felt almost guilty of fostering a kind of distortion.[56]

However, Roseman's suggestion is that, 'although the drama of Marianne's survival was unique, its backdrop was so well illuminated and its cast of players so large that *her story sheds light on the whole theatre in which it took place*'.[57] Marianne's exceptional story becomes a way for Roseman to explore broader issues of German–Jewish relations and memory.

By focusing on exceptional 'nobodies' as ghettoization and deportation was implemented in Hungary in the spring and summer of 1944, my hope is to cast light on broader themes. I have tried to get inside the heads and reimagine the stories of some of those who enacted, watched, participated in and experienced the Holocaust in Hungary, by working with the traces they have left behind (the lists they drew up, the sketch maps they made, the letters they wrote, the photographs they took). Starting with these largely unwritten about people (and places) and their traces, my hope is that their distinct yet also overlapping stories will generate broader questions about those who implemented, experienced, watched and narrated journeys into and out of the ghettos during the Holocaust. The potential of starting off with the insignificant is something that John Roth commented on, thinking back on decades of teaching classes on the Holocaust to undergraduates. 'Having taught about the Holocaust for many years,' Roth reflected, 'I have discovered that the best learning strategies often involve concentrating on small details, on events that are utterly particular but charged with intensity. As one explores how these details developed, how those events took place, they lead outward in spiralling concentric circles to wider historical perspectives.'[58]

PART I

Places and Spaces: Journeys to and from the Ghetto

1

Entering and Exiting the Ghetto: Name Lists from Veszprém

In the city of Veszprém in western Hungary, as elsewhere in the country, the Jewish authorities were busy in the spring and early summer of 1944 drawing up lists of Jews. On 4 April, the Interior Minister had requested mayors to, 'instruct the Jewish communal organizations to prepare a list in four copies of all Jews with their families, specifying their apartments and places of residence' as well as their mother's maiden name.[1] A few weeks later there was another request, this time from the Minister of Food Supplies, for lists of 'all persons considered Jews from the point of view of food supplies' to be submitted by 1 May.[2] On 3 May, Lajos Kun, chief rabbi and registrar of the city's Neolog Jewish community, sent three copies of typewritten lists of 674 Jews living in Veszprém 'and known to me' to the mayor, having already sent one copy to the police authorities the day before.[3]

Name lists of Jews from 1944 have something of a controversial history to them. Braham argues that the timing of the Minister of Food Supplies decree was not coincidental, given that it came 'on the eve of the large-scale ghettoization and the authorities used the data to supplement the lists prepared on Baky's orders earlier in the month for use by the Gestapo, the gendarmes, and their collaborators in the round-up of the Jews.'[4] Writing of the earlier Interior Ministry ordered lists, Braham sees them as forerunner to the 7 April confidential ghettoization order and 'the first concrete directives for the implementation' of this measure.[5] Not only does he suggest a direct relationship between the drawing up of names lists and preparations for placing Hungarian Jews into ghettos on the part of the authorities, but also claims that, 'the central Jewish leaders were aware that these two interrelated measures were designed to facilitate the isolation and ghettoization of the Jews', and yet chose to leave 'local Jewish communal leaders ... in the dark'. According to Braham, hundreds of men like Lajos Kun, 'faithfully prepared the lists' because they were 'unwarned and unguided' by the Central Jewish Council in Budapest.[6] His ire is not directed at the likes of Kun, but the coterie of Jewish leaders in the capital who he sees as myopic at best.

However, Braham's insistence on the direct link between these lists and ghettoization remains unsubstantiated. We do not know enough about how they were used. They certainly contained information that the authorities could use, but according to the authors of a report on the current whereabouts of the April 1944 name lists, the copies sent to the Interior Ministry were passed on to Zoltán Bosnyák at the so-called 'Hungarian Institute of Research on the Jewish

Question' (an antisemitic pseudo research institute), where 'the "scientific" processing of the lists began, meaning, for example, attempts to analyze the name-giving habits of the Jews'.[7] This report came after the Hungarian Minister of National Culture established a committee in December 2003 to investigate press claims that a full copy of what became known as 'deportation lists' from 1944 were being secretly held by the Hungarian archives. The committee rejected the descriptor 'deportation lists' and concluded that archival losses – whether accidental or deliberate – meant that no complete national run of name lists of Hungarian Jews survived.[8]

But name lists do survive from place to place, including Veszprém.[9] Here, the list from early May can be compared with lists of Jews living in the city's two ghettos six weeks later and a number of other shorter lists,[10] in order to see who ended up in the ghettos in this city, who did not, and who was removed from the ghettos during their shortlived existence. These lists reveal a gendered inflow into, and outflow from, the ghettos in this city in the spring and summer of 1944.[11] But alongside this major story are two other stories of absences and presences that reveal the short-term urbanization associated with ghettoization and the importance in 1944 of a much longer history of the Hungarian state defining who was 'Magyar' or 'Christian' enough to no longer be a 'Jew' which is where I want to begin.[12]

TOO 'CHRISTIAN' OR 'MAGYAR' TO BE A GHETTO 'JEW'?: LAJOS KUN'S 'JEWISH PERSONS IN MIXED MARRIAGES', DR AND MRS ALADÁR B. AND MRS LÁZÁR S.

The most obvious difference between the name lists drawn up at the beginning of May and in the middle of June was the absence from the ghetto of all those described by Lajos Kun as 'Jewish persons in mixed marriages with those of Christian faith living in Veszprém'. When he drew up lists of Jews living in the city in early May, the rabbi sent not one but three separate typed lists, each with their own cover sheet. The first, and longest, entitled 'Name list of Jews of the Israelite faith living in Veszprém', included 608 names. The second list was much shorter, with just forty-three names, of 'Jewish persons of Christian faith living in Veszprém'. The third and final list was shorter still, containing twenty-three names of 'Jewish persons in mixed marriages with those of Christian faith living in Veszprém'.[13] Not only did Kun list these three groups separately, but also he distinguished between them linguistically. The first were 'Jews' (zsidók) but the other two were different types of 'Jewish persons' (zsidó egyének).

Kun reflected a typically assimilated Neolog position in seeing Jews as members of the 'Israelite faith', and thus a religious rather than a racial category. Broadly speaking, Neolog communities in the late nineteenth and early twentieth centuries had seen themselves as Hungarians who were members of the Jewish faith, in a similar vein to the way that other Hungarians were members of

Catholic, Reformed or Lutheran faith communities.[14] However, in contrast to this self-definition, the Hungarian state had adopted pseudo-racial definitions of Jewishness in antisemitic legislation enacted in the late 1930s. Although Hungary gained the dubious distinction of being the country to introduce 'the first major anti-Jewish law in post-World War One Europe',[15] Law XXV of 1920 limiting the number of students enrolling at universities to the proportion of their ethnic group within the population as a whole made no specific references to Jews, sidestepping the vexed question of definition, and was ultimately never fully implemented, being repealed in 1928.[16] Ten years later, Law XV which set a quota (20 per cent) on Jewish participation in the professions and businesses was enacted. While it referred to Jews directly, the law failed to provide a thorough-going definition, simply assuming that Jewishness was a largely unproblematic category based on religious affiliation.[17]

It was not until 1939 that Law IV restricting Jewish participation 'in public and economic life' to their proportion (6 per cent) in the population as a whole, gave the first detailed definition of the Jew as someone who was a member of the Jewish denomination, or had at least one parent who was a member of the Jewish denomination, or at least two grandparents who were members of the Jewish denomination at the point of the law coming into force.[18] In short, Jewishness was not simply a personal denominational choice, but extended back to the religious affiliation of the previous generations. Two years later, what Braham describes as 'the most openly and brazenly racist piece of legislation Hungary ever adopted'[19] was passed by Parliament: Law XV of 1941.[20] Amending a previous marriage law, this prohibited marriage and extra-marital sexual relations between Jews and non-Jews, and defined Jews (either a member of the Jewish denomination or anyone with two grandparents who had been born members of the Jewish denomination) in both religious and racial terms. It was this 1941 definition that determined who the raft of anti-Jewish legislation issued in Hungary in the spring and summer of 1944 was directed against.[21]

Alongside this history of the evolution of the 'Jew' as a pseudo-racial legal category was another history of the evolution of exemptions from antisemitic legislation. Although the 1938 law sidestepped the issue of defining the Jew, it did not hold back from listing 'Jews' exempt from the remit of the legislation. These included war invalids, combatants, and the widows and children of the war dead, those who had converted to Christianity prior to 1 August 1919 (the end-date of the short-lived Bolshevik regime of Béla Kun), and maintained unbroken membership of a Christian denomination and those born to converts who were not themselves members of the Jewish denomination.[22] These broad categories of exemptions – patriotic Magyars and converts – continued to crop up in one form or another in subsequent legislation. The 1939 law extended exemption from those with distinguished military service in the First World War, to those who 'risked their life or suffered for the national movement during the 1918/1919 revolution' as well as other wars fought for the nation.

Exemption on such grounds saw in military service the ultimate show of (masculine) patriotism and a badge of successful assimilation.[23] However, there were clearly other routes into Magyar society, with the 1939 law introducing a long list of exempt individuals – interior privy councillors, royal privy councillors, university lecturers at the Sciences, Technical or Economic universities, pastors in a Christian denomination and Olympic champions.[24]

Away from patriotic service, the other major set of exemptions revolved around conversion. In Hungary, as elsewhere, the much-debated question was what about those with Jewish parents or grandparents who had converted to Christianity: were they still Jewish? In many ways the response in 1939 was 'it depends'. In particular the law sought to distinguish between 'old' – perceived as true – converts and 'new' – potentially spurious – converts. Recent converts were seen by the law as still Jewish. Conversion alone was not enough. As the ministerial justification articulated while the bill was being prepared asserted, '[A] person belonging to the Jewish denomination is at the same time a member of the Jewish racial community and it is natural that the cessation of membership in the Jewish denomination does not result in any change in that person's association with the racial community.'[25] It was only those whose parents had converted prior to their marriage or prior to 1939, those who had been a member of a Christian denomination from birth or prior to their seventh birthday if their parents had also converted before 1939 or themselves had converted before 1919, that were seen for legal purposes as 'non-Jews'. The 1941 law also provided exemption to some converts, although this was now limited to those born and still members of a Christian denomination provided that their parents were also members of a Christian denomination at the time of their marriage.[26]

This complex history of overlapping and competing categories of exemption continued into 1944,[27] leading Minister of Justice István Antal to call for a streamlining of what he saw as the 'muddle' of Jewish exemptions at the 26 April Council of Ministers meeting that discussed ghettoization.[28] Around two weeks later, a decree was ready that provided a single guide to who was, and was not, exempt from what.[29] In Veszprém, it is clear that this nationally issued regulation formed the basis for determining who was, and who was not, to be placed into the city's ghetto. Local officials here played things by the book. Among the long list of Jews exempted from anti-Jewish measures on 10 May were 'those living in marriage with non-Jews who were a member of a Christian denomination before 22 March 1944 at the latest, and the children of such marriages who are not Jewish'. Their inclusion in this decree drawn up in Budapest meant that the 23 persons that Kun had listed as 'Jewish persons' living in mixed marriages on 3 May were not in the ghetto set up in Veszprém at the end of May.[30]

It was not only 'Jewish persons of the Christian faith' in mixed marriages who were absent from the Veszprém ghetto as a result of the new decree issued on 10 May. Also benefiting were Dr and Mrs Aladár B. A clue to their absence from the ghetto comes on the initial list of names, where, just below Dr

Aladár B.'s name was inserted a note that he was '75% war disabled'.[31] This was obviously something seen as important enough for inclusion in the list of names forwarded to the authorities at the beginning of May 1944, given the longer history of the war disabled being exempt from a series of anti-Jewish laws. In the decree issued on 10 May, 75 per cent war invalids and their immediate families were amongst those exempt from wearing the yellow star, and therefore from ghettoization.[32] That exemption extended to immediate family members meant that Mrs Aladár B. joined her husband in staying put, living literally down the street from, but most crucially outside, the ghetto.

But another Jewish women whose two husbands had fought in the First World War was not so lucky. Mrs Lázár S. wrote to the Mayor on 25 April requesting that she be exempt from all government decrees relating to Jews.[33] Her case rested on being a 'war widow of Jewish origin' not only once, but twice over. This was, she reminded the mayor, a basis for exemption in the so-called 'second anti-Jewish law' of 1939 which she drew his attention to. She then went on to tell her story of the heroic death of her first husband – an 'old Christian' rather than a mere convert – in the First World War. Her second husband, Lázár S., had also served in that war, dying afterwards, she claimed, as a direct result of his wartime injuries. Hers was a tragic story of two husbands' lives cut short by war.

It was a story that the mayor wanted fact checking, so he forwarded it to a clerk at the welfare organization for disabled servicemen and their relatives (*hadigondozó*) on 5 May.[34] Three days later he received a report back confirming that Mrs Lázár S. was on their files as receiving a pension payable to the war widows of non-commissioned officers.[35] However, the clerk drew attention to the recent legislation requiring Jews to wear the yellow star which he noted referred to exemptions to those widowed in the present war only. By the time the deputy mayor had made a final decision on the case, which he did on 17 May, the situation had changed again, with the issuing of the new decree aimed at streamlining the complex web of categories of exemption on 10 May. Mrs Lázár S.'s request for exemption was refused on the grounds that her husband was not 75 per cent war disabled and that he had died before 1 January 1939.[36]

Her story reflects a number of things. First, it reveals the shifting and contested nature of the category Jew. Mrs Lázár S. was considered Jewish enough by Lajos Kun to be included on his list of 'Jews of Israelite faith' drawn up in early May, but by her own self-description, she was a war widow first, and of 'Jewish origin' second. Her two husbands had done enough to prove not only their, but also by extension her, patriotic credentials and so she should be exempt from all measures impacting Jews in the city, hence her letter to the Mayor. Her claim was based on the category for exemption that excluded war widows like her from the scope of the 1939 law. However, things had moved on as the clerk at the welfare organization for disabled servicemen and their relatives signalled on 5 May by specifically referencing the decree requiring Jews to wear the yellow star, issued less than a week earlier. In fast-changing circumstances, by the time the deputy mayor had made his final decision, a new decree had been issued, which formed the basis for his rejection of Mrs Lázár S.'s claim for exemption on the grounds of her dead husbands' wartime service. In his letter, he repeated more or less word for word an extract from the newly published decree. Mrs Lázár S. may have been exempt from anti-Jewish measures in 1939 but she was no longer exempt at the end of May 1944. She ended up in the ghetto, from where we can assume she was taken at the end of June, two weeks after the ghetto list was completed, to Pápa, and then less than a week later to Auschwitz-Birkenau. Here it is unlikely that a fifty-seven-year-old woman would survive the initial selections for labour.

Second, as the paperwork around Mrs Lázár S.'s case makes so clear, decisions on the ground were being made in a context of rapid change. In the time lag between Mrs Lázár S. first writing her letter, a clerk investigating the matter and the mayor finally reaching a decision, two critical pieces of national legislation were issued, which changed the situation. This rapidly changing legislative context is particularly important given the implementation of ghettoization and deportation on a zonal basis. Broadly speaking, ghettoization began in the north-east and south-east of the country in April before moving westwards gendarme district by district before ending up in the capital Budapest where ghettoization was implemented in mid-June. Likewise, deportations followed a similar pattern of early implementation in Transylvania and Carpatho-Ruthenia in May, before reaching western Hungary in early July. This time lag in the west of the country was critical. It meant that these twenty-three 'Jewish persons in mixed marriages with those of Christian faith living in Veszprém' along with Dr and Mrs Aladár B. escaped the ghetto – established as it was *after* 20 May – and therefore also Auschwitz. This was not the case everywhere. In some places, Jews who were exempt from ghettoization according to national decrees were placed into ghettos on local initiative going against national directives, or if national exemptions were recognized, this came too late.[37] This picture of, broadly speaking, greater chronological opportunity in western Hungary to escape ghettoization and deportation was even more marked with a greater number of ghetto absentees: Jewish men called up from the ghettos for labour service by the Hungarian army. Their story, like that of exempt Jews, is one with a longer history than simply the critical year of 1944.

TOO VALUABLE TO BE A GHETTO 'JEW'?: THE CALL-UP OF JEWISH MEN FOR LABOUR SERVICE IN MAY AND JUNE 1944

When Hungary entered the war on the side of the Axis powers on 27 June 1941, plans for separate Jewish labour battalions were implemented and Jewish men aged between twenty and forty-two years called up to serve in auxiliary labour service units for a period of two years. In what can be seen as a compromise solution of sorts, Jewish men were to serve in the military like non-Jewish men, but – critically – they were to be unarmed. Hungarian Jewish men were sent to the Eastern Front, where they suffered especially harsh conditions and high casualty rates.[38] Tom Kramer claims that the mortality rate for Jewish labour servicemen attached to the devastated Second Hungarian Army was over 85 per cent compared to a figure of 65 per cent for non-Jewish combatants. This disparity came, he suggests, because 'whereas the Hungarian Second Army was decimated by enemy action in the theatre of battle, the Jewish Labour Service casualties resulted largely from the deliberate actions of nominally friendly forces'.[39]

Not only were death rates higher among Jewish labour servicemen, but also their wartime deaths were not deemed heroic by the Hungarian state. The decree issued in May 1944 which provided a single list of those Jews exempt from anti-Jewish regulations, while it extended exemptions to those who were 75 per cent war invalids and their immediate families (like Dr and Mrs Aladár B.) from the First World War made an explicit exception for war invalids serving in 'auxiliary labour service companies', and the widows and orphans of men who had served in these companies.[40] This meant that Jewish men like Dr Imré Sz. from Veszprém, who had been buried on the Eastern Front in November 1942, had not died a hero's death, and therefore his widow and orphan were not exempt from the flurry of anti-Jewish legislation issued in 1944, including ghettoization.[41] Unlike Mrs Aladár B., Dr Imré Sz.'s widow and orphaned son György were placed in the ghetto in Veszprém.[42] Dr Imré Sz. had died in the wrong war.

Dr Imré Sz. was not alone in being a wartime casualty of labour battalion service from Veszprém. If you were to walk further along the street, Kossuth Lajos utca (street), where he had once lived, in the early summer of 1944, you would come across a number of other addresses where Jewish families had recently mourned the loss of family members on the Eastern front. At number 14 lived Mr and Mrs László Sz. whose son Imré was killed at Novij Oszkol in January 1943 aged twenty-six.[43] Next door at number 13 lived Mr and Mrs Vilmos P. who had lost their son Rezső in the same month as their neighbours, killed on the Eastern Front at the age of thirty-four.[44] January 1943 was a particularly devastating month, with at least four other Jewish men aged between twenty-three and thirty-nine from Veszprém killed or recorded missing that month.[45] On 12 January, the Soviet Army made a dramatic break-through at the River Don, where the Second Hungarian Army held the Uriv bridgehead near Voronezh. The Soviet victory at the Battle of the Don was swift and crushing, with tens of thousands of Hungarian casualties. Thousands more were taken prisoner by the Soviets, with the remnants of the devastated Second Hungarian Army forced into a chaotic and rapid retreat, with particularly dire consequences for Jewish labour servicemen.[46] The few days immediately after 12 January 1943 left their terrible mark on families living in Veszprém. Mr and Mrs Simón F.'s son György was killed on 15 January;[47] Mr and Mrs Alfred R.'s son Andor died two days later on 17 January;[48] and Mrs Mór D.'s son Ferenc was killed on 20 January.[49]

The experience of gendered separation and death in 1942 and 1943 was recalled by Mrs É.K., a Jewish survivor from Kapuvár in western Hungary, interviewed by Ilana Rosen. Putting right what she saw as the misnomer that 'Hungarian Jews had a peaceful life until 1944', Mrs É.K. remembered 1942 as 'a terrible year', because:

> [M]y brother Jozsi, who until then was in Hungary with his battalion, was now sent eastwards. My mother became sick from worrying about him. She lost her appetite ... My aunt's husband was called to labour service and she was left with a five year old child and didn't know anything about running the firm. A forty year old man who supported his blind brothers was called too, and within six months he was dead. Everyone lived in fear ... In January 1943 we heard that a whole Hungarian regiment was killed in battle. The Russians simply finished them off. No news came from my brother, and my mother got even sicker. She started going to séances like a primitive person, although she didn't use to be superstitious. Eventually a letter came notifying us that my brother had disappeared near Novij Oszkol in January. This was a blow to my parents, but they still hoped that he might be in prison in Russia.[50]

The devastating impact of two to three years of military service on the Jewish community in Veszprém can be seen reading between the lines on Kun's lists of names from early May 1944. Arranged alphabetically by family, it is striking how often the names of husbands, fathers and sons are missing. Women formed a majority of Jews living in the city, with this female majority particularly marked among those in their twenties and thirties.[51] Of the eighteen to forty-two-year-olds living in Veszprém in May 1944, women made up just over seven out of every ten Jews of this age.[52] As the absences and presences on Kun's lists make clear, labour battalion service amounted to gendered vulnerability for Hungarian Jewish men. All Hungarian Jews were subject to an economic onslaught prior to the Nazi German occupation as a result of a number of years of antisemitic legislation, but it was only Hungarian Jewish men in their twenties and thirties who were dying in 1942 and 1943.[53] The initial vulnerability of Jewish men here reflects a broader picture across Europe. While 'in the final tally, women were most probably more than half of the dead,' concluded Raul Hilberg, 'men died more rapidly.'[54]

However, this story of labour battalion service as gendered threat changed dramatically during the early summer of 1944. Not only did the ghettoization decree issued at the end of April 1944 explicitly exempt Jewish men already serving in labour battalions from being placed into ghettos,[55] but also, as ghettoization was implemented, new waves of conscriptions took place. On 20 May, thirty-seven men aged between eighteen and forty-nine were called up in Veszprém, their names listed, in alphabetical order, on a typewritten sheet of 'Jewish persons' called up for labour battalion service by the Third Army.[56] On 4 June, 11 men aged from twenty-five to forty-six were conscripted from the 'Komakuti Jewish Camp' where Jews from rural communities around the city were concentrated.[57] On 12 June, another seventeen men, aged twenty-three to forty-eight, were called up from the Horthy Miklós utca ghetto.[58] Aware of ongoing call-ups, the vice president of the Jewish Council in Veszprém wrote to the deputy mayor on 23 May with the request that men aged between twenty-one and forty-eight awaiting the draft be allowed to take a backpack full of extra clothing and equipment into the ghetto with them.[59]

The call-up of Jewish men for labour service was not only taking place in Veszprém in May and June 1944. Gendarmerie Lieutenant Colonel László Ferenczy (whose reports form the basis of chapter seven) noted on 10 May that draft papers were being delivered to the newly established transit camps. On 29 May, he pointed out that Jewish men were continuing to be called up by the Ministry of Defence from transit camps and ghettos.[60] A few weeks later, on 12 June, he reported 'new attempts to call Jews up for labor service'.[61] It seems that 12 June was a particularly busy day. On that day, seventeen men were called up in Veszprém.[62] A short distance away, in the town of Körmend, Jewish men aged between eighteen and forty-eight were also conscripted.[63] It was not only in the gendarmerie district of Szombathely – which included Veszprém and Körmend – that Jewish men were being called up in May and June 1944. They were also entering labour battalions in the Budapest, Székesfehérvár and Miskolc gendarmerie districts following a decision in April to conscript older Jewish men.[64] Jewish men were leaving ghettos in a large number of towns and cities: among them Hajdúböszörmény, Kecel, Kecskemét, Keszthely, Kiskunhalas, Ózd, Rosznyó, Szeged, Szentes and Szombathely.[65]

As a result of these call-ups, hundreds and hundreds of Jewish men were removed from those ghettos that had not yet been liquidated. Instead of being deported, Jewish men in the twenties, thirties and forties served out the war in labour battalions. This represented a dramatic turnaround in fortunes for young Hungarian Jewish men. While their absence from the May 1944 name lists points to their vulnerability, their absence from the June 1944 ghetto list signals their escape from both the ghetto and the deportation train. It would be wrong to equate the call-up of Jewish men to labour service as simply akin to rescue. Conditions in these units varied from place to place, but were generally harsh.[66] But, as Braham has reflected, 'it is one of the ironies of history that the Ministry of Defense, which had been viewed as one of the chief causes of suffering among [male] Jews during the previous four to five years, suddenly emerged as the major governmental institution actively involved in the saving of Jewish lives'.[67] Although arguing that what motivated the new rush of conscription in the early summer of 1944 remains 'not absolutely clear',[68] Braham does claim that, 'it is safe to assume that many local commanders, aware of the realities of the ghettoization and deportation program and motivated by humanitarian instincts, did everything in their power to rescue as many Jews as possible', although he does also point to more pragmatic motivations resulting from 'the manpower shortage from which the country was suffering at the time'.[69] This, for Krisztián Ungváry, was more critical than any notion of humanitarianism.

He argues that the agreement reached between the Hungarian and German authorities that 80,000 Jewish men be retained to work in Hungary, which meant that, 'many men ... drawn out of the ghettos into the workforce', should not be interpreted as 'a deliberate rescue attempt'. As he suggests, '[S]paring the Jews certainly was not the intention of those Hungarians responsible, but rather exploiting Jewish work power and expertise (physicians, pharmacists, etc.) "for free" and for as long as possible.'[70]

This picture of the initial vulnerability of Jewish men being overturned once mass deportations commenced is one that can be seen elsewhere in Europe.[71] As Hilberg noted, '[T]he comparative advantage afforded to women was limited to the labor recruitment and expansion drives of 1940, 1941, and 1942. With the onset of deportation there was a reversal of fortunes. Labor became numerically the most important reason for deferment or exemption during roundups. More women than men could now be considered "surplus."'[72] In Hungary in the spring and early summer of 1944, it is clear that Jewish men were seen as more valuable than Jewish women by the Hungarian state. It was only several months later, in October 1944, that Jewish women were called up en masse in Budapest, when the fascist Arrow Cross (Nyilas) government was increasingly desperate for labour.[73] But in May and June 1944, Jewish women were seen to be dispensable. This meant that Jewish men in their late teens to late forties from a city like Veszprém experienced a very different 'Holocaust' from women of the same age, as can be seen in two families' stories.

Dénes S., who was forty-five years old, lived with his thirty-eight-year-old wife Ilona and their three children at Völgyikút utca 13. Their eldest child, György (aged eighteen), was an apprentice. His younger sister Éva was sixteen years old and still at school. The baby of the family was eight-year-old László. Dénes, had been born in Székesfehérvár, but his wife was from Veszprém and her seventy-three-year-old mother Karolin still lived in the city, just a few doors down from where the S. family lived.[74] At the beginning of May 1944, when Kun drew up his lists of Jews in the city, this was a family of five that had remained together despite the war and anti-Jewish measures. However, all this was about to change for this family, as for many others. On 20 May, Dénes and György were both called up for labour service. They were not the only family members to be called up together on 20 May.[75] Mobilized together we don't know whether Dénes and György S. managed to stay together during the last year of the war. But Dénes was separated from his wife and two children, and György was separated from his mother and younger siblings. With Dénes and György gone, this family shrank to one so typical of many on the ghetto name lists – a mother and her children.

Taken to the Horthy Miklós utca ghetto, we find Ilona, Éva and László's names on the list drawn up in the middle of June, just a few days before deportations from this ghetto took place. Also in the ghetto, was Ilona's mother Karolin.[76] Like many families, ghettoization meant the coming together of an extended family minus adult male family members within one place. Taken first to Pápa, and then on to Auschwitz-Birkenau, we know that sixteen-year-old Éva survived the initial selections and ended up at the camp of Stutthof,[77] ultimately listed among a group of other girls of a similar age from Veszprém who survived the camps.[78] For Éva, Auschwitz was a clearing house that funnelled her into the Nazi slave labour system. But for her grandmother, Karolin, Auschwitz was the place of her death. It would seem that Auschwitz-Birkenau was also where her eight-year-old brother László and her mother died.[79] This was the terminus on their journey from their family home on Völgyikút utca to the ghetto on Horthy Miklós utca, on to the fertilizer factory on the outskirts of Pápa, and from there to Auschwitz-Birkenau: a journey completed within less than two months.

Just over three weeks after Dénes and György were drafted into labour service, the cantor in the Jewish community in Veszprém, Oszkár F., was called up on 12 June along with sixteen other men from the Horthy Miklós utca ghetto.[80] Oszkár, like Dénes, was forty-five years old, and therefore young enough to fall within the age cohort of both younger and older men called up by the Hungarian Army in the late spring and early summer of 1944. But his two sons, Tibor and Tamás, were too young. In early May, Oszkár F. was listed living with his forty-year-old wife Malvin, at Horthy Miklós utca 13, close to the synagogue where he was the cantor. Three children lived at home with them in early May – the oldest, Judit, aged sixteen, was a dressmaker's assistant. Her younger brothers, Tibor (aged fifteen) and Tamás (aged eleven), were both still at school.[81]

Unlike the S. family, the F. family had all moved into the ghetto just around the corner where they briefly lived as an intact family. However, on 12 June, Oszkár was drafted from the ghetto leaving his wife and three children behind. While he was enlisted, Malvin, Judit, Tibor and Tamás stayed in the ghetto for another couple of weeks, before being taken to Pápa and on to Auschwitz-Birkenau. Here the F. family's story parallels in many ways that of the S. family. Like Éva S., Judit F. was a sixteen-year-old who survived the initial selections, entered into the slave labour system ending up in Stuffhof and survived the camps.[82] However, her mother and brothers, it would seem, were not selected for labour at Birkenau. According to the 'pages of testimony' submitted by Judit to Yad Vashem in 2006, all three were killed in Auschwitz in July 1944.[83]

The stories of the S. and F. family highlight a number of things. First, they point to the significance of gender and age in understanding the very different experiences of Hungarian Jews during the Holocaust.[84] Those experiences were not only gendered. It was not as simple as the male members of the S. and F. family experiencing one thing, and the female members another. Eight-year-old László S. was placed in the ghetto and deported whereas his brother ten years his senior was not. Aged fifteen, Tibor F. was a couple of years too young to be mobilized with his father and so remained in the ghetto with his mother, sister and younger brother, and was deported alongside them. Rather than gender alone being critical, it was the intersections of gender and age that were of central importance in determining who experienced what. Sixteen-year-old Éva may have been deemed less valuable by the Hungarian state than her eighteen-year-old brother, but she was valuable enough to the Nazi state at this point in the war to enter the slave labour system, rather then the gas chambers. Also deemed of value to the Nazi state was another sixteen-year-old, Judit. And it is clear that these teenage girls were not alone.[85] It is the names of women in their upper teens and twenties that dominate the postwar lists of Hungarian survivors of the camps.[86] But missing from those lists are the names of older men and women and younger children. While Éva and Judit entered into the slave labour system, Éva's grandmother, and both Éva and Judit's mothers and younger brothers were deemed of little value by both the Hungarian and Nazi German state.

But second, these stories also point to the separation of Hungarian Jewish families before the trauma of arrival at Auschwitz where Éva was separated from her grandmother, mother and younger brother, and Judit was separated from her mother and younger brothers. Before this separation, another separation had already taken place, in the city of Veszprém. On 20 May, Éva had been separated from her father and older brother. On 12 June, Judit saw her father, for what appears to have been the last time.[87] These separations worked two ways. For Éva S. and her mother, grandmother and younger brother, ghettoization and deportation was experienced without her older brother and father being there. For her older brother and father, no doubt the news of the deportation of the rest of their family, when they found out about it, came as a blow. Certainly finding out about the deportation of family members from Pápa for the first time was remembered by one labour battalion survivor as a devastating experience for the men.[88]

Many Hungarian families had already been split up prior to arrival at Auschwitz, where selections separated out those deemed fit to work from those sent immediately to the gas chambers.[89] Given that barracks in Auschwitz were divided by sex, those teenagers and young adults who survived the initial selections were subject to a second separation, this time from surviving family members of the opposite sex. This was one of the striking differences between the camps and the ghettos, which in the case of the latter generally meant that families remained together. Indeed as I explore in Chapter 4, in Tolna county there was a self-conscious policy to place extended families together in the ghetto. However, in Tolna, as in Veszprém, Jewish families in ghettos in Hungary were families with husbands, fathers, sons and brothers missing. In short, the trauma of families being split up – something that as I suggest in Chapter 8 was being actively avoided – had already taken place prior to deportation. In the case of most of these families, they would never be reunited.

Third, the splitting up of Jewish families from Veszprém and other Hungarian cities in the weeks immediately prior to deportation meant that in effect, 'selections' had already taken place prior to those on the ramp at Auschwitz-Birkenau. As it turned out, a pre-selection of sorts had been taking place since Hungarian Jewish men aged between twenty and forty-two had been called up for labour battalion service from the early 1940s onwards, with new waves of selections of younger and older men taking place in the spring and early summer of 1944. The Hungarian state had already selected Jews that it deemed fit for labour. The end result was, as both the stories of the S. and F. families and the sheer statistics of the June 1944 list reveal, that the Jews arriving at Auschwitz-Birkenau from cities like Veszprém were primarily made up of children, women and the elderly. Looking at the list of Jews concentrated in the Horthy Miklós utca ghetto in Veszprém, women accounted for roughly seven out of every ten ghetto inhabitants and a staggering 97.4 per cent of twenty- to twenty-nine-year-olds and 90.8 per cent of thirty- to thirty-nine-year-olds.[90] While there were 187 women aged between eighteen and forty-nine living in the Horthy Miklós utca ghetto, there were only thirteen men of the same age.[91] An almost identical picture emerges when attention shifts to the other ghetto in the city, in the Komakuti barracks ghetto where rural Jews were concentrated. There, women also made up roughly seven out of every ten inhabitants, 96.7 per cent of twenty- to twenty-nine-year-olds and 97.4 per cent of thirty- to thirty-nine-year-olds. Putting these two ghetto lists together, as was indeed the case once deportations commenced from Veszprém, it is clear that out of the more than 300 adults aged between eighteen and forty-nine deported from this city, only twenty-one were adult men.[92]

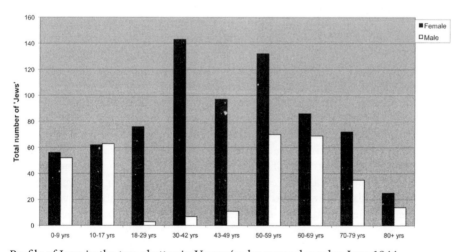

Profile of Jews in the two ghettos in Veszprém by age and gender, June 1944.

The impact of what in effect amounted to pre-selection of Hungarian Jewish men within Hungary was that young women aside, the numbers of Hungarian Jews who survived the initial selections were very low. The majority – as the stories of the S. and F. families point to – were killed immediately on arrival. The death rates of Hungarian Jews at Auschwitz were so high in large part because adult males were not on the deportation trains. If the estimate that only around fifty Jews from Veszprém returned from the camp is accurate,[93] then a little over 10 per cent of those deported from the Horthy Miklós utca ghetto survived, in the main young Jewish women who were joined in postwar Veszprém by Jewish men returning from labour battalions. In 1946, 106 Jews lived in the city, which included some who had moved in from smaller communities in the surrounding area, a continuation of the urbanization begun by ghettoization.

GHETTOIZATION AS URBANIZATION

Throughout Hungary, ghettoization meant temporary urbanization for the country's Jews. The ghettoization decree issued at the end of April stipulated that Jews were to leave small towns and villages and move into towns and cities with a population of more than 10,000 where ghettos were to be established by the local authorities. This cut-off figure of 10,000 was not always adhered to (chapter four). However, the principal was that ghettoization meant that Jews from rural Hungary moved into urban ghettos. In Veszprém, this meant that the Jewish population in the city, temporarily at least, effectively doubled in size.

Some of the Jews brought into the city in May 1944 were housed with the 576 Jews from Veszprém. The names of fifty-one 'Jews transferred from the countryside and placed in the Horthy Miklós utca ghetto' were listed alongside the names of 576 'Jews currently living' in the 'Veszprém synagogue premises'.[94] But the number of Jews being brought into Veszprém from surrounding towns and villages was so large that it required the creation of another ghetto set up in the former Komakuti barracks in the city with its own name list. Rather than a typewritten list in alphabetical order, the Komakuti ghetto list was handwritten and made use of a blank marriage register with the title 'Marriage Register' crossed out and replaced with 'Komakuti Jewish Camp Name List'.[95] Instead of listing the names of brides and grooms and the date of their wedding, the names of Jews brought into the ghetto established in Veszprém were written in, starting with those brought in from the town of Siófok, on the other side of Lake Balaton. It was a case of recycling what was at hand for new realities. A pre-printed ghetto list simply did not exist. Listing ghetto inhabitants was a new requirement for Jewish authorities more used to registering births, deaths and marriages.

This reflected the massive changes that Jewish leaders like Kun experienced in 1944. By the time that he was drawing up lists of Jews in the ghettos, the name of the institution that he represented had changed to the Veszprém Jewish Council. Jewish Councils were set up throughout Hungary, as elsewhere in occupied Europe, playing the major liaison role between the State authorities and the Jews.[96] In Veszprém, as in many other places, there was a strong degree of continuity between the existing Jewish community leadership and the membership of the Jewish Council, with the chief rabbi, Lajos Kun, assuming the role of head of the Jewish Council.[97] It was a new role, with responsibility for a new group of people. He was now responsible for hundreds more Jews from the surrounding towns and villages, as well as a group of ghettoized 'Jewish persons of Christian faith' that he clearly never saw as 'Jews'. Although these converts were placed in the ghetto as 'Jews', the distinction in Kun's mind that led to the issuing of separate lists on 3 May continued. In mid-June, there was only one ghetto for Jews from the city and only one ghetto list. Gone were the separate cover sheets, but the jump from number 524 on the ghetto list – Mrs Jenő W. who was the last of Kun's 'Jews of the Israelite faith' – to number 525 – Dezső A. the first of Kun's 'Jewish persons of the Christian faith' – suggests that the distinctions from May between 'Jews' and 'Jewish persons' persisted both on the list and on the ground.[98] Special dispensation was made to allow clergy from the Christian churches to enter the ghetto to visit converts housed there.[99] Kun did not take over pastoral responsibility for those he saw as 'Jewish persons of Christian faith' although he now exercised considerable authority over their day-to-day lives in the ghetto as head of the Jewish Council.

But writing of 'Jews' and 'Jewish persons' in the ghettos in Veszprém in gender-neutral language hides the reality that those living in the ghettos in Veszprém were almost entirely women, the elderly and children. Ghettos across Europe tended to be female dominated, especially prior to the onset of mass deportations, and among young adults.[100] But the overrepresentation of women in Hungarian ghettos like those in Veszprém was particularly marked given the longer history of labour battalion service which became all the more significant in the summer of 1944. The intersections of age and gender are absolutely central to radically different experiences of what we call the Holocaust in Hungary. The name lists drawn up in Veszprém in May and June 1944 reveal a gendered outflow from, and inflow into, the city. Leaving the city were Jewish men for labour battalion service in military camps. Entering the city were Jewish women, children and the elderly from rural communities. It is that process of spatial concentration into another city to the northeast – and the journeying involved in achieving it – that I now turn to consider.

2

Journeying to and from the Ghetto: Receipts from Nyíregyháza

Thinking about Holocaust journeys conjures up images of trains pulling freight cars tightly packed with hundreds of Jews. Trains dominate Raul Hilberg's pioneering account of the implementation of the 'Final Solution of the Jewish Question', frequently travel across the screen in Claude Lanzmann's epic *Shoah* and have entered the postwar imagination as one dominant symbol of what has been seen – perhaps rather mistakenly – as the most modern of crimes.[1] Trains are certainly part of the story of the Holocaust journeys taken by Hungarian Jews. Every few days between mid-May and early July 1944, trains left Hungary, laden with Jews, the majority headed to Auschwitz-Birkenau. Prior to this, local train networks had been used to move Jews to ghettos and entrainment points. As I explore in Chapter 6, a number of amateur and professional photographers made their way to railway stations to record scenes of Jews being loaded into wagons.[2]

But journeys to and from Hungarian ghettos did not only involve railway stations and trains. In some places they involved farmsteads and horse-drawn carts. When he issued the confidential ghetto order on 7 April 1944, Secretary of State in the Interior Ministry László Baky informed local officials not only where Jews should be housed, but also how Jews were to be transported to these new segregated living places. 'Transportation as prisoners' was, Baky wrote, 'to take place by train, or should it prove necessary by horse-drawn coaches ordered by the city or respective municipal authorities'.[3] Whether trains, or horse-drawn carts were used to transport Jews to and from ghettos depended on where in the country you were. In urbanized areas with good rail connections, Jews were transported using Baky's preferred method of mass travel – the train. However, in rural areas there was not the same density of rail connections, and so horse and carts were used for the initial waves of Holocaust journeys.[4]

To give just one example, Aranka Siegal who lived in Beregszász, recalled being

> awakened by strange sounds of movement in our street. We came out onto the porch in our nightshirts to see our street lined with slowly moving wagons and walking refugees – mostly women. We went back inside and quickly dressed ourselves and the children. Mother told Sandor to keep Joli inside while she, Iboya, and I went down to the gate and watched as the carts and wagons, pulled mostly by oxen, with an old horse appearing occasionally, crawled by. In the wagons, heaped high with bundles, rode the infants, the old, and the sick. Hungarian policemen and German soldiers with bayonets fixed to their rifles walked alongside the wagons.[5]

A short time later Siegal was taken to the brickworks ghetto herself, along with her mother and siblings. Like the rural Jews before them, they travelled there by horse drawn cart, 'at a very slow pace', with a driver who looked 'tired and bored'.[6]

My focus here is on Holocaust journeys by horse and cart in Szabolcs county – the neighbouring county to that where Aranka Siegal lived – due to the survival of traces of those journeys around the county seat of Nyíregyháza.[7] Working with lists of expenses incurred in transporting Jews along with orders from a mayoral official, Dr Gönczy, requesting farmstead leaders to supply carts to ghetto camps set up outside Nyíregyháza, I tell stories of mass participation in the events we know as the Holocaust.[8] Horse-drawn carts were a means of transport lacking the efficiency of mass rail travel. It only took seven trains – and their drivers – to transport the more than 20,000 Jews from Szabolcs county to Auschwitz between 15 May and 5 June.[9] But prior to this, concentrating Jews in this rural county necessitated thousands of shorter journeys by horse and cart, driven by hundreds of carters. Here I am interested in uncovering who these men – and women – were, as well as exploring what we can find out about what motivated their participation. But I want to start by focusing not on those driving the carts, but rather on the rural Jews journeying to and from ghettos in hundreds of carts in April, May and June 1944.

TAKING JEWS TO THE GHETTO
(AND THE GHETTO TO THE JEWS)

The story of the rapid spatial concentration of Jews in Szabolcs county began with the decision of the deputy prefect on 13 April 1944, to relocate all the county's Jews into just two cities.[10] Effectively the county was split into two, with Jews from southern and central districts sent to Nyíregyháza, the geographical (as well as political) centre of the county, while Jews from the northern districts were concentrated in the town of Kisvárda. These ghettos were established well before the issuing of national legislation at the end of April, which was the basis for implementing ghettoization in the towns and cities of western Hungary such as Veszprém.[11] The deputy prefect in Szabolcs county responded to an earlier confidential ghetto order issued on 7 April, after a meeting three days earlier in the Ministry of Interior, attended by Interior Ministry officials such as László Baky and László Endre, gendarmerie officers such as László Ferenczy and Győző Tölgyesy, as well as by Adolf Eichmann and other German officials.[12] This national level meeting was followed by a regional meeting, chaired by Endre, held in Munkács on 12 April. Here, the concentration of Jews in Carpatho-Ruthenia and north-eastern Hungary, the area including Szabolcs county, was discussed in the presence of relevant regional officials.[13]

What is striking is how quickly the concentration process was implemented in the locality. On 14 April, the mayor in Nyíregyháza published an order that

Jews were forbidden from leaving the city limits from the morning of 16 April onwards.[14] A week or so later they were prohibited from leaving their apartments from 5 am on 23 April.[15] Simultaneous with this restricting of Nyíregyháza Jews first to the city itself, and subsequently to their apartments, Jews in rural communities were being rounded up, generally in the local community building, and then transported to either Nyíregyháza or Kisvárda.[16] For Jews in Szabolcs county, the noose was tightening. In Nyíregyháza, thousands of Jews from rural communities were placed into the ghetto established in the city, where Jews from the city itself were taken between 23 and 28 April.[17] By 3 May, the central Jewish council was reporting that over 10,000 Jews were gathered in the Nyíregyháza ghetto, a figure made up of 4,120 Jews from the city itself and around 6,600 from the surrounding towns and villages.[18]

The ghetto in Nyíregyháza became so severely overcrowded that makeshift ghetto camps were set up on farms at Varjúlapos, Nyírjes, Simapuszta and Harangod on the outskirts of the city in the second half of April and first half of May.[19] By 5 May, the deputy prefect reported that 15,220 Jews were housed in the ghetto and camps in Nyíregyháza and 7,012 Jews in the Kisvárda ghetto, with 'no Jews in the countryside'.[20] Over the next few days the reported figures changed marginally,[21] with the deputy prefect putting the number of Jews in the ghetto and camps in Nyíregyháza at 16,606 and in the Kisvárda ghetto at 6,932 on 11 May.[22] By this point, deportations had already been discussed, at a meeting held at Munkács on 8 and 9 May, and these commenced on 15 May, when the first train of 3,200 Jews left Nyíregyháza on its way to Kassa, and then on to Auschwitz. Another four trains left Nyíregyháza and two trains left Kisvárda, before the deputy prefect announced, on 5 June, that Szabolcs county was now free of Jews.[23]

While ghettoization involved spatial concentration for all Jews in Szabolcs county, initially it did not involve dislocation for all. For some urban Jews, the ghetto came to them. Nyíregyháza and Kisvárda were home to more than a third of the Jews living in the county and there was a demographic logic behind the deputy prefect's decision to concentrate the county's Jews in these two cities with the largest Jewish populations in the county.[24] Moreover, within Nyíregyháza it was the area of the city traditionally occupied by Jews that was chosen as the site of the ghetto.[25] Concentrating Jews where they already lived was a pragmatic solution to the problems thrown up by ghettoization. Bringing the ghetto to the Jew limited the number and distance of Holocaust journeys, but more significantly for local authorities conscious of non-Jewish opinions, it limited the number of non-Jews living in the ghetto area who were forced to relocate (Chapters 3 and 4).

For the victims, whether the ghetto came to you, or you went to the ghetto – via a series of journeys – was a matter of considerable significance. Interviewing Judit Brody – whose story I tell in the epilogue – I was struck by her reaction when I asked whether her family's experience of remaining where they were when ghettoization was implemented in the capital mattered. Of course it mattered she told me. Staying put meant you had access to 'your own stuff', 'your own food' and a network of existing connections. In short, remaining in your former home meant 'everything'.[26] Something of the privileges of staying put was seen from the other side by a teenager living outside Kállósemjén who was taken with her family to the Nyíreghaza ghetto. According to her,

> Those in the ghetto who had been its tenants all along were able to exercise a social leverage over those of us from the outside. To be able to remain in their homes with the means to sustain life, their food, their clothing, their creature comforts, gave the permanent residents advantages that set them apart from the masses of new arrivals. Besides not having been driven from their homes, they had been spared the marches, the beds of straw, and the mysteries of unknown surroundings during journeys of no discernible purpose.[27]

For this survivor, there were two different groups of Jews in the Nyíregyháza ghetto – urban 'permanent residents' (memorably dubbed by Gottlieb writing of the Pest ghetto, 'the armchair royalty' given that they had managed to hang on to their own furniture)[28] and rural 'new arrivals'. These 'new arrivals', who made up the majority of the 15,000–16,000 Jews gathered in the ghetto and ghetto camps in Nyíregyháza, experienced multiple journeys by horse and cart in the spring of 1944. Ghettoization for them involved dislocation and not just concentration and segregation.

The first Holocaust journeys for Jews living in towns and villages around Nyíregyháza began in the middle of April 1944. It would seem that in general, the practice was that Jews were woken early in the morning, forbidden from leaving their homes, and then over the course of the day gathered in some central point such as the synagogue courtyard. From here, they were taken by cart to the ghetto in Nyíregyháza accompanied by armed gendarmes.[29] However, many of those Jews taken to the ghetto in Nyíregyháza were, because of the overcrowding there, relocated – again by horse-drawn cart – in late April and early May to one of the camps on the outskirts of the city. With the commencement of deportations in mid-May to early June, the flow of journeys for these Jews was reversed, as they were taken by cart from these ghetto camps to the entrainment point at Nyíregyháza railway station.

A survivor, from the town of Ibrány in Dadai felső district, recalled these three separate journeys in the spring and early summer of 1944. She and her family were among the thirty to thirty-five Jewish families in Ibrány taken the twenty-five or so kilometres to the Nyíregyháza ghetto in carts drawn by an assortment of horses, oxen and cattle, accompanied by gendarmes. Upon arrival, she recounts that their cart driver was simply asked which village this 'shipment' had come from, and they were directed to the appropriate area of the ghetto for Jews from their town.[30] Later, her family were transported out of the city ghetto to the makeshift ghetto camp set up in tobacco drying barns at Simapuszta. Again the journey was by cart, but this time horse drawn. Her final journey in Szabolcs county, took place on a 'glorious ... sunny spring day', a welcome change from the cold, wet weather that had marked journeys in open carts at the end of April,[31] when farm carts delivered her and her family on the second of the two transports out of Simapuszta bound for the railway station in Nyíregyháza.[32] Across the course of these three journeys, the number of fellow travellers increased. In the words of another survivor from Szabolcs county, reflecting on the later stages of multiple journeys, 'Now we were 3,000 instead of the 250 who had begun to the walk from the temple in our town.'[33] The sheer numbers of Jews being moved around the county in these three waves of Holocaust journeys meant that a very large number of carters were mobilized to ensure that ghettoization and deportation were swiftly and effectively enacted.

CARTING JEWS AROUND NYÍREGYHÁZA

During the six-week period when the last two sets of journeys referred to by the survivor from Ibrány were carried out, over 2,500 days of horse-drawn cart transport was mobilized to shift Jews around Nyíregyháza.[34] Rather than being spread evenly over the period from late April to early June, there were frenetic peaks of activity. In the first phase of journeys to the ghetto camps set up on farms outside Nyíregyháza, over 1,000 days' worth of cart-drawn transport was used between 23 April and 11 May,[35] focused around a number of particularly busy days. On 2, 3 and 4 May, around 150 carts were in use each day.[36] A couple of days later, on 6 and 7 May, just under 100 carts were being used to transport Jews on both days. A little later, on 10 and 11 May, the number of carts mobilized reached a peak of just under 250 each day.[37] As deportations commenced, there was again considerable demand for carts to transport Jews. It was rural carters who took thousands of Jews to the railway station at Nyíregyháza, from where they were then taken, by train this time, to Auschwitz-Birkenau. The five waves of deportations from Nyíregyháza are reflected in the receipts. On 14 May, just over 50 carts were in action,[38] with just under 200 used on each of the following two days.[39] Between 20 and 22 May, there was another peak of activity.[40] A few days later, on 24, 25 and 26 May, came another wave of transports.[41] The final peaks of activity come on 30 and 31 May, and then again on 4 June, when over 150 carts were mobilized.[42]

These carts had to be driven by someone. Over the course of the six-week period from the end of April to early June, close to 1,000 individual cart owners from more than sixty farmsteads transported Jews to and from the ghetto and ghetto camps. Most of these carters spent on average anywhere between two to four days transporting Jews in late April, May and early June 1944. Ghettoization and deportation was not just something that relatively large numbers of the local population witnessed, but actively participated in and profited from, with individuals paid 6 pengő 40 per cart per day for their services.[43]

The total cost of these multiple journeys was considerable, reaching at least 16,000 pengő, at a time when a one- or two-bedroom apartment in central Budapest cost around 10,000 pengő.[44] This sum was not paid by the local authorities. The costs of transporting Jews were met, as elsewhere, by the Jewish community in what Gábor Kádár and Zoltán Vági dub 'self financing genocide'.[45] However, the Jewish Council in Nyíregyháza put up a fight against demands that they pay these transport costs. On 12 May, they wrote to the mayor asking for exemption from the request that they pay 10,000 pengő into the city account to cover the costs of transporting Jews into the camps established in the outskirts of the city, on the grounds that they were already footing the bill of buying foodstuffs for these camps, transporting these there, and removing rubbish from the camps. Their suggestion was that the costs for transport be covered from the accounts of rural Jewish communities instead of from their own account.[46]

While the total cost of transport was sufficiently steep to mean that the Jewish Council in Nyíregyháza sought to shift the burden of payment elsewhere, the sums paid to individual carters themselves were relatively modest, given that this task was one shared out among close to one thousand people. The most that any individual received appears to have been 153 pengő 60, paid to the aristocrat Count Gyula D. who obviously owned a large number of carts. Even this was not a massive sum, but most were paid considerably less: on average around 20 pengő each. These sums were dwarfed by those being earned, according to the press in Szeged, by 'hyena' hauliers moving Jews and non-Jews in and out of the ghetto area who were reportedly charging double or triple the going rate of 20–30 pengő for a day's labour.[47] Transporting Jews did not make any single individual carter living around Nyíregyháza rich. It brought a little additional cash to these individuals, but the mass participation of rural farm workers cannot be explained primarily in terms of material enrichment, given the low sums involved. For carters living around Nyíregyháza the carrot of payment was less influential than the stick of compulsion wielded by the mayoral official Dr Gönczy who oversaw the whole operation.

In some ways, Gönczy had a problem. Finding 200 or 250 carters with their carts on any one day was no small task, especially in the context of a country at war. Some 150 miles south of Nyíregyháza, the problem of finding both vehicles and people was a matter of concern to the local press in Szeged that advocated mobilizing a workforce of Jewish labour battalion members to move Jews into the city ghetto, given that, they claimed, 'it is impossible to get a day worker these days for reasonable wages'.[48] In Nyíregyháza, Gönczy's solution to the problem of transporting Jews to and from ghettos and ghetto camps was to draw upon the pool of carts and carters in nearby farmsteads. Reading through the orders he issued, it is clear that he simply went through an alphabetical list of local farmsteads and called on each in turn to do their bit. Thus, it was Halmos, Horfát, Jakus, János, Kordova, Kovács and Vajda, Kisteleki and I Rozarét, Kazár and Szeles, Lakatos and Lóczi and I Manda farmsteads that were required to provide carts at 9 am at the ghetto camp at Harangod on 20 May.[49] Also on that same day, the farmsteads of I Manda 2 district, II Manda, Nádasi and Nagylapos were to supply carts to the ghetto camp at Felsősima.[50] Two days later, it was the farmsteads beginning with the letters P through T – Polyák, Róka, Salamon, Sváb, Sipos, Sulyán, Szélső, Szekeres and Tamás – that were to provide carts to Felsősima.[51] Once the bottom of the list was reached, and transport demands still existed, Gönczy returned to the top of the list and began again with the farms starting with the letter A.[52]

Although all farmsteads were called upon in turn to provide carts, the numbers of carts required varied from place to place, presumably based on Gönczy's reckoning of the size of individual farmsteads. Some were called upon to provide only five, most ten or fifteen, and a few twenty, twenty-five or thirty carts. Gönczy did not deal directly with the hundreds of individual carters, but rather with the heads of more than sixty farmsteads. It was left up to these middle-men to deliver the required number of carts and drivers at the right time to the right place. In some cases it would seem that these middle-men simply went down a list of names like Gönczy himself did, in ensuring that orders were met. In the relatively large farmstead of Alsópázsit, the foreman seems to have worked his way down names on a list, calling the first batch one day, then the next another, before returning to the first group again.[53]

But, initially at least, Gönczy did not always get the number of carts that he needed. For example, his request that eleven farms supply anything from ten to thirty carts each (155 in total) at Varjúlapos at 6 o'clock on the morning on 2 May was not met by the majority of farms.[54] Three came up with the goods, but the other eight fell short of target. This appears to have led Gönczy to take stronger action. When he wrote to farmstead leaders requesting carts, on 13 May, he threatened them with 'legal consequences' if they failed to provide carts at the required place and time.[55] This language was used again on 23, 24 and 31 May.[56] On 19 May, Gönczy reminded community leaders that he would hold them 'personally and materially' responsible if they defaulted in providing transport at the right time and the right place.[57]

Broadly speaking, Gönczy's threats appear to have had the desired effect. In comparison to the widespread failure to deliver the goods on 2 May, the picture as the month went on was of an increasing number of farms managing to deliver to target. On 14 May, half of the farms delivered the number of carts ordered to the Nyírjes camp.[58] On 20 May, eight out of ten farms delivered either the required number or just above, to Harangod camp.[59] On 22 May, eleven of twelve farms provided the carts ordered, or more, to Felsősima camp, with a similar picture at the same camp two days later, when the majority of farms appear to have delivered, a couple of exceptions aside.[60] On 26 May and 4 June, it seems that only small numbers of farms were failing to provide the required quantity of carts to Nyírjes camp, and those that did not supply what Gönczy requested included a number of repeat offenders.[61] Reading through the orders and receipts it is clear that the majority of farmsteads fell into line and delivered the numbers of carts requested as the weeks went on.

THE RELUCTANT FARMSTEAD OF KORDOVA, THE DISAPPEARANCE OF JÁNOS M. AND STORIES OF REFUSAL FROM I MANDA AND BUNDÁS

However, there were a small number of farms that continued, consistently, to fail to deliver what Gönczy asked for. Out of the more than sixty farmsteads called upon to provide carts, six – Alsósima, Kordova, Lakatos, I Manda 2nd district, II Manda and Marko – all failed to come up with the goods, not just once, but again and again.[62] The farmstead of Kordova provided only eight of the ten carts requested on 2 May.[63] Just over two weeks later, it was Kordova's turn again. Their name had come back round. This time, perhaps following the failure to provide ten carts earlier on in the month, the number of carts requested was halved. Only five carts were called for, but in the event just three carters turned up at Harangod camp at 9 o'clock on the morning of 20 May.[64] All three, András T., Pál T. and András J., had transported Jews for three days at the beginning of the month. They had done this job before, and returned to do it again. But none of the other five men who had worked alongside them at Varjúlapos camp on 2 May turned up. Their absence is surprising given that Gönczy had made farmstead leaders 'personally and materially' responsible if they did not deliver. It would seem that this threat was not sufficient to ensure compliance on the part of this farmstead leader – as well as a small number of others – bucking the broader trend towards increasing provision of exactly what was asked for.

A similar picture of non-compliance can be seen within individual farmsteads, where small numbers refused to turn up for work. Some individuals quickly withdrew after working for just one day and did not return to transport Jews when their farmstead again provided carts.[65] An example comes from Lakatos farmstead which provided carts on the 2, 3, 4 and 15 May and then again on the 4 June. On the first day, János M. turned up for work. However, he disappears from the record after this point, not providing transport again unlike the other eleven carters who accompanied him that first morning.[66] All of them returned again to transport Jews, which appears to be the norm across the paperwork. While János M.'s story of non-return is one that comes from reading between the lines, a few individuals were explicitly named and shamed by their farmstead leaders as refusing to turn up to transport Jews. The farmstead of I Manda had been asked to provide ten carts on 2 May; however, only nine carters showed up because one – Mrs József R. – refused to carry out the assigned work. The next day the number of carters dropped to just eight, as a result of János K.'s refusal to return for this work.[67] A little over two weeks later, farmers from I Manda were once again called upon to transport Jews. By this point, Gönczy was threatening consequences on farmstead leaders who failed to deliver the required number of carts. While János K., who had earlier refused, did turn up to transport Jews on 20 and 21 May, and then again on 4 June, Mrs József R. did not.[68] From her continued non-appearance it would seem that local pressure was not insurmountable. Although farmsteads in Hungary in 1944 should be contextualized within the continuation of what amounted to almost quasi-feudal relationships in a country where land reform had never been fully implemented, we should not cast those power relations in overly monolithic terms.[69] For refuseniks like Mrs József R., the power of the foreman was not total.

Overall, the number of individuals who refused to turn up to transport Jews are a tiny fraction – less than 1 per cent – of the close to 1,000 men and women who complied with Gönczy's orders mediated through their farmstead leader.[70] Most of those who did refuse were, like János M., individuals who turned up once, but then refused to turn up again having found out what the work entailed. A smaller number were people like Mrs József R. who refused, never having carried out the task. Examples of both can be found at the farmstead of Bundás. There, fourteen carters turned up to transport Jews on 10 May. However, when Gönczy requested twenty carts on 15 May, two refused and one absented herself on the grounds that her horse was sick.[71] One of those who refused – Mrs József H. – had previously transported Jews a few days earlier on 10 and 11 May. It was obviously a job she did not want to do again. But joining her in refusing to turn up on this occasion was another woman, Mrs János K., who had no personal experience of transporting Jews herself.[72] Her refusal suggests that what happened on 10 and 11 May had been talked about in this small community. Stories must have circulated of just what such transporting entailed, and these were obviously enough to put her off.

The presence of Mrs József R. from I Manda and Mrs József H. and Mrs János K. from Bundás among those refusing to turn up at the ghetto camps on the outskirts of Nyíregyháza reflects the marked over-representation of women among the small number of carters who refused to transport Jews. Women made up a minority – less than 6 per cent – of the carters paid for transporting Jews around Nyíregyháza, but they made up half of the carters explicitly recorded in the accounts as refusing to transport Jews, or providing an excuse for their non-compliance.[73] It would seem that women were more likely than men to refuse to carry out mayoral – and farmstead leaders' – orders. That is not to say that all women refused. Far from it. But as a proportion, more women refused than men. But more significant I think than the over representation of women amongst those refusing to provide carts to transport Jews is another gendered story. In the main, women were not asked to do this job.

CARTING JEWS AS GENDERED WORK

Gönczy appears to have been unconcerned about whether it was men or women who turned up with their carts to the makeshift ghetto camps on the outskirts of Nyíregyháza. He cared only about the number of carts rather than the gender of their drivers. This contrasted with the attitude of the mayor of Nyíregyháza when he had requested help in registering Jews as ghettoization got underway in the city.[74] On 22 April he wrote to the principals of nine schools in the city, asking them to send teachers and trainee teachers who were not tied up with examinations to a meeting to be held that evening in the Council House. There they would receive orders for registering Jews from the city over the following few days. In the letter, he stressed that only male teachers should be sent. Registering Jews was clearly seen by him as men's work.

Gönczy made no such distinction. Carting Jews around Nyíregyháza was not considered by him to be men's work. But it seems that most of the farm managers who received his requests thought otherwise. It was these farm managers who made decisions about who supplied and drove the carts ordered by Gönczy. Six out of ten of them never called upon women in their community, and while four out of ten did not discount women from involvement in transporting Jews, in none of these places did women make up anything close to a majority.[75] Where women were called upon, it tended to be one or two women, with just a few places where the numbers crept up to three or four. The one exception was Bundás, where eight women transported Jews, alongside fifteen men.[76] This single farmstead was one place where twice as many women participated in transporting Jews as any other community in the vicinity of Nyíregyháza.

On 10 May, five women from Bundás – Mrs András G., Mrs Mihály Cs., Mrs József H., Mrs András Cs. and Julia N. – supplied carts alongside nine men.[77] On 15 May, the foreman in this community called upon six women – and fourteen men – to provide transport.[78] He did so knowing the full nature of the job required. It is clear that these women were not simply making up the numbers in a tiny community. Bundás was somewhere with over fifty dwellings, and a place large enough to mean that when it came to working through his alphabetical list, Dr Gönczy reckoned upon it providing twenty carts.[79] Here was a place – an exceptional place – where the foreman clearly did not see transporting Jews as solely men's work, but something that women carters in the community were to participate in.

When it came to women carters in Bundás, they were more divided over whether they saw this job as something they wished to do. As I have already noted, Mrs József H. and Mrs János K. refused to transport Jews on 15 and 16 May, and another woman excused her absence on the grounds of a sick horse. Mrs János K., did not turn up on the basis of the stories circulating in the farmstead. But these stories were clearly not enough to put off Mrs András Sz. and Mrs Mihály M. who both provided carts on 15 and 16 May for the first time. Nor did Julia N.'s own experience of transporting Jews a few days earlier put her off providing transport for another two days. However, for one woman that earlier experience was not one to be repeated on 15 and 16 May. While Mrs Mihály Cs. had worked for two days earlier on in the month, on 15 and 16 May, it was her husband, Mihály Cs., rather than her who turned up to transport Jews.[80] She did not refuse, but it seems that she passed this job over to her husband. Perhaps we should not read too much into this. In the farmstead of Polyák, husbands and wives appear to have shared transport duties between themselves as well.[81] But this may point to decisions about whether this was men's work or women's work being ultimately made within the domestic space of the home.

Bundás was exceptional in its policy of relative equality of opportunity. Its exceptionality is a little surprising given that large numbers of non-Jewish adult males were serving in the military. The demographics of female dominated Jewish populations that I have examined in Veszprém are ones that could be replicated amongst the non-Jewish population. In that context, women played an increasingly important role, as did adolescent boys and girls and older men, in farm work. It was not farm work that Gönczy required, but country carts – the normal day-to-day run around vehicles in use throughout rural Hungary – and their drivers. This was a driving job first and foremost which could be undertaken by anyone from adolescents upwards, whether male or female. But it was a particular kind of driving job given the passengers and the destinations. It would be impossible for local farmers, living so close to these makeshift ghetto camps where conditions were so terrible, not to know at least something of what these places were like. Certainly once they had been there for the first time, this would be the case.

Perhaps this provides the backdrop to the decisions being made, not by Gönczy, but within localities – including the domestic space of individual homes – that transporting Jews to and from ghetto camps was men's work. These decisions may have been influenced by longer standing assumptions about gendered work. But I wonder if they also reflected a certain disquiet about this activity. Transporting Jews was a job to be done, but it was being seen in the locality as a job to be undertaken in the main by men. However, this is not to suggest that it was only Hungarian men who participated in event we know as the Holocaust. Hungarian women were being mobilized, but in smaller numbers and at times for specific tasks. One of these was to undertake body searches of Hungarian Jewish women, as the state sought to expropriate every last piece of Jewish wealth. In Nyíregyháza, the police wrote to the Mayor on 24 April requesting that at least five or six women, preferably midwives, be provided in order to undertake intimate body searches on Jewish women arriving in the city ghetto.[82] The numbers of women needed for such work was even greater in the much larger city of Szeged, where ten midwives and ten nurses worked for ten days undertaking 'the necessary medical examination, or rather body searches' alongside three male doctors.[83] For this, they were paid 20 pengő per day. The doctors earned ten times that sum – 200 pengő per day. This sum was clearly on the high side, but was seen by local officials as 'absolutely necessary' given that these individuals 'performed such a responsible and tiring job without any rest,' and worked long days from 5 am until 'late at night'.[84] Carters in Szabolcs county were clearly not performing 'such a responsible and tiring job' and were to be compensated at a far lower rate.

The involvement of hundreds of cart owners in transporting Jews around the county is not first and foremost a story of material enrichment. Rather, it is primarily a story of the way in which hundreds of rural carters were effectively mobilized to move thousands of rural Jews from place to place as concentration and deportation were rapidly implemented. There was clearly a degree of compulsion, as Gönczy's threats for non-compliance reveal. This seems to have been the case outside of Hungary, with Patrick Desbois noting the use of carts 'driven by requisitioned peasants' to take Jews from villages to killing sites in Novozlatopol.[85] However, despite the evidence of a degree of compulsion, there was still some room for manoeuvre. Small numbers of individuals and farmsteads were reluctant to transport Jews. But the overall picture is one of a remarkable degree of complicity. Farmsteads, in the main, provided the numbers of carts they were asked to. Individual carters, in the main, turned up again and again to transport Jews. It would seem that some of these carters sought to help the Jews they transported. In the community of Nagykálló, food was hidden by carters and passed on to their passengers.[86] But despite offering such assistance, carters in a place like Nagykálló were still engaged in facilitating the Holocaust journeys so central to concentrating and deporting Szabolcs county Jews.

In September, the chief constable in Nagykálló submitted his half-yearly report to the deputy prefect of Szabolcs county. On the second line of his report, which outlined the major events that had taken place during the first half of the year, he reported that 'the collecting and removal of the Jews happened peacefully without disturbances'.[87] This has something of the ring of a stock phrase about it, echoed in Ferenczy's reports (see Chapter 7). However, the brevity with which the chief constable dealt with this matter is striking. From its placement high up his report, it is clear that the concentration and deportation of Jews in this district was the major event in the first half of 1944. But it was not something he dwelt upon at length. His brief reporting suggests that this major event took place with surprisingly few problems. That this was the case, owed at least something to carters living in farming communities around Nyíregyháza who transported Jews around Szabolcs county. These ordinary Hungarians – small numbers of women, in the main men – played their part in ensuring that the concentration and deportation of Szabolcs county Jews was, in the mind of this local official, such a straightforward event.

However, for one of those farmers at least, carting Jews around Szabolcs county had been more of a problem. In mid-May, József R. wrote to the mayor with a request for compensation. He was one of the many farmworkers mobilized to transport Jews on 25 and 26 April. The weather, he reported to the mayor, had been atrocious. On both days it was cold and wet. His concern was not with the impact of the weather on his passengers, but his pregnant horse that had caught colic and died on the evening of 26 April. He reckoned the value of the horse to be around 3,000 pengő, and assumed that it was only fair that someone pay him for his loss. That someone was, he suggested, the Jews. Drawing upon a widely used phrase in 1944, he wrote to the mayor asking for compensation 'from the Jewish wealth'.[88] József R. was someone who not only participated in one aspect of the events we term the Holocaust, but was also personally impacted by these. He was far from alone. Nowhere was this more the case than in urban areas where ghettoization was seen as too close for comfort. Non-Jewish city dwellers were – broadly speaking – not anti-ghettoization *per se*, but they did not want it in their backyard. Ghettoization was being seen as an opportunity for personal enrichment – to use József R.'s phrase – 'from the Jewish wealth'.[89] But it was also being seen as a problem that almost everyone appears to have had an opinion about.

3

Debating the Ghetto: Newspapers from Szeged

On 7 June, the deputy mayor in Szeged – a large university city in the south of the country – wrote to the editors of three local newspapers asking them to publish an announcement the following day.[1] This informed the newspaper-reading public in the city that Jews could only shop between 11 am and 1 pm, with those caught shopping outside of this two-hour window, as well as the shopkeepers serving them, liable to prosecution. As elsewhere, newspapers played an important function in disseminating national and local anti-Jewish measures to the local population.[2] In the case of this specific announcement, the line of command was very much from the top down. Jewish access to shops and markets had been discussed by the Council of Ministers – the Hungarian cabinet – on 1 June, when the Minister of Trade and Transport Affairs had complained that shopping provided space for Jews and non-Jews separated by ghetto walls to come into contact with each other for extended periods of time, opening up opportunities for unrest and rumours to spread. In order to combat this, it was decided to limit the time period that Jews could shop to two hours a day, leaving local authorities to decide which two hour window that would be.[3] The ministerial decree, published on 4 June, was flagged to the Mayor in Szeged on 7 June by county officials.[4] His decision to permit shopping by Jews only between 11 am to 1 pm was then made public in the local press. You could not find a clearer example of the top-down implementation of an anti-Jewish measure, with the mayor following national and regional orders and the press simply reporting this.

However, even in the case of this particular measure the situation was more complex than this flurry of paperwork from early June would suggest. In Szeged, the local authorities had already seized the initiative and restricted Jewish shopping hours a month earlier. On 8 May, the Deputy Chief of Police stipulated that Jews in Szeged were only permitted to shop for one hour each day, between 10 and 11 in the morning.[5] This was outlined in the press the following day,[6] and two weeks later *Szegedi Új Nemzedék* reported the arrest of a forty-seven-year-old Jewish man who tried to buy a packet of cigarettes at 9.30 in the morning.[7] Similar restrictions to Jewish shopping hours can be seen in other Hungarian cities during May 1944.[8] All were implemented prior to, and without, national legislation to back them up. It is clear that in a place like Szeged, local officials were taking initiative in implementing anti-Jewish measures, something applauded by national government officials. On 3 May, *Szegedi Új Nemzedék* reported on the recent visit of Secretary of State in the Interior Minister, László Endre, to Szeged on an inspection tour of sorts to check on progress in implementing anti-Jewish measures by local authorities.

Endre was reported as being 'pleased to understand that Szeged is ahead of other country towns in eliminating Jews from communal life' and to learn of the 'initiative' being taken by the municipal authorities.[9] This picture of local initiative is one that historians have long recognized across Hungary.[10]

But my focus here is not primarily on initiative being taken in the locality by municipal authorities, but rather the initiative taken by the local press.[11] A newspaper like the Catholic-influenced *Szegedi Új Nemzedék*[12] did more than simply report anti-Jewish measures and dutifully publish official pronouncements. This paper also publicized the ideas of political parties on the extreme Right that were outside the governing party – for example reporting and endorsing fascist Arrow Cross Party proposals[13] – provided a forum for individuals' views in its 'the voice of our readers' column and wholeheartedly threw itself into debates over what to do with the city's Jews. This was nowhere more the case than with plans for the Szeged ghetto. Here the paper sought to influence events by offering its own and other's solutions, which brought it into conflict with local officials.

Reading through *Szegedi Új Nemzedék* as ghettoization was planned and implemented in the city, it is clear that this was not a secretive measure, but something that was widely reported and discussed.[14] Ghetto plans in Szeged may not always have been the leading story, but the sheer number of column inches point to it being very much newsworthy in May 1944. In this chapter I explore what the press was saying about ghettoization as it was planned and implemented. While the pages of *Szegedi Új Nemzedék* do not give us direct access to the slippery concept of public opinion, they do provide an opportunity to explore how ghettoization was imagined by individuals other than simply city officials implementing anti-Jewish policy on the ground (Chapter 4). But before I focus on the counter-voice offered by the paper to municipal ghetto plans in mid-May, I begin with the ways in which *Szegedi Új Nemzedék* played a far more supportive role in reporting and policing earlier anti-Jewish measures.

REPORTING AND POLICING THE MARKING OF JEWS WITH YELLOW STARS

The national legislation ordering all Jews over the age of six to wear a canary-yellow six-pointed star on the left side of their outer clothing from 5 April onwards,[15] was applauded by *Szegedi Új Nemzedék*, as it was by other rightist papers.[16] On 6 April, it published a letter from a 'Christian Hungarian refugee from Southern Translyvania', which countered a tendency among some 'Christian Hungarians' to feel sympathy for Jews in Szeged now forced to wear a yellow star through a mixture of rational argument – the Star of David was to Judaism what the cross was to Christianity and therefore not a shameful symbol – and outright antisemitic attack on Jews as the enemy of the Hungarian nation and therefore undeserving of sympathy.[17] A little under a week later, the paper praised the recently introduced legislation in a full-page article that offered the chance for an outpouring of antisemitic rhetoric.[18] In part it was a situation report of the way in which the streets of Szeged had changed in the preceding week from an initial absence of Jews on the streets, to a scene where yellow stars had 'blossomed', a chance to praise the 'wisdom' of the framers of this legislation and an opportunity to urge the speedy prosecution of Jews who sought to evade the decree. But this was also seized upon as a moment to launch an antisemitic attack on Szeged's Jews. Jewish fears that the yellow star only now made their Jewishness visible were dismissed as a naïve belief in the possibilities of emancipation and assimilation. In language revealing deeply held views of the Jew as a racial 'Other', the paper suggested that these misguided Jews should take a good look in the mirror and realize that their Jewishness was all too visible: their 'Semitic faces, the characteristic look of their eyes, their sing-song voices and rocking gait' gave their 'race' away like 'the smell of a negro'.[19] Marking Jews with a yellow star was not interpreted as distinguishing who was Jewish, but rather taken to be an interim measure to 'separate' Jews from 'Christian Hungarian society' prior to 'the Jewish question being finally settled with us and in the other European countries'. That there was a 'Jewish question' requiring action was obvious to *Szegedi Új Nemzedék*.[20]

In its reporting of the scene on Szeged's streets now that Jews were marked with a yellow star, the language of physical, racial difference was combined with assertions of moral differences between Jews and 'Christian Hungarians'. The paper contrasted what it claimed was the dignified response of Hungarians over the last few days, with that of Jews who had either flamboyantly sported expensive silk stars as fashion items, or tried to dodge the regulations by covering up the yellow star with scarves, briefcases and handbags, or refusing to wear it claiming for themselves exemption. However, all attempts at evasion were seen to be doomed to failure, with *Szegedi Új Nemzedék* enthusiastically endorsing the punishment of those caught not wearing the yellow star. Three days after publishing this initial page-length article applauding this legislation, *Szegedi Új Nemzedék* reported that the first group of Jews from the city had been fined for failing to wear the yellow star, publishing their names, addresses and the size of their fine, and pointing out that any further attempt to evade the law would result not in a further fine, but internment.[21] In providing its readers with the names and addresses of the six Jews who had been arrested and fined, there was an invitation to a more public policing of these individuals whose next punishment would be transfer to an internment camp. Their very public naming and shaming meant that Péter Sz., Jenő K. and his wife, Dr Sándor W., Ferenc W. and Sándor Sz. were now under the surveillance of more than simply the city police.

Szegedi Új Nemzedék continued to urge its readers to play an active role in policing the wearing of the yellow star. On 30 April, it reminded them that all Hungarians were duty bound to ensure that anti-Jewish laws were being adhered to. In a lengthy article, the paper sought to educate its readers on who should be wearing the yellow star, and who was exempt from doing so.[22] Delving into a series of clauses within anti-Jewish legislation was not simply reporting the various categories of exemption. Rather it was self-consciously offered as the basis for a more effective policing of these laws by the population at large. Anti-Jewish measures were not simply something that the Hungarian government was doing, but were a far more broadly shared fight against the Jewish enemy which the paper wholeheartedly threw itself into and urged its readers to do likewise. This was nowhere more the case than with the physical separation of Jews, which the marking with the yellow star prefigured.

REPORTING AND CONTESTING THE SZEGED GHETTO

Initially the paper seemed happy to leave ghettoization to local and national officials. At the end of April it simply reported that plans were being drawn up in the City Hall to create a ghetto in an as yet unspecified part of the city within eight days.[23] A few days later, it referenced the visit of Endre who was touring towns and cities across the country to inspect the ghettoization process. He had, the paper noted, visited a number of sites in the city which were being considered as potential ghetto locations.[24] On 3 May, the paper returned to Endre's visit, reporting that he was in broad agreement with the ghetto plans being developed in private by mayoral officials. The precise whereabouts of the ghetto was reported to be a matter of considerable debate among the city's Jews, but it was also clearly of concern to the paper, which took its first tentative steps in highlighting some issues that it felt needed consideration.[25]

By 5 May, *Szegedi Új Nemzedék* was reporting that ghettoization was a growing source of concern to the city's non-Jewish population, having already received plenty of 'in large part legitimate and well-founded' complaints from readers about rumours over the likely location of the ghetto. However, at this stage the line taken by the paper was to reassure its readers of the commitment of the local authorities to implement ghettoization with an eye to safeguarding 'Christian and Hungarian interests' and urge them to take a long-term view. This was, the paper announced, a historic moment:

> Our most feared internal enemies have now been fully cornered. So we must not bemoan and complain about certain regulations that ultimately uphold Hungarian interests. The best opportunity is here to gather our opponents into a closed, well-demarcated place. We need self-discipline, and if needs be a little self-denial or discomfort, in order to achieve our great goals …[26]

On 3 May, *Szegedi Új Nemzedék* had confidently announced that details of the ghetto would be decided by Saturday 6 May.[27] However, Saturday came and went without a final decision. In the week that followed, ghettoization was an unresolved and increasingly contentious issue in Szeged. *Szegedi Új Nemzedék*'s earlier calls for 'self discipline' on the part of the non-Jewish population of the city went unheeded. According to a newspaper in a nearby city, 'tumultuous scenes' were taking place in Szeged over 'the plans for the ghetto' to be located in 'the most finely built district' of the city, with a public meeting held by the mayor to discuss the matter reportedly cleared by police when it descended into uproar.[28] *Szegedi Új Nemzedék* no longer exercised the restraint urged on its readers a few days earlier. It waded into the very public debate over the nature and location of the ghetto in the city.[29]

On 7 May, *Szegedi Új Nemzedék* reported that the Party of Hungarian Renewal (*Magyar Megújulás Pártja*) was collecting signatures for a petition opposing the plans emerging from the City Hall to locate the ghetto in the heart of Szeged. According to the paper, the Party planned to go over the heads of the local authorities and appeal directly to the Interior Minister.[30] The Party of Hungarian Renewal had been formed in October 1940, after a group of rightist members of the governing Hungarian Life Party (*Magyar Élet Pártja*) had seceded under the leadership of Béla Imrédy. The new party they formed was pro-Nazi and called for the settling of the 'Jewish question' which they primarily interpreted in economic terms. In the aftermath of the Nazi occupation, three members of the Party took cabinet posts, including the post of Deputy Prime minister and Interior Minister, and were wholeheartedly supportive of the anti-Jewish legislation introduced in the spring of 1944.[31] Thus, in threatening to go over the heads of the local authorities in Szeged and appeal directly to the Interior Minister, the Party was threatening to go to their own man, who they assumed would offer them a sympathetic hearing.

In the days following 7 May, *Szegedi Új Nemzedék* wholeheartedly threw in its lot with the Party of Hungarian Renewal, supporting and publicizing their proposals that the ghetto be located on the outskirts of Szeged rather than in the city centre. For both the Party and the paper, placing the ghetto in the heart of the city was deeply problematic. It was claimed that it would negatively impact non-Jews living in the heart of the city. According to the paper, an estimated 3,600 'Christians', including 100 families who owned their properties, would be forced to leave their homes compared to a smaller number – 3,200 – of Jews. This simply did not seem fair. But their opposition revolved around a bigger fear that a city centre ghetto would not just negatively effect several thousand non-Jews who lived there, but the entire city, given that it would 'completely ruin' Szeged and create problems in accessing the central market square. Alongside these concerns over the impact of ghettoization on the non-Jewish population of the city, the paper was quick to point out an additional problem with mayoral plans. Bringing the ghetto to the Jews, by choosing a part of the city where 3,800 Jews currently lived was seen to be a big mistake because it would offer ample opportunities for those Jews to hide their valuables.[32]

The paper clearly saw ghettoization as a measure that had an economic dimension to it, and was more than simply about separating out Jews from non-Jews. Here they shared the understanding of ghettoization as expropriation central to Ferenczy's reporting of the concentration process to his superiors in the Interior Ministry (Chapter 7). As with Ferenczy, underneath such thinking lay an assumption that Jews formed a wealthy elite, who would be asset-stripped as they were placed into ghettos. Back on 3 May, when the paper had reported on Endre's visit to Szeged, they had informed readers that Jews would 'naturally take their personal property necessary for everyday life with them' to the ghetto, but not luxury items or comfortable furnishings since they would not live in 'unnecessary luxury' in their new living places.[33] Yet this widely shared goal of stripping Jews of their personal property was seen as threatened by mayoral plans to bring the ghetto to the Jews. Moreover, it was simply incomprehensible to *Szegedi Új Nemzedék* that the local authorities were planning a ghetto in the heart of the city, when 'Christian Hungarians' were living in poor housing on the outskirts. Ghettoization was seen as the once-in-a-lifetime opportunity to solve a long standing housing problem in the city, which the city authorities appeared to be about to miss.[34]

   Szegedi Új Nemzedék lobbied for Jews to be removed to the outskirts of the city, where they could live life at the periphery, separate from the non-Jewish population, out of sight and out of mind. On 7 May, two major options were being offered by the paper. One was to place Jews in the outlying settlements of Somogyi-telep (settlement), Újsomogyi-telep, Aigner-telep, Kecskés-telep and Klebelsberg-telep, which were currently occupied by non-Jews. The other was to create a purpose-built barracks ghetto outside of Szeged. Arguing the case for both brought the paper into conflict with the city authorities. However, far from backing down the paper responded vigorously and in considerable detail to the deputy mayor's dismissal of their two plans for out-of-town ghettos as impractical.

   Responding to his rejection of using the five settlements on the outskirts of the city on the grounds that moving the 10,000 non-Jews currently living there was impossible, the paper pointed out that if only the 500–600 houses of Aigner-telep, Kecskés-telep and Klebelsberg-telep were used to house the 7,000 Jews requiring accommodation, then this would mean that the 8,000 non-Jews living at Somogyi-telep and Újsomogyi-telep could remain in their homes.[35] But what the paper had not, perhaps, reckoned on, was opposition from its own readers. On 11 May, it published a letter to the editor from the management of the Citizen's Club at Klebelsberg-telep. They portrayed their home as nothing less than a 'paradise' of family houses surrounded by small vineyards and orchards, where the 'industrious' inhabitants of the settlement had, 'established by their scarce money a nice little open-air bath on the banks of the Tisza, so as to offer an amusement park and sports place for their children'. From the perspective of these residents, siting a ghetto here would amount to 'rewarding' Jews and 'punishing' non-Jews who would be forced to leave their own 'healthy, cosy' homes for the 'infested and unhealthy' Jewish houses in the centre of the city.[36]

   Rather than seeing ghettoization as an opportunity for upward mobility on the part of non-Jews in the city as *Szegedi Új Nemzedék* did, these inhabitants saw ghettoization as something to be personally avoided. Underlying this reticence was another way of viewing Jewish properties and Jews. They saw Jewish houses not as large, centrally located properties to be sought after, but 'infested' properties to be avoided like the plague, and perceived Jews not so much as a privileged social and economic elite that *Szegedi Új Nemzedék* articulated, but rather as dirty and diseased. Of course, it may simply have been the case that the non-Jews living in Klebelsberg-telep wanted to stay put and would argue anything in support of their case. According to the deputy mayor, speaking at a public meeting, the reticence of these 'people of modest means' to leave their homes was driven by a refusal to exchange their garden houses for large, centrally located apartments with far higher rents.[37] This may well have been a decisive factor, but in arguing their case, non-Jews living in Klebelseberg-telep adopted a stereotype of the dirty and polluting Jew, which was something that *Szegedi Új Nemzedék* itself was to focus upon a few weeks later.

In the end the idea of relocating the city's Jews to settlements on the outskirts of the city was not pursued much further by the paper. Instead, it was the Party of Hungarian Renewal plan to create a purpose-built barracks ghetto that the paper seized upon and ran with. These ideas were aired by Dr László L., the chairman of the Szeged branch of the Party of Hungarian Renewal at a public meeting held in the city to discuss ghetto plans, attended by 4,000–5,000 people that dissolved into chaos. This meeting was thoroughly reported by the Hódmezővásárhely paper *NépÚjság*, which clearly had half an eye on what was being done about ghettoization in neighbouring cities.[38] However, as was the case with plans to make use of settlements on the outskirts of the city, these plans were dismissed by city officials on practical grounds: this time the lack of the necessary materials to construct a purpose-built ghetto.

In the face of opposition from City Hall, *Szegedi Új Nemzedék* leapt to defend the practicalities of these plans, going into considerable detail in order to convince its readers – and municipal officials – of the ready availability of materials. The paper had done its sums, and offered what was in effect a shopping list for a city embarking on building an out of town ghetto to house 7,000 Jews. This would require 4.5 million sun-dried adobe bricks and 1 million bricks at a cost of 400,000 pengő; 1 million kilograms of sand at a cost of 40,000 pengő; 10,000 kilograms of lime at a cost of 15,000 pengő; 3,600 roof beams, 10 cubic metres of roof timbers and 38 cubic metres of wooden lining for the ceilings, planks for building fences 2 metres high and 1,570 metres long, and 450 cubic metres of wooden posts at a cost of 450,000 pengő; 1,700 windows, 570 external doors and 1,130 internal doors at a cost of 200,000 pengő; 150 lavatories, 1,750 chimneys and sufficient thatch and reeds to roof the barracks.[39]

The sheer quantity of materials and cost of a purpose-built ghetto – the very thing that reportedly put the deputy mayor off the idea – was seen as far from insurmountable. Wooden beams and planks were available at a number of sites across the city. Seizing the opportunity to take a swipe at what the paper saw as an earlier misconceived plan of the municipal authorities, they pointed out that the large recreational structure at the Fehértó fishing lake was a white elephant that remained unused and the wood could be usefully recycled for constructing the ghetto. The local branch of the Party of Hungarian Renewal had reportedly identified some 40,000 bricks owned by Jews along with planks, nails and tar paper, but if these supplies proved insufficient, *Szegedi Új Nemzedék* reminded its readers that sun-dried bricks could be made cheaply and thatch could be found for roofing. If adobe houses were acceptable for Hungarian peasants to live in, then they were also perfectly acceptable for Szeged's Jews.[40] Cinders were readily available for making roads, saplings could be taken from the nursery owned by H. – a Jewish gardener – and if push came to shove, then the planned brick foundations for the barracks could be dispensed with entirely. Moreover, the paper suggested that voluntary contributions would be forthcoming from the non-Jewish population of the city. Ghettoization in part was to be achieved through the beneficence of a population that was seen to be eager to separate themselves from the Jewish population in Szeged.[41]

The estimated total cost of the project – around 1.5 million pengő to cover the materials, construction costs, haulage, administration and costs of digging wells – was reckoned to be around a year's worth of rents of the Jewish apartments that would be emptied out as a result of ghettoization. Jewish money was to finance the ghetto and Jewish labour was to build it. The paper argued that 1,500 Jews fit for suitable labour, helped by Jewish women and adolescents, could make the adobe bricks, cut the reeds and build the barracks and fences under the watchful eye of the Hungarian Army or the German *Organisation Todt*. With the mass mobilization of Jewish labour, it reckoned that the work could be achieved in five or six weeks. As an incentive to ensure 'proper work discipline' they suggested that Jews be informed that they would move into the barracks after six weeks regardless of whether they were ready or not. Jews were to build their ghetto with their own hands, finance it with the rents from their confiscated apartments, and utilize materials confiscated from Jews.[42] This was envisioned to be the epitome of self-financing genocide.

As well as outlining the practicalities of such a solution to the ghetto question, these articles offer a sense of how ghettoization was being imagined outside city hall. *Szegedi Új Nemzedék* visualized the ghetto to be a self-contained Jewish settlement on the outskirts made up of 150 wooden barracks on a fenced site between twenty-eight and thirty acres in size. Constructed around a central square, the ghetto camp would be made up of 144 barracks in which 7,000 Jews would live. Each barracks – fifty metres long, 4.5 metres wide (225 square metres) and three metres high – was to be broken down into eight single-room flats, with four shared kitchens. Within an individual barracks block, forty-eight Jews were to be housed, with six people in each room. This was a self-conscious policy of overcrowding. In 1893, the city authorities in Budapest had recognized a figure of more than four persons to a room as 'unhygienic overcrowding'.[43] Half a century later, *Szegedi Új Nemzedék* was putting forward a proposal that a single room was sufficient space to house six Jews. Individual barracks were to be spaced twelve metres apart, but within those barracks, accommodation was severely restricted. Another six barracks were set aside as a synagogue, elementary school, clinic, isolation hospital, bath house and municipal building. These fitted with the earlier assumptions of the paper that there be provision for health care – including for dealing with epidemics – and religious worship within the ghetto.[44] The ghetto was imagined as a self-governing, enclosed community established on the edge of the city.

It was not only in Szeged that alternative ghetto plans were being offered to the local authorities.[45] A parallel set of debates can be seen in the nearby town of Hódmezővásárhely, explaining why the local paper there followed developments in Szeged with considerable interest. The similarities between debates in Szeged and Hódmezővásárhely are marked. In both places the local authorities planned to site the ghetto in the vicinity of the synagogue in the central urban area where Jews had traditionally lived. However, these plans were countered with alternative suggestions that Jews should be removed to the outskirts, and placed in either poor quality residential properties or non-residential buildings. The equivalent in Hódmezővásárhely to Klebelseberg-telep was workers' houses on Iszák utca. The equivalent to purpose-built barracks were plans to place Jews in brickworks.[46] In both places, popular opinion was portrayed by the respective press as favouring the removal of Jews from the city to its outskirts, prior to, at some unknown later stage, according to *NépÚjság*, the expulsion of Jews from the country and not only the city.[47] The precise timescale was unclear. According to the editor in chief of *NépÚjság*, János Szathmáry, no one knew whether the ghetto was a temporary or permanent measure. But regardless of whether it was one or the other, he was still against plans to house Jews in the traditional Jewish quarter in the centre of the town. If a temporary measure, he argued that there was no point forcing hundreds of non-Jews to relocate. If a permanent measure, he suggested that resettling Jews in the centre of the town made no sense.[48]

Ultimately the stand-off of sorts in Szeged between the Party of Hungarian Renewal and *Szegedi Új Nemzedék* and the local authorities came to a resolution. The Party of Hungarian Renewal met with the new prefect of the county and Party of Hungarian Renewal member (and therefore very much their man), Aladár Magyary-Kossa, to discuss the question of ghettoization on 10 May, the day that the fullest iteration of plans for a barracks ghetto outside Szeged was published.[49] The result of their meeting was a decision to postpone sending the threatened memorandum against local ghetto plans to the Interior Minister. Instead they expressed themselves satisfied with the Prefect's plans and urged the 'Christian Hungarian' population of the city to 'calmly wait' for the decision on the location of the ghetto which would be announced by the end of the week.[50] It was a return to the language of *Szegedi Új Nemzedék* less than a week before.[51] This climb down by the Party of Hungarian Renewal was important. The plan to send a memorandum to the Interior Minister threatened to invite

national officials to intervene in ghetto plans in the locality. National intervention was being offered by the Interior Ministry at the very moment that
ghettoization was being so fiercely debated in Szeged. On 11 May, Endre sent
a directive to local authorities informing them that, 'in every city and town in
which the gathering of Jews into ghettos cannot be carried through without
obstacle for any reason, it will be necessary to await the arrival of the advisors
appointed from the Interior Ministry'.[52] That this was offered suggests that
'obstacles' to ghetto plans were present in cities other than Szeged. For example,
it was reported that non-Jewish residents elsewhere were petitioning Endre
against local ghetto plans.[53] In Kistelek, it would seem that Endre directly
intervened after the failure of the local authorities to decide upon a ghetto site,
earmarking a timber yard for this purpose.[54]

The offer of help from Interior Ministry officials that Endre extended was
read, I think, as a threat within the localities. In Szeged my sense is that local
officials did not wish to admit failure to national officials. Once ghettoization
had finally been implemented in Szeged, Endre visited the city again, on 10
June, to see the ghetto for himself. Prior to his visit, the Mayor wrote with
an obvious degree of urgency that the ghetto needed to be fenced in and the
external windows white-washed by the day of Endre's visit, and that the Jewish
police be established to ensure internal order.[55] It was important to put on a
'good show' for the visiting national official, and to convince him of the ability
of the locality to effectively implement ghettoization legislation. After all, on his
earlier visit, the local authorities had been reportedly praised by Endre for their
initiative and zeal in anti-Jewish measures.[56] This reputation was to be guarded.
Anti-Jewish measures provided one sphere among others where mayors and
prefects could assert and safeguard local autonomy vis-à-vis the national state.
They were an opportunity to play local and regional politics (see Chapter 7).

However, as well as an opportunity for local officials, ghettoization also
presented problems. In some ways, they found themselves caught between
pleasing the national officials they were answerable to and appeasing the local
population who contested ghetto plans. The way out of this dilemma was to
adopt a compromise of sorts. An urban ghetto was created, but it would be
relatively dispersed in nature and would house only the city's Jews and not
the thousands of Jews brought into the city from the southern borders of the
country earlier on in the year. The end result was that relatively few non-Jews
would be forced to leave their homes.[57] It was not only here that ghettoization,
when implemented, amounted to a compromise.[58] What is striking is that not
only was ghettoization publicly debated and contested by non-Jewish urbanites,
but their voices appear to have been listened to. In Szeged, the ghetto was
smaller than originally envisioned and largely restricted to properties owned
and occupied by Jews. In Hódmezővásárhely, where the local paper kept a keen
eye on events in Szeged, it would seem that opposition to a centrally located
ghetto was responsible, at least in part, to the abandoning of all ghetto plans
entirely.[59]

After days of uncertainty over the nature and location of the ghetto in Szeged, things sped up considerably. Ghettoization was to be achieved, according to the new prefect in an interview in *Szegedi Új Nemzedék* as quickly as possible with minimal disturbance to the non-Jewish population.[60] A meeting was held on Thursday 11 May to discuss plans, which were finalized two days later and unveiled at a press conference hosted by the prefect on the Saturday evening.[61] The next day, details of the location of the ghetto were published in a lengthy article. As the headline at the top of page three revealed – 'The ghetto is designated in individual houses in the vicinity of the synagogue and near the main station. Moving in will start on Thursday' – the earlier plans of the paper and Party of Hungarian Renewal for an out-of-town barracks ghetto built over a period of six weeks had been shelved.[62] Here, as in many other towns and cities across Hungary, the ghetto was brought to the Jew and therefore built on existing demographic realities, rather than seeking to radically overturn them as the out-of-town ghetto plans had sought to do. When the problem of where to locate the ghetto in Szeged was finally resolved, a pragmatic and speedy solution was adopted.

For the time being at least, *Szegedi Új Nemzedék* ceased its earlier campaigning against mayoral ghettoization plans. On 14 May, and in the following few days, the paper simply reported the location of the ghetto – in apartment buildings in the vicinity of the synagogue, and should they be needed, a cluster of buildings near the railway station, along with another property at Kelemen utca 11 which was specified for housing Jewish converts – and the timescale for moving in.[63] On 16 May it reprinted the list of ghetto properties following, it reported, repeated requests to do so.[64] But it also sought to save face. *Szegedi Új Nemzedék* informed its readers that the ghetto plans were the 'most expedient' solution to the problem of where to place the ghetto. Only some aspects of the original plans had been retained. Jews would live around the synagogue, but only in those buildings where they made up a majority of residents.[65] While 3,814 Jews were reported as having to move, the number of non-Jews was given as just 262, many of whom were tenants rather than house owners given that only 6 non-Jewish-owned houses were included in the ghetto area.[66] *Szegedi Új Nemzedék* may not have succeeded in attaining a barracks ghetto on the outskirts of the city, but it no doubt felt that it had played its part in limiting the impact of ghettoization on the city's non-Jewish population.

Moreover, it would seem that the paper itself had pulled back from its desire for an out-of-town ghetto, given the emergence of new concerns. According to the paper, civil defence considerations had also played their part in determining the compromise solution of a ghetto established in three sites in the city. In the context of aerial bombing, it was decided that Jews should not be placed in one site whether downtown or on the outskirts of Szeged, but should be 'dispersed through the area of the city'. This would mean that Jews would share the dangers of aerial bombing alongside the 'Christian Hungarian population'.[67] In this one sentence, *Szegedi Új Nemzedék* not only suggested that the deputy mayor's earlier plans for a single ghetto in the heart of the city were unthinkable in the context of the threat of aerial bombing, but also their own plans for a barracks ghetto on the outskirts of the city. As was the case elsewhere a connection was made between Allied bombing, Jews and the adoption of a dispersed form of ghettoization.[68]

With concerns about aerial bombing more to the fore, the paper appears to have let its earlier plans go and was happy to report that Szeged would have a ghetto by 1 June at the latest 'and with this the Szeged ghetto question will come to a rest' after a month of contentious wrangling.[69] The separation of Jews and non-Jews that the paper longed for was coming closer to becoming a reality. But before this happened, there were practical matters that became issues of concern to the paper during the rest of May and into June. As had earlier been the case, the paper assumed a role of safeguarding 'Christian Hungarian' interests. Reporting the final ghetto plans, it assured readers that the local authorities were paying attention to the interests of non-Jews in the city. Only those non-Jews who voluntarily offered their homes in the planned ghetto area near to the railway station would have to move, and they would be fully compensated. Not only would non-Jews who did relocate be assured housing on a level with their former homes, but there was the offer of better homes which would be cleaned and newly painted prior to their removal with all costs being borne by the city authorities.[70] In order for this to happen, painters, decorators and hauliers were asked to make themselves available from Thursday onwards.[71] On 16 May the paper assured readers that the city authorities were proceeding with ghettoization in such a way as to protect 'the interests of Christian families' and ensure they were not left out of pocket.[72]

However, it was not quite the end of the 'ghetto question' in the city. *Szegedi Új Nemzedék* soon latched upon another set of problems thrown up by ghettoization. On 20 May, the day after relocations into the ghetto were to commence, the paper pointed to the problem of moving thousands of Jews and their furniture around the city, and were quick to offer a potential solution. As was the case with the earlier adoption of Party of Hungarian Renewal plans, the paper's solution was derivative. This time the source was Ödön F., a local expert given his position as director of the largest removal company in the city. His suggestion was that Jewish labour battalion members be mobilized. If five Jewish servicemen could be assigned to the fifty haulage contractors who were available in the city then he reckoned that all the removals could be accomplished within three weeks. His plans were endorsed by *Szegedi Új Nemzedék*, which not only published them for the benefit of their readers but drew the specific attention of the city authorities to them.[73] However, once again the timescale being offered by the paper did not fit with that which the local authorities were still working to, which continued to be the end of the month.[74] In the end, relocations did take longer, with the deadline being extended to mid June – which fitted more closely with the kind of time period being envisioned by Ödön F.[75] On 15 June, the paper reported that all Jews had been moved into the ghetto and that it would be sealed later that day.[76]

The question of removals continued to be a cause of concern to *Szegedi Új Nemzedék*. They reported cases of overcharging by hauliers, citing non-Jewish families that had been charged 480 pengő and 600 pengő for moving homes: rates well above those set by the authorities.[77] Once again, the paper called the citizens of Szeged to action. This time, it was not Jews without yellow stars who were to be reported – they were by now gathered in the ghetto – but 'profiteers' who were overcharging and should be interned. Here the paper walked a fine line between demonizing 'profiteers' and celebrating the profits that 'honest tradesmen' could make in the aftermath of ghettoization. Separating out the city's Jews and non-Jews was seen as bringing a 'fresh pulse into the economic life of the city', given the increased demand for hauliers, masons, painters and decorators and parquetry inlayers.[78] Not only were large numbers of Jews and non-Jews to be moved around the city (the paper claimed that 50,000 people were moving home although this seems to be something of an exaggeration), but also apartments vacated by Jews were to be renovated. Ghettoization, the paper claimed, had brought an economic 'boom' to the city.

But it was clear that not everyone thought the rates for payment set by the authorities as generous as *Szegedi Új Nemzedék* portrayed them. Not only were there cases of higher rates being charged and some reluctance on the part of hauliers to undertake jobs to be reimbursed by the local authorities,[79] but it would seem that some non-Jews who were moving into vacated Jewish homes were also seizing upon this opportunity as something of a free-for-all. On the same day that *Szegedi Új Nemzedék* denounced 'profiteer' hauliers in the city, they also passed on a message from the City Hall that only the authorized removal, cleaning and painting fees would be paid. Not only were readers reminded of the accepted rates of reimbursement in the aftermath of ghettoization, but also that repainting should amount only to one 'plain' colour and not the 'multicoloured patterns' of a complete makeover.[80] This message was reiterated in a report outlining the closing of the ghetto, published the following day. Readers were reminded to present their bills for removals and tidying up their new apartments to the authorities, but payment would only cover 'unavoidably necessary repairs' that had been officially approved not any 'special work'.[81] Some non-Jews in Szeged were seizing upon this moment as a chance to create an ideal home at Jewish expense as well as refurnish their homes with furniture left behind in Jewish homes. *Szegedi Új Nemzedék* passed on a message from the authorities asking those who had not suffered bomb damage to stop besieging the Housing Office with requests for Jewish furniture. This may be available later on to a broader cross-section of the population, but at present, it was only to be given to those who had lost their homes as a result of the aerial bombardment of the city.[82] That such advice was being passed on to the local population in the pages of the paper suggests that this was a real problem. It would seem that even before the ghettoization process was completed, some were trying to get their hands on Jewish property. And after the deportations had taken place, Judit Molnár claims, 'applications for Jewish flats and possessions were received by the thousands'.[83]

However, on 21 June, *Szegedi Új Nemzedék* offered a contrasting picture of vacated Jewish homes, and by extension, of Szeged's Jews to that which had dominated its pages six weeks earlier. On the one hand ghettoization was still being represented – as it had during the planning process – as an opportunity for 'Christian Hungarian families' to leave small and unhealthy apartments and move into the larger homes vacated by the city's Jews. On the other hand, the way these Jewish homes were portrayed by the paper shifted from earlier rendering of desirable real estate housing wealthy Jews. According to the report, those non-Jews allocated vacated apartments found them to be swarming with vermin which 'scared the most determined from taking up residence'.[84] In describing them this way, the paper adopted the language of the letter penned by the management of the Citizen's Club at Klebelsberg-telep which it had published on 11 May that saw Jewish homes as 'infested and unhealthy'.[85] The paper was now doing the same as it identified another problem thrown up by ghettoization – this process full of problems as well as opportunities for the non-Jewish population. The problem was the lack of cyanide in Szeged which was signalled as the chemical of choice for fumigating vacated Jewish apartments. This issue was one which the paper assured its readers it had raised with the local authorities.[86]

This article was published a matter of days before Jews from Szeged were deported. On 16 June, the day after the ghetto was sealed, the liquidation process began. Ironically, the ghetto here that was so thoroughly debated in the press was extremely short-lived. Jews were transferred from the ghetto to the brick works on Cserzy Mihály utca.[87] They were removed from the heart of the city, as *Szegedi Új Nemzedék* had wished. Ultimately they were removed from the city altogether, in a series of three transports that left the city on 25 June, 27 June and 28 June. The first transport went directly to Auschwitz, but the second two were sent to Strasshof, where many survived.[88] Those Jews in the first transport which left Szeged on 25 June were subject to selections at Auschwitz-Birkenau where those deemed unfit for labour were sent to the gas chambers. There is a macabre irony in the fact that Szeged Jews were gassed with Zyklon B around a week after *Szegedi Új Nemzedék* had called on the local authorities to find cyanide to fumigate the former Jewish apartments in the city. I am not suggesting a direct and simple connection between these two events, aside from a shared perception of the 'dirty' Jew, but it is clear that a local paper like *Szegedi Új Nemzedék* offered its own solutions to what it perceived as a 'Jewish question' and urged its readers to take their part in dealing with the city's Jews. Implementing anti-Jewish measures was a shared concern in this city, rather than simply being something that the authorities did to the Jews and the press merely reported to its passive and unconcerned readership. Non-Jewish neighbours played a far more active role as Jews were placed into ghettos and deported.[89] It is clear that local authorities were both sensitive and responsive to non-Jewish concerns.[90] In particular, as the ghetto maps from Tolna county show, they were concerned with limiting the impact of ghettoization on non-Jewish property rights.

4

Placing the Ghetto: Maps from Tolna County

In May 1944, a clerk in Tolna in central Hungary annotated a street map of the town with the addition of a new hand drawn key and accompanying shading and numbering.[1] The base map they used was one that privileged a particular rendering of the city. As Jeremy Black notes with regard to street maps more generally, 'in the "A–Z"-ing of life, habitations emerge as the spaces between streets. Differences within the city or town, for example of wealth, or environmental or housing quality, are ignored ... in favour of a bland uniform background that is described, and thus explained, insofar as there is any explanation in terms of roads.'[2] But in Tolna, the town clerk reworked this rather bland base map in two ways.

First, and most obviously, they shaded in (and created) a new reality of differentiated living space for Jews and non-Jews in the town. Nine building plots – eight on Árpád utca just south of the main square and the town hall where the clerk worked, and another on Szedresi utca – were coloured in. As the key in the bottom left-hand corner explained, these were 'buildings – residences serving the segregation of the Jews'. Second, the town clerk effectively remapped an entire street – Árpád utca – by sketching in plot boundaries. Rather than being imagined as a single unity as an A–Z street map does, Árpád utca was reworked as a street made up of individually owned plots. As they mapped out ghettoization in their town, it is clear they did so with an eye to who owned what. In the previous chapter, I showed how in Szeged it was not just officials in City Hall who sought to shape the ghetto. Here I extend this story of non-Jewish neighbours shaping the ghetto, by focusing on places like Tolna where patchwork ghettos were constructed to avoid violating non-Jewish property rights.

This town clerk in Tolna was not alone in mapping out a ghetto in May 1944. In neighbouring towns and cities, a further seven clerks were also busy mapping out the segregation of Jews in their patch for the county authorities.[3] They did not do this on their own initiative. Rather these ghetto maps were commissioned. On 11 May 1944, the Tolna county deputy prefect had issued two orders implementing the national ghettoization decree within his county.[4] The first, as was the practice elsewhere, outlined the towns and cities where ghettos were to be constructed. Local officials in these eight places were given some of the practical regulations relating to ghettoization in this order, with further details following in a supplementary order published on the same day that outlined the nitty-gritty of the construction and day-to-day running of the county's ghettos. Point number twenty-eight in a long list of detailed instructions ordered local authorities to provide four copies of a name list of the Jews living in each building in the ghetto along with two copies of a ghetto map.[5]

As with any other map, these ghetto maps from Tolna county offer selective representations.[6] What all show, in one form or another, is something new – the ghettos created in their town sketched out and shaded in on a mixture of pre-existing printed maps, or purpose-drawn sketch maps. These maps not only represented the new realities of ghettoization, but also constituted those realities. They were works in progress. On the map drawn up in Bonyhád on 15 May 1944, last-minute changes to the shape of one of the two ghettos in the town were made.[7] The three shaded-in buildings joined to the central part of ghetto number two by a single pathway were crossed off the map and removed from the ghetto as the process of mapping out segregation on paper shifted to bricks and mortar – from the discursive to the material.

While my main focus is on the map from the town of Tolna and the motivations behind adopting a patchwork ghetto and the implications of this for Jews living there, I want to compare the mapping of ghettoization here with other places in the county in two ways. First, as becomes clear from even a cursory glance, the shape of ghettoization varied from place to place. Here is a story of local differences in the degree of concentration and dispersion adopted as Jews were segregated from non-Jews.[8] In some towns a single, closed ghetto was constructed. Elsewhere, two closed ghettos were established. In other places a far greater number of separate premises were utilized, as was the case in Tolna. But second, it was not only the ghettos sketched out by eight town clerks that differed from place to place. So also did the ways in which these clerks represented these new entities cartographically. As in Chapter 6, where I am interested in getting inside the heads of those who took photographs of deportations from towns in western Hungary to understand the 'bystander gaze', here I am interested in what visual representations of ghettoization through mapping might say (and I realize I am on more speculative ground here) about how municipal officials saw the ghettos that they mapped out. But before focusing on the maps themselves, I begin with the broader story of why it was that clerks in these eight towns drew up maps in May 1944, given that it is surprising that ghettos were established at all in the majority of these places.

PLACING GHETTOIZATION IN TOLNA COUNTY

Putting Jews into ghettos involved the creation of absences (the places where Jews were removed from) and presences (the places where Jews were relocated to) at a variety of scales, from the national, through the regional to the local.[9] In both national and Tolna county ghetto orders, the creation of Jewish absences came to the fore in opening statements that Jews would no longer live in towns and villages with a total population of fewer than 10,000.[10] Both at a national and county level, the paperwork imagined ghettoization as a process of making rural Hungary *judenfrei*. The implication of this in a largely rural county like Tolna was that the county's more than 5,000 Jews would only be concentrated in the three towns – Szekszárd (14,683), Dunaföldvár (11,480) and Paks (11,776) – technically large enough for ghettos.[11] Yet, when he came to identify where ghettos would be sited in the county, the deputy prefect chose eight places. Alongside Dunaföldvár, Paks and Szekszárd were Bonyhád (8,333), Dombóvár (8,859), Hőgyész (3,541), Tamási (7,222) and Tolna (8,314).[12] Their presence on this list is, as Zsuzsanna Toronyi notes, 'unusual' given their size.[13]

Ultimately, the final list of ghetto sites in the county was odder still. At the end of May the deputy prefect issued a new ghetto order complete with a list of amendments. Central to these was the removal of Szekszárd from the list of ghetto sites, with the small village of Pincehely (3,958) taking its place. This new ghetto, which had been mapped out on 21 May, was one of the places (along with Tamási, Dombóvár, Paks and Bonyhád) where Jews from Szekszárd were sent at the end of May after the failure of ghettoization there.[14] With Szekszárd rejected as a ghetto site, six out of eight of the ghettos mapped out in Tolna county in May 1944 were in places where they should not have been. This variation from the national norm appears to have been because of greater concern in Tolna county with presences rather than absences. Two issues appear to have been key to the choice of eight, rather than three ghetto sites.

First, it seems that the deputy prefect in Tolna county thought at the scale not of the county as national officials did, but the next scale down – the district (*járas*) – which was the way in which he parcelled up the territory under his control. Administratively, Hungary was divided into a patchwork of counties (one of which was Tolna), each with a county seat (Szekszárd in the case of Tolna) where the county administration was based. Each county was further subdivided into a number of districts. In Tolna county, there were six districts that were broadly equal in size, each of which had their own district seat (Tamási, Simontornya, Dunaföldvár, Szekszárd, Bonyhád and Dombóvár) where the offices of the chief constable in the district were located. While national officials were concerned that Jews in each county were concentrated into major urban centres within the county, it would seem that the deputy prefect in Tolna county wanted each district to have its own ghetto, located more often than not, in the district seat. In five of the six districts in the county (Dombóvári, Dunaföldvári, Központi, Tamási and Völgységi) the district seat was either the only, or one of two ghetto sites.[15]

However, in Simontornyai district, the district seat was skipped over, with the ghetto being placed in what was in effect the second town in the district, Hőgyész. Here it would seem that the second, and I think ultimately the more important of the two factors that shaped the choice of ghetto sites, was significant: the size of the Jewish population. Hőgyész appears to have been chosen over the district seat of Simontornya largely because the Jewish population in the former (282 in 1941) was considerably greater than in the latter (fifty-nine in 1941). The list of eight cities, towns and villages identified by the deputy prefect as ghetto sites on 11 May 1944 were neither places with a total population above 10,000, nor the eight largest towns and cities in the county. Rather, they were the eight places with the largest Jewish populations in Tolna county. Ghettos were sited where Jews already lived in relatively large numbers, with at least one ghetto per district. This meant that, broadly speaking, ghettos were taken to the Jews in Tolna county.

While locating ghettos in those places where Jews already lived in Tolna county was a local variation from the national ghetto decree, it did mesh with earlier drafts of the 28 April decree. Cut from the final version of this decree was the proviso that Jews were no longer to live in towns of fewer than 10,000 *if* the total Jewish population there was fewer than a hundred.[16] In Tolna county, the logic of these earlier drafts that ghettos should be constructed where Jews lived, was enacted on the ground. It meant that ghettoization in this county was relatively dispersed (eight ghettos rather than three) and a more intimately local experience. Jews in Tolna county either stayed put or travelled to small ghettos relatively close to home. Across Hungary ghettoization meant rather different things from county to county. But it also meant rather different things from place to place within a single county as the Tolna ghetto maps reveal.

DIFFERENT PLACES, DIFFERENT GHETTOS

Sitting down at my desk to write this chapter, I have copies of the Tolna county ghetto maps pinned to the wall in front of me. Glancing up at them, it is the shaded in areas on each map that catch the eye. From even a cursory glance the different shapes of ghettoization in this single county are striking. This was a place where single, multiple and dispersed ghettos were constructed in May 1944. In Dombóvár, Dunaföldvár, Paks and Tamási a single closed ghetto was set up. In Bonyhád and Pincehely there were two ghettos, in both cases separated by a major street. In Tolna and Hőgyész more dispersed clusters of 'Jewish houses' were created. Local variation owed much to the fact that while it was the deputy prefect who identified the eight towns where Jews from across the county were to be relocated, the job of identifying precisely where the ghetto was sited in the town or city they knew so well, was left to local officials, as it was elsewhere.[17] They were given quite considerable room for manoeuvre by both the national ghettoization decree published at the end of April and the order issued by the deputy prefect of Tolna county in May. According to the ghettoization decree discussed by the Council of Ministers on 26 April and published two days later, mayors in towns and cities with a population greater than 10,000 were to determine which 'parts, or rather specified streets, *or perhaps designated houses*' Jews were to live in.[18]

This provision for ghettoization at the scale of the town, the street or the individual house was conveyed to local officials by the deputy prefect when he ordered that Jews be separated from non-Jews in Tolna county. In the first of the ghetto orders issued by the deputy prefect on 11 May, it would seem that the norm was that Jews be separated into either a single area or street.

However, a concession of sorts was granted in the following paragraph. Jews could be placed into groups of houses bordering onto each other where 'local conditions' made designating a single area or street impossible. In what would appear to be a case of last resort, individual buildings could be designated, but only if the dimensions meant that a large number of Jews could be housed there. The language of 'specified area, or rather specified street, group of houses, or autonomous building' subsequently cropped up in the order, pointing to the variety of practices permitted to local officials on the ground.[19] As the second ghetto order, issued on the same day, made clear, the crucial principles underlying ghettoization in the county were to be the 'strict separation' of Jews from non-Jews and the concentration of Jews. Thus, the deputy prefect stressed that where 'local conditions' meant that it was impossible to establish a 'closed Jewish living quarter' and instead the decision was made to place Jews into groups of houses or blocks of flats, then it was essential to ensure that Jews and non-Jews were separated and had no contact with each other. Likewise, it was left to 'local conditions' to determine the number of persons living in each living space, but the principle was that Jews be housed three to four persons per room, with a view to keeping the number of buildings needed down to an absolute minimum.[20] In short, both national and country officials imagined that the core principles behind ghettoization were segregation and concentration, but that the precise shape of ghettos would vary from place to place.

There was no single shape to ghettos in Tolna county and nor was there one single way of describing them. While those drawing up the maps in Bonyhád, Dombóvár and Tamási used the term ghetto (gettó).[21] in Dunaföldvár it was a 'group of Jewish houses (ghetto)',[22] in Pincehely, it was a 'collective Jewish settlement (ghetto)',[23] in Hőgyész they were 'Jewish houses' and in Tolna 'buildings – residences serving the segregation of the Jews'.[24] This diversity of descriptors on the ground was repeated by a county official who drew up an undated handwritten list outlining the numbers of Jews gathered in each of the eight ghetto sites alongside a brief description of each. Dombóvár and Paks were both described by this official as having '1 ghetto – completely closed', Dunaföldvár and Tamási were listed simply as places with '1 ghetto'. Bonyhád had '2 ghettos', whereas Pincehely was described as having '2 groups of houses (ghettos)', which differed only through the use of parenthesis from Hőgyész with its '2 groups of houses'. For this official, Tolna had '3 groups of houses'.[25] There were multiple descriptions, multiple mappings and multiple forms of ghettos in this single county. To examine why this was the case – and the implications of that for Jews – I would like to return to that map from the town of Tolna that I began with and explore what shaped the ghetto in this town.

BRINGING THE GHETTO TO THE JEW/KEEPING THE GHETTO FROM THE NON-JEW

As they worked out where to place the ghetto in their town, it is clear that local officials in Tolna avoided houses owned by non-Jews. The patchwork ghetto mapped out on Árpád utca neatly sidestepped non Jewish residential properties.[26] The same was true in Bonyhád, where the ghetto fence twisted and turned to avoid including non-Jewish homes, resulting in two abstract-shaped ghettos centred around the synagogues on either side of Rákoczi Ferenc utca.[27] In both Tolna and Bonyhád, private property rights shaped ghettoization, rather than being reshaped by the implementation of ghettoization. It was property ownership, rather than simply tenancy, that was critical. In Hungary, the distinction was a crucial one within broader legislation and practice. These distinctions carried over as housing stock was redistributed between Jews and non-Jews with the implementation of ghettoization. While ghetto orders at both a national and local level made provision for non-Jewish tenants forced to leave their homes,[28] owner-occupiers had greater provision, and it seems that there were attempts to shape ghettos to avoid infringing these rights.[29] Certainly it was the plight of non-Jewish owner-occupiers that was being highlighted by the press in Szeged. Non-Jews leaving homes they owned was clearly seen as something to be avoided where and whenever possible.

One way to do this was to make use of Jewish owned property. In Tolna, eight of the nine ghetto houses were Jewish owned.[30] But another way was to eschew residential property entirely. In Tolna, alongside making use of eight Jewish owned houses, the local authorities also utilized the former gendarme barracks at Árpád utca 7. This building formed the heart of the ghetto. It explains why it was this street rather than others in the town that was chosen as the main spine of the ghetto. After all, Árpád utca was just one of a number of streets where relatively large numbers of Jews (twenty-three) lived in 1944. Roughly equal numbers of Jews lived on Deák Ferenc utca (twenty-three) and Kossuth Lajos utca (twenty-five), with slightly smaller numbers on Bezeredy utca (eighteen) and Ferenc József utca (sixteen).[31] The attraction of Árpád utca appears to have been the former barracks building that was so physically large in this town made up of small family homes rather than large apartment buildings. According to the name lists drawn up once the ghetto in Tolna was established, this one building housed 128 Jews, or just over one-third of the total ghetto population. It dwarfed the next largest ghetto building – Árpád utca 28 – which housed fifty-two Jews and was far larger than the majority of the Jewish houses that were the home to between eighteen and thirty-seven Jews in June 1944.[32] It provided one-third of the ghetto space. Without it, another four to six houses would be needed. In short, it kept the number of Jewish houses to a minimum, which fitted with the concerns expressed by the deputy prefect when offering clusters of houses or freestanding buildings as an option when 'local conditions' made this necessary. In the first ghetto order published on 11 May, the deputy prefect had pointed out that individual buildings should only be used if 'the dimensions and number of living room are suitable for placing a larger number of Jewish people'.[33] Size mattered. Ghettoization was not only imagined as an act of segregation but also spatial concentration.

But segregation and concentration were to be achieved with minimal impact on non-Jews, by making use of Jewish owned and non-residential properties. These strategies can be seen elsewhere, with widespread use of Jewish-owned community buildings. In Bonyhád, Tamási and Hőgyész the ghettos included the synagogues, and further afield ghettos were sited in, or around, synagogues in Veszprém, Szeged and Körmend. Elsewhere, Jews were removed from the town into non-residential properties on the outskirts, seen in the use of the former Komakuti barracks in Veszprém, farmsteads on the outskirts of Nyíregyháza and the plans for an out-of-town purpose-built ghetto in Szeged that dominated the pages of the local press in early May. The whole *raison d'être* in Hungary was that the definition, expropriation, concentration and deportation of Jews should materially benefit the non-Jewish population and Hungarian state (see chapter seven).[34] When something like ghettoization negatively impacted non-Jews, as was clearly seen to be the case by the press in Szeged, there was opposition.

The controversy over ghettoization in Szeged appears to have been mirrored in Szekszárd, the Tolna county seat. Although one of the eight ghetto sites originally identified by the deputy prefect on 11 May, Szekszárd was removed from the list in the amendments published on 30 May and replaced with the village of Pincehely.[35] According to Nándor Erdős, head of the Jewish Council in the city, the decision to cancel plans to establish a ghetto in Szekszárd owed much to the unwillingness of the city's mayor, István Vendel, to implement ghettoization.[36] This explanation, found in *Pinkas Hakehillot*, puts this act of resistance on the part of the mayor down to the efforts of a secret coalition of Jewish community leaders and 'influential' non-Jews, despite the more official explanation proffered being that no adequate ghetto site was identified.[37] However, this may be little more than a post-war playing-up of a wartime role by a key Jewish leader in this locale. The local press, describing the removal of Jews from Szekszárd to its readers on 3 June, began by recapping that, 'it is well known that the settlement of the Jews together into a single closed place according to the issued state order was not achieved in Szekszárd' because of the unsuitability of the vacated homes for non-Jewish rural dwellers with animals and smallholdings who would be relocated in the course of ghettoization.[38] Such concerns with the types of houses that non-Jews were leaving in rural towns, and the kinds of former Jewish homes that they were being moved into, were shared elsewhere. For example, the mayor in Kiskunhalas expressed his own concerns about the unsuitability of former Jewish apartments and houses for non-Jewish smallholders.[39]

Given the difficulties with identifying a single, closed ghetto in Szekszárd, it would seem, at least from the press reporting, that a form of dispersed ghettoization was enacted in the city. According to the report, Jews were moved together into larger Jewish houses, which they were only permitted to leave for the purposes of shopping, throughout the city marked with signs complete with yellow stars and the words 'Jews live in this house'. Such designation was not a local invention, but was specifically outlined by the deputy prefect in his 11 May ghetto order.[40] From the press report at least, it seemed to share much with the solution adopted in Tolna. It begs the question why a relatively dispersed form of ghettoization was tolerated in Tolna, but not in Szekszárd. In Tolna, the use of the former gendarme barracks as something like a super ghetto meant that dispersion was seen as being kept to a minimum, and thus control to a maximum. However, in Szekszárd, it would seem that dispersion was seen to undermine the demands to exercise control through space that was central to ghettoization. The Jews from this city were therefore redistributed to the less dispersed ghettos in smaller towns and villages in Tolna county.[41]

Ghettoization was clearly about more than simply separating out spatially Jews from non-Jews. It was also about concentrating Jews in severely confined living quarters in large buildings in urban Hungary, which in turn meant that greater control could be exercised over the country's previously dispersed Jewish population. As I have suggested, the macro story of ghettoization in Tolna county threatened to undermine this principle. Six of the eight ghettos were in places they should not have been. And at the micro scale, some of those ghettos were multiple or dispersed. In this context, mapping ghettoization was a critical tool in exercising control over Jews in a county where ghettoization was relatively dispersed at both the scale of the county and within individual towns like Tolna. In the second of his ghetto orders issued on 11 May, the deputy prefect requested that alongside producing sketch maps of the ghetto in duplicate, local officials also draw up four copies of name lists detailing who was living in the individual buildings within the ghetto.[42] That four copies of this list were required was due to the broader distribution of these name lists. While the local town council and chief constable of the district were to receive copies of both the map and the name lists, additional copies of the name lists were to be supplied to the Jewish house commanders responsible for ensuring order and cleanliness within the ghetto, as well as to the gendarmerie, or in the case of cities, the police district station.[43] Ghetto maps did not exist in an informational vacuum, but were used in town council offices and the offices of district chief constables alongside detailed lists of who lived where. Armed with the map and housing list, it was possible for local officials to pinpoint the precise whereabouts of Jews from their district and town. As Patrick Joyce notes of a different time and place, 'the modern map is essential to power and to the practices of rule'.[44] The ghetto maps and lists in Tolna county were instruments of territoriality – the exercise of 'power with the help of maps'[45] through spatial control. The local authorities knew where any one of over five thousand individuals were at any one time, which was particularly important in this county where there were rather too many ghettos.

While the ghetto maps survive from all those places in the county where ghettos were created in the early summer of 1944, the survival of ghetto name lists is far more patchy. The sources are richest from Tolna.[46] There, we can metaphorically peer over the shoulder of local officials and – like them – see who lived where. What emerges is both the intimacy of ghettoization in this town, and the ways in which dispersed ghettoization separated Jews from other Jews, as well as Jews from non-Jews. Rather than re-people all of the Jewish buildings in the town, I will focus on one – Árpád utca 12 – which housed eighteen Jews drawn from the town of Tolna itself.[47] It was exceptional of all the ghetto houses in being a place for urban Jews only. Most ghetto houses in Tolna had a mix of Jews from the town itself, alongside those brought in from the surrounding district.[48] The other exception was the outlying building at Szedresi utca 6, on the northern edge of the town, several streets away from the central spine of the ghetto on Árpád utca.[49] Here only one of the thirty-nine Jews living in the house was from Tolna itself. Most were from smaller rural communities around the town, as was the case in the Komakuti barracks ghetto in Veszprém.

THE 'MICRO GHETTO' AT ÁRPÁD UTCA 12, TOLNA

The 'Jewish house' at Árpád utca 12 was owned by the D. family, who lived there prior to ghettoization, as well as after. The four members of the extended D. family – Mr and Mrs Zsigmond D., their daughter in law, Mrs Ödon D. and six-year-old grandson György D. – stayed put.[50] The ghetto came to them. For this family, their place on the town map remained the same, but the remapping of ghettoization meant being squeezed into just one room of the house, and the new experience of sharing a kitchen and bathroom with the other families who moved into their home. The D. family's experience was one common throughout Hungary, and further afield, where ghettoization built upon the demographic logic of where Jews already lived. Describing her own experience of ghettoization in the town of Nagyszölös, Zipora B. recalled that, 'each family now received only one room. We had a house of five or six rooms, and now we had to share it with five or six families. There were many children and many adults there. The children cried, the adults wanted to sleep.'[51] For families like the D family in Tolna, or the B family in Nagyszölös, ghettoization did not involve moving from their home, but moving within their home. It meant concentration, but not relocation.

There were advantages to staying put, even when this now meant living in only one room in a familiar place. As I have noted in Chapter 2, the perception of one teenager forced to move from her home into the ghetto in another city was that, those who stayed put could 'exercise … social leverage',[52] as well as retain their furniture and food. Given the restrictions on what Jews could take with them if they had to move into the ghetto, there were in effect two classes of Jews: those concentrated within their former homes, who still had everything; and those who had moved into new homes carrying only small quantities of clothing, bedding and food. Moreover, these two different groups – those who stayed put and those who had to move – had very different relationships with the physical property. One were *de facto* 'hosts'; the other *de facto* 'guests'. In the case of the D. family in Tolna, Zsigmond D. assumed the role of house commander for the Jewish house.[53] This role was laid out by the deputy prefect in his ghetto orders as overseeing order within the ghetto.[54] Rather than this job being given to a newcomer, it was assigned to the male house owner, who continued to assert his authority over this space.

However, rather than one of the women in the D. family being given the role of shopping for the ghetto house, this task was given to one of the incomers, Mrs Izidor K.[55] The K. family was one of the three families that moved into the rooms vacated by the D. family. Mrs Izidor K. moved in along with her eight-year-old son Zoltán and two-year-old daughter Hedvig. Joining her was her widowed mother, Mrs Ignác K., and her two sisters Ilona and Mária, along with another sister Erzsébet and her three-year-old niece, Julianna. Ghettoization brought the extended K. family under one roof. In May 1944, Mrs Izidor K. and her two children had lived on Bezerédi utca along with Erzsébet and Julianna, while her mother and sisters had lived round the corner from them on Garay utca.[56] Previously geographically close, they now lived in the same Jewish house.

Joining the D. and K. families in Árpád utca 12 were two further families: Nathan M., his wife Julia and their son Mihály, and the widow Mrs Ferenc H. and her son László.[57] Relocating Jews in family units was explicitly spelt out by the deputy prefect in his 11 May ghetto order. Rather than families being broken apart in the process of ghettoization, in Tolna county there was an intentional practice of bringing together extended families within Jewish houses. Where there was capacity for more people in a room or house than within an individual family then others should be brought in to ensure that 'the space is exploited', although this should be done where possible through including 'relations, those connected by marriage or friends'.[58] In the case of Árpád utca 12, there was clearly seen to be enough space once these four families were housed there for at least one more person. Marked down at the bottom of the name list, Mrs Ferenc G. was brought in to make up the numbers.[59]

Her presence brought the number of women in this micro ghetto to 12. As with other ghettos in Hungary, Árpád utca 12 was predominantly a place of women, the elderly and children. Of the six men in the house, two were older men (aged sixty-seven and seventy-two) and three boys (aged six, eight and fourteen). Only one, Mihály M. (aged forty-four), was a member of the generation of Hungarian Jewish men missing from ghettos as a result of their labour battalion service.[60] The population profile of this micro ghetto mirrors the much larger ghettos in Veszprém. While ghettoization in Tolna intentionally brought extended families together, these were families that had already been divided along gendered lines as the state mobilized 'valuable' male labour.

But while sharing an almost identical age and gender profile with the Horthy Miklós utca ghetto in Veszprém, which housed 627 women and men, this was a rather different ghetto and ghetto experience given its size. There was an intimacy to ghettoization at this micro scale which extended to other places where dispersed Jewish houses were adopted. Árpád utca 12 was – according to Hungarian legislation – quite definitely a ghetto. But it was not perhaps what we imagine when the word 'ghetto' comes to mind.[61] This was a ghetto housing just four extended families along with one extra person to make up the numbers. They lived, one family to a room, with a shared kitchen and bathroom.[62] Although the neighbouring two houses (numbers 10 and 11) were also part of the dispersed ghetto, these were entirely separate places. The eighteen Jews living in the micro ghetto at Árpád utca 12 were in reality cut off not only from the non-Jews living in Tolna, but also from the Jews living in the eight other Jewish houses in the town, one of which was just next door. There were limited opportunities for exchange. Only Mrs Izidor K. regularly left Árpád utca 12 to shop along with seventeen other Jews who left their ghetto houses between 10 am and 12 midday on market days and 3 pm and 5 pm on other days.[63] Others left the house more sporadically, as was the case in Körmend, to work in labour gangs. On 30 May, Mrs Ödon D., Mrs Béla P. and her sister Mária K., along with nineteen others from Jewish houses in Tolna, left their homes to undertake agricultural work.[64] It was at moments like these that there was the possibility for some contact between Jews separated out into self-contained micro ghettos.

This segregating of Jews from Jews, as well as Jews from non-Jews, was also the case with the multiple ghettos in Bonyhád. Here, the creation of two ghettos, on either side of Rákoczi Ferenc utca, reflected and hardened the longstanding existence of distinct religious communities in the town. Bonyhád had the largest and longest established Jewish community in Tolna county. In 1781, the census recorded 382 Jews in the town, and the existence of a grave dating back to 1703 in the cemetery points to the early establishment of this community which built its first prayer house in 1764. A new synagogue was built in 1794 and by 1840 the census recorded a total of 1,120 Jews living in Bonyhád, a number that remained more or less constant over the next two centuries.[65] In 1868, seven families left the existing Jewish congregation to establish an Orthodox congregation. In the decades that followed, the town had separate Neolog and Orthodox communities, with the Orthodox congregation becoming the stronger of the two. In April 1944, the Orthodox community had 750 members and the Neolog congregation around half that number (376).[66] One survivor remembers living in a divided town, suggesting that

> [W]e had a cordial business relationship. On the other hand, there were no close social or friendly connections between these groups. Strange as it was, the Orthodox did not appreciate enough, their Neolog counterparts, saying, they are mostly 'amhaaratzim,' lacking in knowledge of the Talmud … On the other side, the Neolog felt, that the Orthodox did not care enough about worldly knowledge. In general, the two groups did not care to visit one another's homes.[67]

Rather than the concentration entailed by ghettoization bringing these two communities into a single ghetto, the divide between the Orthodox and Neolog survived ghettoization and indeed was hardened through it, with two ghettos each with their own Jewish Councils.[68] Multiple and dispersed ghettos separated Jews from other Jews as well as separating Jews from non-Jews.

WORKING UP OLD MAPS, DRAWING NEW MAPS

As is clear, a variety of shapes of ghetto were created in this county, with implications for both Jews and non-Jews. But in closing, I want to suggest that there were also a variety of ways of mapping and visualizing ghettos on the part of local officials. In part, different mapping strategies reflected real differences in the shape of the ghettos from place to place. However, it was not simply the case that all single, closed ghettos were mapped one way, with dispersed ghettos made up of groups of Jewish houses being mapped another. For example, although Tamási and Dunaföldvár both had a single closed ghetto, the way that the clerks chose to map out ghettoization differed markedly. In Dunaföldvár, they shaded in the ghetto onto an existing base map. In Tamási, they created a new map from scratch.[69] The variety of strategies adopted by clerks in these two places reflects broader differences in cartographic practices that suggest there were different ways of seeing ghettoization.

The town clerks in Dombóvár, Dunaföldvár, Paks and Tolna chose to work with standard street maps that imagined these towns as coherent entities made up of a familiar network of named streets.[70] The boundaries of the town and the boundaries of the map coexist. The centre of the town is the centre of the map and the town ends where the map ends. There is a familiarity about these maps, despite the unfamiliarity of the shading, labelling and keys which variously identify a 'ghetto', a 'group of Jewish houses (ghetto)' or 'buildings – residences serving the segregation of the Jews'. The annotation may be new, but the base map was not. These familiar maps could be, after all, annotated differently. Working in the map library at the Library of Congress, I came across another annotation of the same edition of the Dombóvár street map that was reworked in May 1944 to site the ghetto. Originally from the CIA Map Library, this map had been marked up with the major factories in the town which are numbered and listed in a new key placed at the bottom left.[71] Taking an existing map and shading in the ghetto area or Jewish houses was both a quick and easy solution to the request for ghetto sketch maps. But it can, I think, be seen as more than simply pragmatic. It suggests a normalization of ghettoization both on the map and on the ground. In these four towns, ghettoization was not a policy 'Other' requiring a new mapping strategy, but something represented within the existing cartographic norms of visualizing the town. Ghettoization was inserted within that dominant mode of representation, rather than forcing a new mode of representation.

In contrast, in Bonyhád, Pincehely and Tamási, the implementation of ghettoization demanded a new mode of representation. Rather than taking pre-existing town maps, clerks in these three places mapped the ghetto on its own, rather than the ghetto within the town.[72] It suggests that they saw the ghetto as sufficiently new, and other, to be mapped on its own terms, rather than inserted into a pre-existing representation of the town as a whole. In all of these three maps, the ghetto took centre stage. It formed the centre of the mapping, although the ghetto was not located in the absolute centre of the town. Through this cartographic centring on this new spatial form, other parts of the town were excluded from the map. This was less striking in Tamási, where the seven numbered buildings plus the synagogue which are labelled making up the 'Ghetto' were set within a more familiar broader streetscape of a section of the city where other features are also marked: the town hall, the chief constable's office, the Catholic church and an elementary school.[73] While not quite the normalization that I read in the case of the use of pre-existing street maps to place ghettoization within a familiar rendering of the town, I see in Tamási, a mapping that situates the ghetto alongside other labelled places, rather than as spatial *sui generis*.

But in Pincehely, the ghetto was seen as something new – and alien – that stood alone from the rest of the village.[74] Mapping out the ghetto here at a scale of 1:1000, the clerk turned the village on its side, so to speak, mapping the ghetto oriented to the west, rather than the cartographic norm of the north. Entitled 'Sketch of Pincehely collective Jewish settlement (ghetto)', the representation of the ghetto contrasts markedly with the other ghetto maps, and in particular those placed onto pre-existing town maps. On the map, the ghetto takes centre stage. The only broader orientation comes from the naming of the street that separates the two halves of the ghetto (*Dunaföldvár-Dombóvár-i közut*), the signalling of the direction of Dombóvár on the road, the marking of a bridge and the labelling of the river channel (*Kapos csatorna*) that runs along the eastern edge of the ghetto. It is a purpose-built sketching out of a ghetto visualized as a coherent whole made up of two groupings of buildings – five in one, four in the other – with specifically defined boundaries. Eschewing representation of the village as a whole, there is little sense of the ghetto as sited in the wider space of the village. It is a representation of a new institution – a 'collective Jewish settlement' – which is shown as a self-standing entity, even though as the marking of the road, river and bridge reveal, the ghetto was located where the major road running north-east to south-west crosses over the *Kapos* channel on the eastern edge of the village. It is a mapping of the separateness of the Jews – removed visually from the non-Jewish village of Pincehely, into the distinct and separate space of the ghetto.

The 'Otherness' of the ghetto which comes through in its cartographic representation is made all the more clear in the title of this sketch map. It is a 'sketch of Pincehely collective Jewish settlement', with the word 'ghetto' added in parenthesis. Bracketing ghetto after other terms can be seen elsewhere. As I have already suggested there was flexibility in how these places were described. On the Dunaföldvár ghetto map the key identifies one area of shading showing 'group of Jewish houses (ghetto)'.[75] On the undated list of ghetto sites in the county, Pincehely is described as having '2 groups of houses (ghettos)'.[76] However, what is striking is that on this county document and on the Dunaföldvár map the word ghetto is spelt *gettó*, the standard Hungarian spelling of the term, which is the way the term was spelt in national and county directives. In contrast the town clerk in Pincehely, who sketched out the 'collective Jewish settlement' in the village, drew upon the 'foreign' term '*ghettó*' to define this place that he represented existing in, and yet in a sense imaginatively outside of, Pincehely.[77] Both in the mapping of ghettoization here, and the naming of the ghetto in this place, there is a sense of the strangeness (rather than normalization) of ghettoization. These clues on the map make sense given the specific context in Pincehely which was a latecomer to ghettoization. A ghetto was only created here because of the failure to create one in Szekszárd. And it was, the mapping would suggest, seen by this town clerk as an alien entry into this village. Just as not all bystander photographers saw deportations in the same way (Chapter 6), so also the town clerks who drew up ghetto maps in May 1944 did not see ghettoization in the same way. The clerk who sketched the ghetto map in Pincehely saw it in a different way, I would suggest, from the clerk who inserted a rectangular box labelled *gettó* onto a pre-existing town plan of Dombóvár. It is those kinds of subtle differences that I foreground in this book, precisely because I am interested in uncovering the ways in which there were multiple experiences of this event that we tend to think of in rather monolithic ways.

THREE DOCTORS: DR LAJOS K. IN HŐGYÉSZ; AND DR IGNÁC P. AND DR GYULA SZ. IN KÖRMEND

That sense of multiple experiences is something that I want to explore more in the next chapter, which examines the selective porousness of the ghetto boundary in Körmend. There, two doctors – Dr Ignác P. and Dr Gyula Sz. – were uniquely mobile during a time of ghettoization. Their exceptional experience of ghettoization is mirrored by the experience of another doctor – Dr Lajos K. – in the town of Hőgyész. He was unusual in being the only individual named on the one of the Tolna county maps. As I have suggested, name lists of ghettoized Jews were part of the armoury of control exercised through the paperwork being generated by local clerks. But in Hőgyész, the name of Dr Lajos K. and the 'temporary residence' where he lived were marked on the map.[78] Like the two Jewish doctors in Körmend whose stories I tell next, this doctor had an exceptional ghetto experience. In both towns, it is clear that continued access to Jewish doctors by the towns' non-Jewish populations was ensured despite being threatened by the segregation so central to ghettoization. In Hőgyész, the local authorities temporarily exempted a Jewish doctor from living in the ghetto. However, such a practice was explicitly mapped out as temporary, with Dr Lajos K.'s exceptional living situation marked on the map. His transgression of ghettoization was still under the control asserted through mapping. An alternative in Körmend was to permit Dr Ignác P to leave the ghetto to visit patients. But he could do this only through holding a ghetto pass that needed to be shown to the police guarding the ghetto gateways. In both Hőgyész and Körmend, Jewish doctors were seen as indispensable and too valuable to be confined behind a ghetto fence for twenty-four hours each day. But they were still men who were controlled, in the one case through mapping and in the other through the paperwork of passes, which I now turn to look at.

5

Exiting and Entering the Ghetto: Passes from Körmend

On the morning of 6 May 1944, the chief constable in Körmend met with the deputy prefect of Vas county to discuss setting up a ghetto in his town, one of seven scheduled for ghettos in this county.[1] After this initial meeting, things progressed very quickly. Three days later, the ghetto site was chosen – a single closed area bordered by the synagogue, Széchenyi utca, Gróf Apponyi utca, Dienes Lajos utca and Rábamellék utca at the southern edge of the town. Non-Jews living in this area were to vacate their homes by 12 May to make way for Jews from other parts of the town and the surrounding villages.[2] On 16 May, the chief constable ordered the Jewish Council to pay for the construction of a wooden fence around the ghetto, which was to be finished by midday on 20 May. Planning and constructing the ghetto took only two weeks from start to finish. At the end of May, a two-metre high fence – with two closed and guarded gateways – physically separated Jews from non-Jews in Körmend.[3]

But even as they ordered the fencing of the ghetto, the local authorities foresaw some foot traffic out of this closed ghetto. When he wrote to the Jewish Council on 16 May ordering them to pay for fencing in the ghetto, the chief constable also instructed them to nominate Jews who would leave to shop for the whole ghetto population. On 19 May the Jewish Council submitted a handwritten list of 28 names,[4] with a shorter supplementary list following a day later.[5] The first list included four married women in their thirties and early forties – Mrs Miklós F., Mrs Gyula S., Mrs Sándor S. and Mrs Sándor H. – who were to leave the ghetto to shop. But their names came as something of an afterthought at the end of the letter below the signatures of two members of the Jewish Council. More prominent on the two lists were the names of another twenty-seven individuals who the Jewish Council requested were to leave the ghetto on a daily basis for a host of other reasons. The chief constable's specific request that the Jewish Council provide the names of ghetto shoppers had been met by two letters asking that a tenth of the ghetto population be allowed to leave the soon-to-be closed ghetto. Just who the Jewish Council wanted to leave the ghetto, when and why is worth examining – prior to the chief constable's response – as it is suggestive of how the Jewish Council imagined ghettoization.

It is clear that the Jewish Council assumed that the smooth running of a closed ghetto would entail more than simply a shopping group being allowed to exit through the ghetto gates. Far higher up the list than the names of the four-woman shopping group were the names of the men who made up the Jewish Council. They needed to be able to leave the ghetto at any time both night and day to undertake official business. Another group of men needed to exit the ghetto to collect post, urgent medicine and newspapers, collect bread and carry groceries. It was not simply foodstuffs that needed bringing into the ghetto, but also information (mail and newspapers) and medicines. But the Jewish Council did more than simply expand the categories of who needed to leave the ghetto to ensure the continuation of life within its walls during the early summer of 1944. They also reimagined the place.

Dominating the lists sent by the Jewish Council both numerically and in terms of their physical placement were the names of men and women who were to continue working outside the ghetto. Over half the initial Jewish Council requests were that Jews be allowed to continue their pre-ghetto employment as doctors, workers in a steam saw mill, clerks, shoemakers, tailors, hauliers, tinsmiths and plumbers.[6] Rather than being a place where all Jews were to be housed, separate from the non-Jews in the town twenty-four hours a day, the Jewish Council saw the ghetto as a place where a number of Jews of working age would leave each morning to go to work and then return to at the end of the day to sleep. This fitted with the spirit of an earlier order issued by the chief constable on 8 May 1944 that Jews (doctors and vets aside) were only to leave their apartments between seven in the morning and seven in the evening.[7] In Körmend, the Jewish Council assumed that, despite ghettoization, at least some Jews should continue to leave their homes – homes now in the 'ghetto' – during daylight hours to continue working. In the majority of cases it seems that they saw this as more than simply a temporary provision. In short they imagined the ghetto as something like a semi-permanent workers dormitory for at least a part of the town's Jewish population.

However, whatever Jewish Council perceptions, the critical question is how the chief constable responded to these requests which seemed to misread the ghetto. What is surprising is that all but one of the Jewish Council's initial requests was successful.[8] When he first wrote to the Jewish Council on 16 May, the chief constable only intended that a limited number of individuals leave the ghetto to ensure that the ghetto was fed – what the late Raul Hilberg described as 'institutional transactions that had to be maintained if the ghetto was to function',[9] but a week later he signed a series of passes that allowed Jews to leave the ghetto for a much wider set of reasons, including continuing daytime employment in the town.[10]

As a result of the intervention of the Jewish Council, local officials drew up a generic ghetto pass on 23 May allowing the holder to leave only through the Széchényi utca gate and to travel by the most direct route and return as soon as they had finished the task they had been permitted to leave the ghetto for.[11] There was to be no dawdling. Exiting the ghetto was solely for specified purposes, with passes strictly non-transferable. Any abuses which the Jewish Council discovered were to be reported immediately to the authorities. In short, the Jewish Council was to play a policing role within the ghetto. In articulating this it is clear that those drawing up these permits saw them as a system potentially open to abuse, hence the setting out of a series of restrictions on who could go where and when and for what purpose. The pass was not *carte blanche* for a general exodus from the ghetto but the limited loosening of the segregatory confinement of ghettoization for a number of named individuals for a specified period of time.

The ghetto passes issued by the chief constable in Körmend can be seen as part of a much broader phenomenon that Hilberg dubbed, 'a control system consisting of identity cards, papers, and the like ... instituted by a variety of agencies in most regions of German-dominated Europe'.[12] It was not just that Jews across central and Eastern Europe were subjected to territorial control by being placed in urban ghettos *en masse*, but also Jews as individuals were given varying degrees of access to different places during the war through a plethora of regulatory paperwork. The extent of this paperwork can be seen most strikingly in the case of Warsaw, where around 53,000 individuals were permitted to enter and leave the ghetto.[13] Körmend was not Warsaw. Here was a ghetto housing fewer than 300 Jews. But ultimately around one-third of the Jews living in the Körmend ghetto were allowed to leave the confines of this fenced ghetto on journeys regulated through a series of passes issued by the chief constable in the town and checked by policemen at the ghetto gates.

While the generic ghetto pass drawn up on 23 May can be seen as a response to the initiative taken by the Jewish Council a few days before (and a minor victory for the Jewish Council), there was one critical difference between the Jewish Council's wish list and the draft pass. On the latter the expiration date was fixed at 31 May 1944, which was a date that only cropped up on the Jewish Council list for a handful of clerks.[14] Local officials drawing up this generic paperwork on 23 May clearly saw their shelf-life to be limited to just over one week. But, when passes were finally issued later on that day and the days that followed, few had an end date on them. The 34 passes issued on 23 May more or less mirrored the requests made by the Jewish Council on 19 and 20 May, as well as including a number of individuals that did not feature on either of the earlier lists who were also to continue working outside of the ghetto.[15]

THE EXCEPTIONAL MOBILITY OF TWO JEWISH DOCTORS: DR IGNÁC P. AND DR GYULA SZ.

It makes sense to begin with the first pass issued on 23 May, given to the oldest member of the five-man Jewish Council in Körmend, seventy-three-year-old Dr Ignác P., who could leave the ghetto from both gates at any time – both night and day – to go anywhere in the town.[16] His freedom of movement, both temporally and spatially, was unique. His four other fellow Jewish Council members could only leave the ghetto between 7 am and 10 pm through the main Széchényi utca gateway. That the ghetto fence was permanently permeable for Dr P. was not so that he could 'deal with the affairs of the Jews and meet with the authorities' as was stated on the passes issued to his fellow Jewish Council members, but to allow him to visit patients throughout the town. The ghetto was to be the base from which he operated, making frequent forays out of its fenced-in confines to visit the sick in Körmend.

Another Jewish doctor who was issued a ghetto pass escaped the confines of the ghetto altogether. Dr Gyula Sz. was not from Körmend itself, but from the nearby village of Újfehértó, which was one of the many places in rural Hungary too small to have its own ghetto. Jews from Újfehértó were concentrated in the ghetto in Körmend.[17] However, when the chief constable wrote to village authorities on 9 May informing them that Jews were to be moved into the ghetto in Körmend by 12 May, he explicitly excluded Jewish doctors and vets who had been mobilized in the Hungarian army from this directive. They were to remain living in their homes, although their relatives had to relocate to the ghetto.[18] This meant that Dr Sz. and his wife were separated. Jolán was taken to the ghetto.[19] Gyula was not. In early June he was serving at the military base at Nádasd, separated from his wife by a two-metre high ghetto fence and a couple of miles.

On 2 June, Dr Sz. was given permission by the chief constable in Körmend to spend part of the weekend in the ghetto with his wife.[20] He arrived at five on the afternoon of 3 June, leaving at seven on the evening of 4 June. He was the only Jew to receive a pass to temporarily enter the Körmend ghetto. His visit is an extraordinary anomaly. Three weeks after the ghetto had been sealed with the erection of a two-metre high wooden fence, permission was granted for a Jew from Körmend district to enter the ghetto for the weekend and then simply walk away. Like Dr P., Dr. Sz. had an exceptional story. What both shared was a profession. They – like Dr Lajos K. named as living in a 'temporary residence' outside the ghetto in Hőgyész – were medics.

It is not surprising to find Jewish doctors in towns like Hőgyész or Körmend in 1944. In the 1930s, over half of all doctors in Hungary were Jews, with the proportion even higher in towns and cities outside the capital.[21] The perceived over-representation of Jews in the medical profession drew the ire of radicals who pressed for limits on the numbers of Jewish doctors in interwar Hungary.[22] However, the realities of large numbers of Hungarian communities being reliant on Jewish doctors posed a dilemma once ghettoization and deportation got underway in the late spring and early summer of 1944. In the city of Nagyvárad in Transylvania, local officials reported that placing Jewish doctors into the ghetto there 'had temporarily aggravated the healthcare situation in the city', which was a complaint echoed elsewhere.[23] But despite local murmurings, national officials took a hard line. On 23 June, when Jews across the country were housed in ghettos, national legislation was introduced forbidding Jewish doctors from treating non-Jewish patients and László Endre rejected calls that Jewish doctors be spared from deportations.[24]

In Körmend in May and June 1944, a temporary local solution was adopted that allowed Dr P. to continue treating non-Jewish patients despite ghettoization, as part of a broader local policy of Jews continuing to work outside the ghetto. He may have been the only doctor in the town by the early summer of 1944 and so the segregatory logic of ghettoization was pragmatically done away with to ensure that the sick in the town could continue to see a doctor. He was too valuable to be closed off behind a ghetto fence night and day. But he was not too valuable to the Hungarian state to escape deportation. His name is there on the ghetto list drawn up in the middle of June 1944, just a couple of days before Jews from Körmend were taken from the ghetto to the railway station and then on to the ghetto in Szombathely.[25] And here his story differs from that of Dr Sz.. Although Dr P. and Dr Sz. shared a medical training in common, they were a generation apart. Dr P. was a man in his seventies. Dr Sz. was probably in his fifties.[26] And while Dr P. treated the civilian population in Körmend, Dr Sz. treated the military at their Nádasd base. When push came to shove, it was the healthcare of the Hungarian military that trumped that of the civilian population. Dr P. was deported. Dr Sz. was not.

But while Dr P. did not escape deportation, he did escape the full segregatory logic of ghettoization. And here he was not alone. The flurry of passes on 23 May was merely the beginning of paperwork permitting exit and entry through the ghetto gates. By the time that the last pass had been issued on 18 June, sixty-five had been granted.[27] The majority of this paperwork allowed Jews to work outside the ghetto and non-Jews to work in the ghetto. In short, the ghetto fence was permeable in order to allow the local economy to continue functioning. The local authorities permitted fifteen men and nine women to exit the ghetto in order to continue working in Körmend as plumbers, cobblers, tinsmiths, commercial clerks, tailors, dress fitters and pleaters as well as ladder menders, hauliers, watchmen, workers in the saw mills, and in the case of Dr P. as a medical doctor.[28] This economic traffic was two-way. In the same period, the authorities allowed nine men to enter the ghetto to work as painters, repairers, electricians, cleaners, teachers, barbers and pastors.[29]

Issuing ghetto passes was a local pragmatic solution to the problem thrown up by creating a closed ghetto. As Isaiah Trunk noted of ghettos more generally, the walling in of the ghetto brought about 'the final, mortal blow' to Jews within the economic sphere, who were now 'entirely cut off from hundreds of years of economic ties to their gentile neighbours.'[30] It was not only placing Jewish medics in fenced off ghettos that created problems, but placing a host of Jewish professionals and craftspeople behind two-metre high wooden fences. Doing so threatened the viability of the local economy.

The question of how to deal with the long history of economic relations between Jews and non-Jews had been a source of debate between moderate and radical antisemites in interwar Hungary. While there was widespread agreement that Jews should be removed from dominant positions within the Hungarian economy, there was disagreement over the pace of this change. Radicals advocated the rapid removal of Jews from the Hungarian economy, but moderates feared economic collapse if Jews were to be removed from the economic sphere too quickly. These concerns were heightened during the war years. The result was, as Yehuda Don has demonstrated, that the 1939 anti-Jewish law, aimed at restricting Jewish participation in public and economic life, was never fully implemented during the premiership of the relatively moderate Miklós Kállay. This was not because of the nature of the law itself. As Don stresses, '[I]deologically, Act IV 1939 remained impeccable. Pragmatically, it was not implementable.'[31] This clash between antisemitic ideology and economic pragmatism can also be seen in the consistent rebutting of German demands for mass deportations of Hungarian Jews – prior to 1944 – on the grounds that this would damage the Hungarian wartime economy, with the knock-on impact of damaging the German wartime economy.[32]

However, with the enacting of ghettoization from April 1944 onwards, Hungarian Jews were, in principle at least, suddenly and completely removed from economic life, segregated as they were behind a ghetto fence. This temporary removal became more permanent with physical removal from Hungary as deportations commenced in May 1944. That ghettoization meant the removal of Jews from the local and national economy was a cause of concern to some. A board member of the Financial Institution Centre noted that, 'the economy has ground to a halt' in the Kassa district as a result of the implementation of ghettoization in April 1944.[33] However, in Körmend, the impact of ghettoization was moderated through a *modus vivendi* of sorts that allowed for a degree of continuing economic exchange between Jews and non-Jews brandishing their ghetto passes.

CONTINUING ECONOMIC EXCHANGE BETWEEN JEWS AND NON-JEWS: SÁNDOR F. AND JÁNOS G.

On 23 May, the seventy-year-old, Sándor F., was given permission to leave the ghetto for twelve hours each day to work as a tinsmith and plumber throughout Körmend.[34] However, it would seem that within a week, some of his equipment broke down and therefore, on 31 May, a non-Jew, Károly K., was allowed to enter the ghetto for an hour on that day, and the two following days, to mend the machinery in Sándor F.'s workshop within the ghetto.[35] It was clear from both passes that Sándor F.'s continuing plumbing and tinsmith services were very much in demand in the town, and the ghetto wall was permeable enough to allow this to continue to be the case. Rather than being self-sufficient and separate communities, it is clear that Jews and non-Jews in Körmend were linked through a network of economic relationships, whose significance was, no doubt, heightened during wartime.

Not only were Jews still working outside the ghetto fence, but also a small number of non-Jews entered the ghetto in order to work there during daylight hours. On 26 May, two painters and decorators spent the day in the ghetto painting and decorating. Within a week they returned for another two days work.[36] In the days that followed, others entered the ghetto. Alongside the painters and decorators, and the man mending machinery in Sándor F's workshop, came two electricians, a man to clean out the toilets, a teacher, a Lutheran pastor and a barber.[37]

The entry of a barber into the ghetto is somewhat ironic, given what we know of the events a couple of weeks after he first started cutting hair within the ghetto's two-metre high wooden fence. I suppose that after a month in the ghetto, there was a need for a barber. Presumably there was no barber in the ghetto, and so János G.'s skills were needed. He first started work in the abandoned barbershop in the ghetto at 7 am on Wednesday 14 June 1944, cutting hair for six hours, before returning again on the morning of Friday 16 June. On Monday 19 June, the ghetto was liquidated and the majority of the town's Jews marched through the main street to the railway station. They were first taken by train to Szombathely. From there they were taken to Auschwitz-Birkenau, where all of János G.'s work would be undone. But presumably, those living in the ghetto in Körmend in mid-June 1944, knew little or nothing of Auschwitz-Birkenau, and certainly did not expect to be sent there, shaved, and for the majority of the ghetto inhabitants, gassed and cremated there within a couple of weeks. It would seem that the ghetto was viewed as enough of a medium-term measure to mean that by mid June, after being in existence for around a month, peoples' thoughts were turning to their hair, and the need to make arrangements for getting it cut.

WORKING AT, AND WINDING UP, THE FRIM STEAM SAW MILL

However, not all of the ghetto passes point to continuity despite ghettoization. In their initial approach to the chief constable on 19 May, the Jewish Council had put in requests for a number of men to leave the ghetto to continue working at the Frim steam saw mill.[38] From 23 May onwards, Samu L. left the ghetto each morning at 5.30 for the mill.[39] An hour later, Sándor W. left to join him.[40] A little later – at 8 each morning – another two men left the ghetto to walk to the mill. Gyula G. worked there as a clerk.[41] Accompanying him was his boss, Géza F., who owned the saw mill.[42] The fifth man permitted to leave the ghetto to work at the mill was Lájos R., who worked as a daytime watchman there on Sundays and major holidays.[43] In part, this daily exodus of men from the ghetto to the saw mill, mirrored the broader daily exodus of Jews permitted to leave the ghetto to go to their workplaces, which amounted to some extent at least a case of business as usual in spite of ghettoization. However, in the case of Géza F., the reason for his daily journey was somewhat different. He had originally been given permission to leave the ghetto to travel to the saw mill only until the end of the month.[44] His journeying there was not simply for ongoing work, but for a specific task with an end date. As became clear in a request made at the end of the month that Géza F. be allowed to leave the ghetto for a further three weeks, his daily activities in late May 1944 involved the process of inventorying the steam saw mill – a process that had taken longer than the initial week assigned for this task.[45]

Géza F. was one of several Jews living in the Körmend ghetto who were given permission to leave the ghetto walls not to continue their work in the town, but to wind up their businesses. All Jewish businesses had been forced to close by 21 April 1944,[46] but it is clear that there was still work associated with this legislation outstanding at the time that ghettoization measures were implemented. It was not only Géza F. who left the ghetto to tidy up his affairs. A former lawyer left each afternoon in order to visit the lawyer who was administering his business affairs.[47] Another two left the ghetto for a few hours on four separate occasions in order to visit the lawyers who were acting as the guardian/receiver for the administration of their business affairs.[48] On 10 June, one Jewish woman left the ghetto for the day in order to empty out her former apartment outside the ghetto walls.[49] On the same day, a Jewish man left the ghetto for two hours in the afternoon in order to settle accounts at a vinegar factory.[50] Two days later, another Jewish man left the ghetto for half a day in order to settle accounts with his former employer.[51]

Alongside allowing Jews to continue working outside the ghetto (and non-Jews within the ghetto), officials in Körmend were also concerned to ensure the successful implementation of other earlier anti-Jewish measures. Given the rapidity of anti-Jewish measures implemented in Hungary in the aftermath of the German occupation, it is perhaps not surprising that there were times when measures conflicted, institutions collided, and a degree of chaos characterized the early summer months. As Kádár and Vági have shown, this was particularly the case with measures implemented to expropriate Jewish wealth, goods and property, where 'the dynamics of expropriation could not keep up with the speed of the deportations'.[52] Ghettoization was enacted in the midst of the rather chaotic expropriation of Jewish wealth, leading Finance Minister Lajos Reményi-Schneller to complain at the Council of Ministers meeting on 1 June that, '[M]ost of these [ghettoized] Jews could not declare their wealth at all, and on the other hand the assets (valuables and movable property) that were left at the flats, shops, warehouses, etc., of Jews who had been relocated from their homes were left uncared-for and unattended, and so some of these – according to the reports of various financial directorates – were lost.'[53] Although it is clear that ghettoization meant expropriation (Chapter 7),[54] it also threatened – as the finance minister noted – the orderly completion of earlier measures enacted by the Hungarian state. In order to ensure that expropriation such as the confiscation of Jewish businesses were effectively implemented in the locality, Jews were allowed to leave the Körmend ghetto to complete the necessary paperwork. But, as the pass given to Géza F. makes clear, this was a task with a clear end date, unlike the ongoing job of continuing work in the town outside the ghetto fence.[55]

Here are two rather different stories. Both point to solutions adopted in the locality to mediate the segregatory logic of ghettoization. But the critical difference between the passes issued to Géza F. and the workers who also left the ghetto each morning for the steam saw mill is that Géza's pass – initially at least – only ran until the end of the month, because his job there was temporary. He was simply tidying up the paperwork of his business that had been confiscated by the Hungarian state. By contrast, Sándor W. and Samu L. continued working in a saw mill which was in the midst of changing ownership.[56] In short, these passes point to histories of continuities of work and histories of change of ownership. Jews were no longer owners, but they continued – here at least – to be workers as ghettoization was implemented. Indeed, for increasing numbers of Jews in Körmend, labour outside the ghetto became a day-to-day experience in June 1944.

LEAF COLLECTING AT THE NÁDASD CAVALRY GROUND

Once the ghetto had been established in Körmend, it was no longer just the Jewish Council that approached the local authorities with requests that Jews be allowed to leave the ghetto to work. Just days after the ghetto was closed off, the leaders of the Körmend branch of the *Levente* organization, a paramilitary youth organization for twelve- to twenty-year-old boys, wrote to the chief constable. They were raising 51,000 silk worms – presumably for parachute silk – which meant a constant need for massive quantities of mulberry leaves. These were available from the mulberry trees at the Nádasd cavalry ground, but the issue was one of labour. This is where Körmend's Jews came in or, more specifically, twelve Jewish boys aged between twelve and nineteen, who were needed to collect these leaves.[57] On 24 May, these boys were permitted to leave the ghetto each morning and afternoon, from 1 to 15 June, to collect mulberry leaves.[58] On 15 June, a new pass was issued, extending the expiry date from 15 June until 28 June.[59] During June 1944, this group of Jewish adolescents travelled from the ghetto to the *Levente* house and then on to the Nádasd cavalry grounds, which lay a couple of miles south of Körmend, for eleven to twelve hours of leaf collecting each day.[60] Before embarking on this ongoing daily task, the group of twelve boys left the ghetto on 25 May to carry rags and paper at the local *Levente* headquarters, which was presumably a single-day's work that needing doing and the answer to the problem of finding manpower was met in the ghetto.[61]

It was not just Jewish teenagers who were mobilized en masse for one-off tasks or ongoing jobs. The army headquarters in Celldömölki asked for twenty Körmend Jews to carry timber from a wood on the outskirts of the village to the railway station in Nádasd,[62] and on 27 May, a group of twenty was duly dispatched from the ghetto in order to accomplish this task.[63] By early to mid-June, Jewish women were also being requested to work outside the ghetto. On 10 June, twelve fifteen- to twenty-eight-year-old Jewish women started gardening work for thirteen hours each day in the Prince Batthyány garden in the town.[64] On 12 June, a group of five thirty-seven to forty-six-year-old

Jewish women started gardening work for thirteen hours each day at the garden of Arpád H.,[65] and another five Jewish women aged between eighteen and twenty-eight years old started working on Imre J.'s farm.[66] On 15 June, the leaf-collecting group mobilized by *Levente* swelled in numbers with the recruitment of a younger boy – eleven-year-old Jeno B. – and nine nine- to fourteen-year-old girls. By the last week of the ghetto's existence, a little over one-sixth of the female population was leaving the ghetto early each morning in order to do gardening, agricultural work and leaf collecting: jobs that one survivor from Körmend remembers as fuelling a rumour that if you worked very hard then you would not come to any harm.[67]

In Körmend, the story of the ghetto passes is one that is about more than simply the interventions of the Jewish Council in ensuring that Jews could keep on working outside the ghetto. It is also about the interventions of other institutions and individuals who saw in the ghettoized Jews in Körmend a potential labour force. Jewish boys, girls, men and women were seen as too valuable to be simply left behind the ghetto fence in this town, but could be put to work outside the ghetto in organized labour gangs. It seems that this is something that was happening elsewhere in the early summer of 1944.[68] In part, this was an extension of broader concerns that Jewish men of military age played their part in the war effort that predated 1944 and resulted in the setting up of labour battalions. In Körmend in May and June 1944, Jewish boys, girls and women were also to do their bit for the war effort, and that meant removing them from the ghetto temporarily. But more permanent removals took place here, as in Veszprém, with the military call up of Jewish men in the middle of June.

MOBILIZING JEWISH MEN: ERNŐ H., ZOLTÁN M., SÁNDOR G. AND IGNÁC N.

On 9 June, the chief constable informed the Jewish Council in Körmend of the Defence Ministry decision to mobilize all eighteen- to forty-eight-year-old Jewish men. They were to ensure that all men born between 1896 and 1926 gathered at 8 am on the morning of 12 June in a suitable place in the ghetto to undergo a medical.[69] One man, Sándor G., had already been given permission a few weeks earlier to leave the ghetto for three hours in the afternoon in order to buy equipment necessary for joining the military, suggesting that there was knowledge that a new wave of call-ups was imminent.[70] Mobilized on 12 June were two of the older boys in the group of teenagers that had made their way to the Nádasd cavalry grounds to collect mulberry leaves each day. Ernő H. and Zoltán M., born in 1925 and 1926 respectively, no longer collected leaves for the *Levente* organization, but were part of the Hungarian Army.[71] They left the ghetto permanently alongside thirteen others.

We don't know how these fifteen men – given three days' notice of their impending call-up – interpreted leaving the ghetto for the military on 12 June.

But there is a hint that for at least one of them this was not welcomed; rather, it was something he actively sought to avoid. When the Jewish Council received the letter from the chief constable on 9 June informing them that Jewish men should report for a medical in three days' time, this news had a personal impact on one of their number. Most of the five-man Jewish Council were too old for this call-up, aged between 52 and 73, but Ignác N. was only 46.[72] On 12 June, it seems that he turned up at the prescribed place in the ghetto brandishing a letter from the chief constable officer confirming his date of birth, as well as his Jewish Council membership credentials.[73] We cannot tell for sure what this letter was intended to achieve, but it seems likely that it was intended as a means of releasing Ignác N. from military call-up, so that he could continue serving in the Jewish Council in Körmend. However, his strategy failed. This letter – and Jewish Council service – was not enough to keep him in the ghetto. Ignác N. was no longer in the ghetto on 16 June. The five-man Jewish Council had lost one of its members to the Hungarian army.

With hindsight, it appears surprising that one of the Jewish Council members would seek to escape the draft on 12 June 1944. After all, what we know is that a week later, the 286 Jews living in the Körmend ghetto – of which Ignác N.'s wife was one – were taken to Szombathely, and then on to Auschwitz-Birkenau a few weeks after that.[74] By contrast, men serving in military battalions escaped not only ghettoization, but also deportation (Chapter 1). But for Ignác N. in mid-June 1944 it seems that ghettoization was seen as preferable to military service. This certainly raises questions about what a Jewish Council member in a provincial town like Körmend knew in the summer of 1944 of the ultimate fate of the ghetto. Of course it may be that Ignác N. knew what ghettoization meant and had a strong sense of duty and wished to remain a part of the leadership of his people. But my sense is that he would not have known, and was more concerned with staying with his wife. As can be seen elsewhere, familial separation was a traumatic experience (Chapters 1 and 8). Whatever his motivations for seeking to avoid mobilization, Ignác N.'s membership of the Jewish Council meant little to the military. What mattered was that he was a man born in 1897, and so he was conscripted on 12 June given his perceived labour value to the Hungarian state.

MATYÁS R.'S TWO JOURNEYS OUT OF THE GHETTO FENCE

Another man, Matyás R., left the ghetto on 12 June, but unlike Ignác N. and the other Jewish men mobilized with him, Matyás returned to the ghetto later that day to join his forty-five-year-old-wife and leaf-collecting thirteen-year-old-son István. Matyás had been born on 12 December 1895, and so was just eighteen days too old to be mobilized by the military.[75] He left the ghetto on 12 June not to join a labour battalion, but for a few hours to settle accounts with his former employer.[76] By this point in mid-June 1944, it is clear that the reasons

for granting *new* permissions to leave the ghetto were less about continuity –
continuing to work – than they were about closure. Jews were busy clearing out
apartments, and settling accounts. Perhaps the clearest example of this comes
with a surprising pass, issued on a Sunday, the day before deportations from
Körmend took place. On Sunday 18 June, one Jew was allowed to leave the
ghetto in order to go to the savings bank to undertake official business.[77] What
this amounted to does not emerge from the bland wording of the pass. But a
man going to the town's savings bank on a Sunday is a strange occurrence, to
say the least. This was no ordinary Sunday. It was the last day that Körmend's
Jews lived in this town. That Sunday visit to the bank was no doubt the final
transaction relating to the Jewish collective account in this community. After
the issuing of strict controls over Jewish bank accounts in April 1944, all Jewish
accounts were combined into a collective account[78] that paid for the costs
associated with the anti-Jewish measures such as ghettoization and presumably,
in the case of Körmend, the mass transport of the entire town's Jews, by train,
to Szombathely the following day. On 19 June, the Jews of Körmend left the
ghetto for the last time. As they crossed the main street of the town someone
took two photographs of this column made up mainly of women, children and
the elderly. I want to turn to look at those photographs in the next chapter to ask
what bystanders saw as well as how they understood the events of deportations.

PART II

People's Stories: Narratives of Ghettoization and Deportation

6

Viewing Deportations: Photographs from Körmend, Kőszeg and Balatonfüred

Körmend's Jews, carrying suitcases and bundles of possessions, were escorted by gendarmes out of the ghetto around midday on 19 June. They were marched along Vida József utca, over Rákoczi Ferenc út and down Thököly Imre utca in the direction of the railway station. As they crossed Rákoczi Ferenc út – the main street in the town – they were photographed by an unknown photographer watching this procession from their vantage point at a first floor apartment window in Rákoczi Ferenc út 8.[1] These images are just two of an estimated more than two million surviving photographs of the Holocaust, which is 'one of the visually best documented events in the history of an era marked by a plenitude of visual documentation'.[2] Photographs of deportations survive from a small number of other Hungarian towns and cities,[3] as well as from elsewhere in wartime Europe, with the richest collections coming from Germany where the local authorities in some cities commissioned photographs.[4] However, only a tiny fraction of Holocaust photographs have been subjected to academic scrutiny with photographs taken by perpetrators receiving the most sustained attention.[5] Snapshots of Jews taken by German soldiers in the East have been interpreted as evidence both of widespread antisemitism,[6] and feelings of cultural superiority.[7]

Largely absent from academic reflection are photographs taken by bystanders, the photographs taken by Allied photographers at the liberation of the camps aside.[8] But that is not to say that these two photographs from Körmend are entirely unknown. They have been reproduced in books and integrated into a recent memorial erected at the site of the former ghetto.[9] The inclusion of deportation photographs within memorial works can also be seen in a better-known set of images from Kőszeg that I also work with in this chapter.[10] However, they have largely been used as illustration, rather than receiving more sustained analysis.[11] One way for historians to work with photographs of deportations was signalled by Sybil Milton, writing of the images pasted into War Chronicles (*Kriegschronik*) created in a number of German cities. These images, she suggested, 'provide visual evidence of Jewish behaviour confirming Raul Hilberg's thesis of "survival by acquiescence"' and 'in rare instances, the visual record of the deportation of the Jews … allows us to analyse the behaviour of the bystanders, the native population occasionally visible in the background or purchasing the abandoned property of deported Jews'.[12] The behaviour of victims, bystanders and perpetrators during deportation are visible in the two photographs taken of the deportation of Jews from Körmend and the other photographs that I look at, and I would like to examine them in such terms.

But there is so much more to deportation photographs than simply reading them as capturing a moment of the past frozen in time. 'To state the obvious,' wrote Alan Trachtenberg, 'photographs transcribe, not "reality," but the world as it was seen and recorded.'[13] The photographs taken in Körmend do not simply record the presence of non-Jewish townspeople at the deportations, they also point to the actions of one of them who chose to photograph. Photographs are not simply images of historical events, but 'are themselves the historical.'[14] Looking at photographs, we are initially drawn to the image itself. But then we – metaphorically – step out of the frame, in order to turn our attention to the photographer looking through the viewfinder and pressing the shutter, given that 'all photographs tell stories about looking'[15] or to draw on Peter Burke's description of historical images more broadly, 'they record acts of eyewitnessing.'[16]

It is here that photographs are particularly useful as historical evidence. It is the very partiality of a photograph – framed to exclude as well as include, with the shutter depressed at a particular moment in time, focused on a particular something or someone – that allows us to ask questions about what was recorded and not recorded by the photographer, when and why. The 'distortion' which results from any image reflecting the 'point of view' of the producer is, rather than a problem, a possibility.[17] Images – as with any other text – are useful precisely because they offer the historian, in Burke's words, 'evidence of phenomena that many historians want to study: mentalities, ideologies and identities.'[18] Not only does a photograph offer evidence of what the photographer saw, but also how it was seen: In Susan Sontag's words, '[P]hotographs are … not just a record but an evaluation of the world.'[19] In this chapter I work with a handful of deportation photographs taken by non-Jewish neighbours to ask how they viewed and interpreted events of the Holocaust that unfolded on urban streets and in railway stations. In short, I am interested in using photographs to examine the bystander gaze.[20]

THE ORDINARY SPACES OF DEPORTATIONS

Taking the two photographs from Körmend, it is striking how ordinary both the time and place of deportations of Jews from this town were. The images show the main crossroads at the middle of the day. There was no attempt to hide this event either temporally or spatially. Rather than taking a circuitous route from the ghetto to the station very early in the morning or late in the evening, the most direct route was taken around noon. It is hard to say with any certainty whether the choice of deportation through the central crossroads in the town in the middle of the day was simply about the functional pragmatics of getting the Jews from point a – the ghetto – to point b – the railway station – by the most direct route possible to make a scheduled train, or whether it was motivated by a concern with display. Whatever the motivation, the route and timing meant that deportation was a highly visible event enacted in a busy market town around midday when the streets were thronged with shoppers.

Photographs of deportations from Körmend, Yad Vashem Photo Archives, courtesy of United States Holocaust Memorial Museum (USHMM) Photo Archives.

The unknown photographer was far from alone in observing the scene, even if it appears that they were the only one to photograph it. In an apartment across the road – at Rákoczi Ferenc út 1–3 – two people lean out of their apartment window, mirroring the vantage point of the photographer. More numerous by far are those who watch from the street. In particular, the pavements of Rákoczi Ferenc út and Vida József utca that are visible in the photographs appear to be thronged with people watching the column of Jews in the middle of the street. Körmend was not a large town. In 1941, just over 7,400 people were recorded in this town where 300 Jews lived. In this small market town where, as the ghetto passes point to, there were strong and ongoing economic relationships between Jews and non-Jews, it is clear that large numbers of townspeople witnessed and watched the deportation of Jews known to them as neighbours. What is harder to say is whether they simply happened to be at this central crossroads in the town as the line of Jews was marched from the ghetto to the railway station or whether they heard that this event was taking place, and came to watch.

What the presence of two photographs, taken in quick succession, does allow is an animation of sorts of the scene. Placed together, it becomes clear who in the image was moving and who stayed still. The most obvious movement is the central column of marching Jews and accompanying gendarmes, who journey out of the town. But there is also some movement among a few of the non-Jewish neighbours. In the second photograph, a man walks, purposefully, head down, on the pavement, in the same direction as the line of Jews – although he appears to be ignoring their presence and has the air of someone who just happened to be headed in the same direction. Close to him, another man on a bicycle is frozen, cycling along Rákoczi Ferenc út, towards the column which halts his progress. You imagine him waiting, and then once the column is gone, continuing his journey. (Or was it that he was cycling quickly to get there in time in order to see what was happening?)

But while there are glimpses of movement among a few of the non-Jewish neighbours who also occupy the streets of the town around midday on 19 June, the vast majority are revealed in the two photographs to be stationary. Most townspeople stopped what they were doing that day to watch as the Jews were marched to the railway station through the centre of Körmend. In the photographs not everyone looks at the line of the Jews. Some look at each other, seemingly engaged in conversation. Some have their heads down. But most do look. It is children who stand closest to the line. Two boys stand only eight feet or so from the marching Jews, and two girls, one carrying a younger child, run along the side of the road, keeping pace with the marching line. Adults stand a little further back on the pavement or in doorways of buildings rather than in the road. Their distance may well be due to the presence of gendarmes marching along, parallel to the column of Jews in the no-man's land of sorts that separated the line of Jews from their watching neighbours: a no-man's land that these gendarmes in a sense police. Beyond this no-man's land many townspeople stand grouped together in clusters. Watching the procession was a shared – a communal – event, rather than a solitary activity in Körmend.

The collective gaze of non-Jewish townspeople on the line of Jews is not, in the main, reciprocated. The majority of the Jews being marched to the railway station look straight ahead or walk with their heads down. Their focus is on the journey and in some cases on those immediately around them. One couple appear to be talking, their heads bent towards each other. A man pauses while the person next to him stops to adjust the packages they are carrying. One woman turns round to check on those immediately behind her, perhaps the man who walks, head down, seemingly supported by the man on his left. Another woman holds a parasol to shade her from the midday summer sun; yet another wheels a child in a pushchair.

Only a small number of Jews in the column look to the sides of the roads, where the pavements are thronged with observers. One child, in a pushchair, directs their eyes along the main street of the town. In the second photograph, a woman and boy about a third of the way along the line both look to their right. The movement of their heads is mirrored in the rightward gaze of a boy in a cap a couple of rows in front of them. His glance in the same direction suggests that something or someone captured the attention of all three. But that something or someone is excluded from the frame. Also outside the frame is the photographer. It would seem that only a very few in the line realized that they were being photographed. A handful look directly into the lens, and their eyes meet ours as we look at these photographs taken over six decades ago. But from the visual evidence in the photograph there appears to be little sense of reciprocity of gazes. While the majority of non-Jewish townspeople on the streets looked at this procession of Jews, most of those Jews being marched to the railway station did not return the gaze.

The clusters of non-Jewish neighbours standing on the pavements in central Körmend a 'safe' distance from the line of deported Jews appear the very epitome of the passive bystander to the Holocaust. The tendency has been to see the wide variety of individuals and institutions dubbed as 'bystanders' to the Holocaust having a shared experience of inaction in common. In his survey of Holocaust historiography, Michael Marrus described bystanders to the Holocaust in terms of what they did not do: '[I]nformation on the Holocaust was not digested, Jews were not admitted, Jewish communities failed to unite, Allied governments spurned rescue suggestions, and access to Auschwitz was not bombed.'[21] Presumably 'townspeople failed to protest the deportations' is something that could be added to this litany of inactivity. Indifference is often seen lying behind this inactivity, something which has emerged within popular tellings of the Holocaust as the critical moral lesson offered by examining Holocaust bystanders.[22]

However, historians have pointed to the dangers of an overly condemning tone in writing on bystanders to the Holocaust and a tendency to jump too quickly to assume that inaction reflected indifference, rather than attempting to grapple with the context within which non-Jewish neighbours encountered the events of the Holocaust.[23] In the Yale University Fortunoff Video Archive for Holocaust Testimonies, there is a moving interview with a Catholic priest who was in his early twenties when Hungarian Jews were deported. In this rare interview with a bystander, Father John S. recalled peering through a hole in the fence at the railway station and seeing one of the deportation trains – which was for him, 'my train, my deportee train'. He described seeing 'literally ... what you see in pictures, mothers with children and people and old people and little children and all ... the impression was terrifying, it was really ... packed, I mean compressed' and a man who 'looked a bit like my father' being clubbed by a German soldier. 'And then I ran away,' recalled Father John, 'I was so scared and I was so upset, I never saw anything like this in my life, I simply ran away ... and you know, this, I see it, personally, as the greatest tragedy of my life, that ... there Jewish people were deported all around me, I didn't do anything, I panicked, I ... not even panic, not even fear, I just didn't know what to do.'[24]

For Father John, recalling the events of decades earlier, his greatest regret was that he 'didn't do anything' because he 'didn't know what to do'. His inactivity was, in his own words at least, not a result of indifference but an inability to know how to respond. He saw, but then did not know what to do with what he saw. But it is clear that at least one person in Körmend who saw the deportations decided to do something – to photograph these events. In doing this, did they cease to be those who 'didn't do anything' and therefore were no longer a passive bystander? As can be seen from other traces that I work with in this book, non-Jewish neighbours in Hungary participated in the elements that make up what we know as the Holocaust, including taking photographs, and the blanket term 'bystander' with its suggestions of inactivity is hardly appropriate to describe the variety of forms of participation by ordinary Hungarians in 1944.[25] I want to shift now from the photograph itself to the act of photographing deportations, to ask what these traces suggest of the positioning of ordinary Hungarians vis-à-vis these events.

CHOOSING TO PHOTOGRAPH DEPORTATIONS

The survival of these photographs shows that not only were the deportations from this town something that was watched, but they were also a visual spectacle,[26] reckoned by at least one individual to be important enough to photograph.[27] In choosing to photograph, this was clearly seen as 'an Event' worth recording.[28] Indeed, it was an event important enough to be photographed twice. Having what in effect is the same photograph taken twice is not unusual photographic practice in attempting to secure the desired image. As Colin Westerbeck and Joel Meyerowitz note, '[W]hen a street photographer shoots, he tends to make one exposure after another in rapid succession, varying the composition only slightly each time, looking for the image that will be the best expression of the subject matter.'[29] In Körmend, the photographer took one shot pointing down at the line of Jews being marched along the street below, and then raised their camera slightly to take a second shot, to make sure they captured this scene.

In both photographs, it is clear that what they wanted was the line of Jews being marched below them. They are centrally framed, walking from top right to bottom left across the image. It is their marching through the town that was seen as significant. Looking at the photographs you have the sense that the gendarmes who march to the side were included because of their proximity to the marching 'Jews', and the same was true of the 'non-Jewish' townspeople who stand and watch from their vantage point in an apartment window over the street or from the street below. In a sense the perpetrators and bystanders trespass into the frame by sheer fact of their proximity to this central column of marching Jews.[30] But in the midst of these intruders is the central element in this image taken twice – the line of Jews. It would seem that the photographer neither wanted to photograph any one individual, nor the entire group with a sequence of photographs that included everyone within the frame. Sections of the line were excluded to both left and right of the frame. This was not the totality of the Jews being marched through the town in a single frame or a series of frames. Instead it was the event in process in the general – rather than the individuals in particular – that was deemed important enough to photograph.

Why the photographer chose to photograph the deportation of the town's Jews under their window is hard to say with any degree of certainty. But the fact that they photographed the middle of the line of deportees, rather than the beginning suggests that this was a snatched, rather than carefully planned image. Moreover, the framing – in the first photograph, an out-of-focus section of balcony intrudes at the bottom of the image and in the second photograph, with the camera raised slightly, it is power cables running down the centre of the street that intrude at the top of the frame – suggests that these were rapidly taken images. You can imagine the photographer, looking out of the window, seeing the line of Jews being marched towards them and running to fetch a camera. Or perhaps it was the sound of close to 300 people being marched through the streets of the town that brought them to their open window to see what was happening, and then deciding to run and get their camera. They chose to pick up their camera and hurriedly take two photographs before this line of Jews disappeared out of sight. This was not a photograph that had to be sought out, but quickly taken before the moment passed. It was a shot that came to them.

Perhaps it was the sheer number of Jews – all the town's Jews – that was deemed worth photographing. Smaller groups of Jews had been walking to and from the ghetto along the town's streets during the weeks of its existence, as the ghetto passes attest. But compared to these smaller groups of Jews, this procession of the entire remaining ghetto population clad in their winter coats at midday on a summer's day, carrying suitcases and bundles of clothes, was obviously seen by this photographer to be something rather different. Whether there was a sense of this as a temporary or permanent disappearance or not, the line of Jews was certainly seen as an Event worth photographing, or even needing to be photographed.

As they framed the scene of deportation through the streets of Körmend through the viewfinder and depressed the shutter, it is hard to say what the nature of the involvement of this person to the act of deportation was. Having a camera to your eye is something that Susan Sontag has suggested puts the photographer in a position of power. Writing of seeing an advertising image for cameras showing a crowd of people with only one man among the crowd holding a camera to his eye, Sontag notes that the lone photographer, 'wears a different expression … he seems self-possessed, is almost smiling. While the others are passive clearly alarmed spectators, having a camera has transformed one person into something active, a voyeur: only he has mastered the situation.'[31] With her self-conscious use of the term 'voyeur', Sontag points to the power relationships at play in the act of photographing others. 'Like sexual voyeurism,' writes Sontag, 'it is a way of at least tacitly, often explicitly, encouraging whatever is going on to keep on happening. To take a picture is to have an interest in things as they are, in the status quo remaining unchanged (at least for as long as it takes to get a "good" picture), to be in complicity with whatever makes a subject interesting, worth photographing – including when that is the interest, another person's pain or misfortune.'[32] Sontag argues that 'photographing is essentially an act of non-intervention,'[33] noting that 'the person who intervenes cannot record; the person who is recording, cannot intervene,'[34] Indeed, far from intervening to stop whatever is happening, the photographer has a vested interested in its continuing, whatever 'it' may be. She points to a long tradition of documentary photographers 'hovering about the oppressed, in attendance at scenes of violence' and engaged in 'the gentlest of predations'.[35]

However, I am not sure that this notion of photography as 'the gentlest of predations' works as a blanket interpretation of all deportation photographs taken by non-Jewish neighbours. Those who photographed were certainly more than simply passive bystanders. But how and why they photographed differed from person to person. Here I would like to shift my own gaze a little broader than these two images from Körmend, to compare them to photographs taken elsewhere. Multiple photographs of deportations also survive from a number of other towns in Hungary. Here I would like to take collections of photographs from another two towns – Kőszeg and Balatonfüred – to explore the way in which these images of what was effectively the same kind of event differ from each other. Those differences are, I think, suggestive of a variety of motivations in photographing deportations and a range of bystander gazes in the summer of 1944.

PHOTOGRAPHING DEPORTATIONS IN KÖRMEND, BALTONFÜRED AND KŐSZEG

The two photographs taken from an apartment window in the centre of the town are not the only photographs taken of the deportations from Körmend. Another photograph, taken at the railway station, shows the Jews from behind walking towards the waiting train. Alongside this image, a photograph of the wooden-plank ghetto fence in Körmend also survives. Whether these images were the work of one photographer, two or more, is impossible to say definitively. If they were the work of the same photographer – although it seems unlikely – it would place the photographs that I have looked at into a new context, as part of a sequence of images of the ghettoization and deportation of Körmend Jews. In this context two quickly framed images of a line of deportees walking beneath the photographer's apartment window would become part of a photo story with a beginning (the ghetto), a middle (the line of Jews walking through the centre of the town) and an end (the railway station). While this does not seem to have been the case in Körmend, it was in Kőszeg, where an extensive photo essay of the entire deportation process from start to finish survives, taken it would seem by a professional photographer in the town who then displayed them in the window of his studio on a main street of the town in the spring of 1945.[36] It was not simply that deportation was a spectacle to be watched, but subsequently reviewed (and consumed) through the images on display, in a manner akin to the presence of deportation photographs in the war chronicles put together in some German cities.

The collection of photographs from Kőszeg records the process of deportation of just over a hundred Jews on 18 June 1944 from start to finish.[37] The first image shows the Jews being gathered outside the town's ghetto where a truck waits – as becomes apparent from the later photographs – to transport luggage to the railway station. The second was of the first few yards of the journey of a line of Jews, led initially by two gendarmes along the pavement of Schey Fülöp utca. The photographer then accompanied them on that journey, taking three photographs as the line of Jews made their way through the tree-lined streets of the town. In all three, as in the initial photograph of the line of Jews leaving Schey Fülöp utca, the photographer was in a position to photograph either the gendarmes leading the line of Jews or the first of the little more than 100 Jews marching through the town. The photographer did this again, as the line of Jews – now more stretched out – passed by a house with advertising hoardings which still stands close to the railway station on the outskirts of the town. Here they photographed the Jews gathered at the station with the loaded lorry in the background.

What is so striking about this sequence of photographs that record the process of deportation from start to finish is that the photographer appears to have known either beforehand or very early on that this process was happening. The photographer was therefore able to photograph the initial gathering of Jews outside the ghetto, their first few steps out of Schey Fülöp utca and then accompany them through the town all the way to the station, consistently focusing on capturing the beginning of the line of deportees or whenever possible, the entire group of waiting or walking Jews. The photographer appears in control of events, both in terms of individual images and the photo essay as a whole. The photographer is in the right place at the right time to frame an image that is complete or captures the beginning of something. And here these images appear unique among the surviving photographs of deportations from Hungarian towns and cities. The majority of these fall into two categories, characterized by the images of Körmend and Balatonfüred that I look at in this chapter. One set of images, as in the case of the two photographs taken in Körmend, shows deportation in progress. These are street scenes, with lines of Jews either from above as in the Körmend, or from street level.[38] The second set of photographs that survives tends to show the first stage of deportation completed, and hint at a new journey about to commence. These, like the images from Balatonfüred, are photographs taken at railway stations of Jews waiting by trains or being loaded on to them.[39]

Working with this complete photo essay of the deportation of Jews from a small town in western Hungary it would seem that while the photographer

Four of the seven photographs of deportations from Kőszeg. Photo [4], Yad Vashem
Photo Archives, courtesy of USHMM Photo Archives; photo [5], Magyar Nemzeti
Múzeum Történeti Fényképtár, courtesy of USHMM Photo Archive; photo [6] USHMM,
courtesy of Lydia Chagoll; photo [7], Magyar Nemzeti Múzeum Történeti Fényképtár,
courtesy of USHMM Photo Archives.

did photograph each stage of this journey, they appear to have repositioned themselves vis-à-vis this line of Jews led by a gendarme. The initial image of Jews gathering outside the ghetto was taken from the end of Schey Fülöp utca, with the photographer stood looking down the street from the junction. There is a sense of distance between the photographer and his subjects in this initial image, which is breached in the second image showing the line of Jews being marched along Schey Fülöp utca towards the photographer. Looking at the first and second photograph it is clear that the photographer moved a few feet to their left and repositioned themselves on the opposite corner of Schey Fülöp utca and Várkör from the approaching line of Jews to take the second shot. Standing there, they were only a few feet from the head of the line with nothing in between their lens and the Jews being marched from the ghetto. The photographer was exposed. Not only did their presence, camera to their eye, draw the gaze of the Jews at the front of the line but also it seems that one of the two gendarmes leading the line was aware of their presence and appears to point their finger directly at the lens. The pointing finger of this official may well have been read as a prohibition because it is noticeable that in the following sequence of photographs taken in the main streets of the town the photographer maintained a greater distance from their subject. In all three images of the line of Jews making their way through the tree-lined streets of the town, the photographer positioned themselves on the pavement on the opposite side of the road and photographed from behind the trees that appear in the foreground. This position was less exposed, with cover provided not only by the trees but also by others who come between him and the line of Jews. In one, a man with an umbrella stands in front of one of the trees lining the road. In another, a man cycles past. In the third, where the photographer appears to be the most distant from the line of Jews, a sign crops up in the foreground and, in the middle distance close to the deportees, stands a small boy.

At every stage of his journey the photographer was not alone in witnessing the deportation of the Jews from Kőszeg. On every photograph we see non-Jewish neighbours also watching.[40] In the first, a small crowd has gathered outside the ghetto gate and watches from the pavement opposite where the Jews stand. A little further along the street, just above where the photographer stands, a face peers from a first floor window. By the time that the gathered Jews had walked underneath that window the face had gone. But, from the cracked open gate on the building next door a face watches the Jews just a foot or so away from the shadows. As the Jews made their way through the main streets of the town their deportation was witnessed by others. In one image this comes across particularly strongly, given the photographer's positioning, behind the line of trees and framing the shot with the back of a man holding an umbrella and watching the deportation in the foreground. He is not a bystander who trespasses onto the edge of the frame, but is centrally positioned in the foreground. The end result is a photograph of a bystander watching the deportations. This man with an umbrella was clearly not alone. The other photographs of Jews making their way through the streets of the town show small clusters of townspeople standing watching from the pavement. Those who stand closest to the line of Jews tend, as in Körmend, to be children. A girl stands on the roadside of the tree-lined pavement and looks directly at the line. In another photograph, a boy stands, legs apart, rooted to the spot in the middle of the road just a few feet away from the Jews. He appears to be set on a collision course with the gendarme who marches to one side of the column, and is headed directly towards him.

The presence of the gendarmes, at the front of the line and to the sides, clearly did not put off this boy from standing as close to the line as he did. However, the presence of armed gendarmes may go some way to explaining the greater distance between most groups of adults and the line of Jews. The placing of the gendarmes between the Jews and watching townspeople is particularly striking on the initial image taken by the photographer in Kőszeg. One of the gendarmes stands some distance from the group of gathered Jews, right beside the pavement and only a foot or so from those who stand close to the wall on the opposite side of the road. In rural Hungary, the gendarmerie was a force that inspired fear among the local population.

But the shift to semi-covert photography seen in the central images in the main streets of the town lessens in the final images from this photo essay. Once the line of Jews reached the outskirts of the town, the photographer was more exposed on roads that were no longer tree-lined. The photographs of Jews passing a house on the outskirts of the town, close to the railway station, are taken from a distance but with no cover between the photographer and their subjects. When the photographer reached the station, it would seem that there was no attempt to hide the act of photographing. The photographer stood close to the crowd of waiting Jews and shot from an elevated position, it seems from the waiting train. In the bottom right of the photograph two gendarmes mill around and railway workers talk.

Taken together, the sequence of photographs reveals a mixture of concern with concealment on the part of the photographer in some, compared with an apparent lack of concern in others, which are taken in the open a short distance from the Jews and gendarmes. It is hard to say with certainty how photographing deportations was viewed by the authorities. László Ferenczy, whose reports I turn to next, clearly saw photographing deportations to be problematic, and let his superiors in Budapest know that he had confiscated a camera and film.[41] Yet on the ground, it may well be that things were less clear about whether this was an event to be photographed or not. A photograph survives showing a line of horse-drawn carts transporting Jews from Balassagyarmat. The line of carts runs along the left edge of the frame, and a group of onlookers stands on the opposite side of the road watching from the right edge of the frame. In the centre, looking directly at the camera, are three figures. Two are gendarmes; the other is also dressed in uniform but not that of a gendarme. They pose for the camera, mid-deportation. One leans on the laden cart. One smiles.[42] But their welcoming of being photographed, perhaps by a colleague, is something that may not have been a universal experience. It is here that I want to turn to another town where a sequence of deportation photographs was taken – Balatonfüred – which provides a marked contrast with the apparently open photographing of Jews at the railway station that you see in the final two images from the photo essay taken in Kőszeg.

Two photographs survive from Balatonfüred, taken at the railway station as the last of the Jews from the town were loaded onto a train that took them to Tapolca on 15 May, just over a month prior to the photographs taken in Körmend or Kőszeg.[43] The photographs show the very final stages of the deportation process, suggesting that the photographer somehow got word of deportations and headed down to the railway station, just in time to see the last of the Jews from the town being helped up into the cattle car, their luggage already loaded. Not only was this photographer less clearly in control of the situation than the photographer in Kőszeg who was there from the beginning of the process and quite literally at the head of the line, but also this photographer positioned themselves at the railway station strikingly differently from the photographer in Kőszeg who photographed the Jews from the train itself with gendarmes and railway workers in between. Both photographs in Balatonfüred are taken from behind a wooden fence, which dominates the foreground. Not

One of the two photographs of deportations from Balatonfüred, USHMM, courtesy of Lydia Chagoll.

only did the photographer maintain a distance from the train, but also they appear to have crouched down to take the photograph from behind the safety of the fence. The result is that in the first photograph the events are not in the centre but at the very top of the frame and the roof of the train is cut off.

It is clear that the photographer was not alone in coming to the station to witness this event. Like the other photographs I look at, deportation was something that non-Jewish townspeople stopped to watch. In the first photograph a couple of men stand watching the scene from a short distance while a small boy stands closer still to the train. On the far left-hand side of the frame, an elbow leaning on the fence that the photographer crouches behind, signals the presence of at least one other viewer beside the photographer. In the second photograph, as the photographer turned to the right and photographed the rest of the train stretching into the distance, groups of people are seen standing close to the train. However, while it appears that it was acceptable to watch this scene, the clues in the photograph suggest that for this photographer at least, it was less clear whether taking a photograph was permitted or not. These two images and in particular the first of the act of loading Jews on to the train, appear as covertly taken photographs.

In both Körmend and Balatonfüred there is a snatched and surreptitious quality to the images of deportations. In the case of the former, the images were taken from above. In the case of the latter they were taken from below. Neither photograph was taken on the street at eye level, but either from a first floor apartment building or behind a low fence. This suggests a self-consciousness at photographing this event, if not a sense that this event was perceived to be inappropriate to photograph and therefore that the act of taking photographs needed to be hidden. This is particularly noticeable in the case of the photographer in Balatonfüred. It could be that in Körmend the raised-up position of the photographer, looking down on these events from the 'safety' of a first floor apartment window, owed less to a conscious act of photographing covertly than it did from the fact that that is where the photographer happened to be when the line of Jews passed by. They did not choose to run down the stairs, and out of the door of the apartment building to get a closer shot from street level. Perhaps they decided that in doing so they would miss the action. Or their positioning could owe something to the aesthetics of the view from above popularized in the 1930s by Hungarian émigré photographers such as André Kertész or László Moholy-Nagy.[44] The position of shooting from above that you see in the Körmend photographs does lend the image a sense of a detached view of the process of deportation, but it is hard to be definitive about the intentions of the photographer.

But in the case of the photographer in Balatonfüred they appear to have positioned themselves more intentionally in a semi-hidden position, with the fence between them and the deportations. It was not simply that this is where they happened to be – crouching behind a fence – nor were obvious aesthetic traditions being aped. Rather, this photographer was positioned low behind the fence to photograph the last of the Jews from the town being loaded on to the train. But this attempt at hiddenness on the part of the photographer was clearly not shared by the other townspeople who turned up to watch. In the first photograph we see some standing the other side of the fence, closer to the train to get a better view. Others clearly did stand behind the fence, like the photographer, but they did not crouch down; they stood there leaning on the wooden beams. The presence of these other viewers, right next to the semi-hidden photographer, makes it clear that they were not trying to conceal the act of photography from fellow viewers. Rather, it seems that they were trying to hide their camera from officials.

There is a paradox about these images. It is clear that the photographer saw deportations as an event that demanded photographing. Having found out about what was happening they set out to the station, camera in hand, reaching it in time to take this photograph. However, reaching the station they positioned themselves not just behind a fence, but crouched low behind that fence to take this shot. This photographer saw deportations as something to be photographed and yet also something that they assumed was not to be photographed. But it was the push to photograph that won out. Perhaps I go too far, but I read these images as acts of resistance of sorts: resistance to an officialdom that were shown deporting the town's Jews and perceived as opposed to the photographing of this event. Despite this perception of the inappropriateness of what they were about to do, the photographer took two snatched images. These were not images to be displayed in a photographers' studio window, but were photographs that were hidden in both production and consumption.

Taking the photographs from Körmend, Kőszeg and Balatonfüred together it is clear that deportation through the main streets of the town to the railway station accompanied by gendarmes, and with townspeople looking on (children tending to get closest to the line of Jews) was something that took place in all three towns. In all three towns this event was photographed. However, taking a closer look at those photographs suggests differences in the ways that these photographers 'saw' and interpreted these events. Rather than a single 'bystander gaze' in Hungary as Jews were deported, there were multiple gazes. Indeed the term 'bystander' is perhaps not terribly useful in capturing the range of responses by non-Jewish neighbours. As I have explored throughout this book, ghettoization and deportation were very visible events in Hungary in 1944. They were also events which both rural and urban neighbours partici-pated in, in a variety of ways. Perhaps forms of participation by non-Jews neighbours is a more productive way of writing about those who have tended to be dubbed 'bystanders' and remain the most understudied of Holocaust actors. Far more widely studied are the perpetrators, given the tendency in Holocaust historiography to privilege questions of causation. I would like now to look at one perpetrator, touching on the question of causation, through a focus on narrativity. Working with the reports written by a senior member of the gendarmerie to his superiors in Budapest as he oversaw the ghettoization and deportation process, I explore both how he saw the unfolding events that he was involved in as well as how he wanted his bosses in the capital to see those events and his own role in them. In short, I am interested in the stories of ghettoization and deportation that he told in the early summer of 1944.

7

Narrating Concentration and Deportation I: László Ferenczy's Reports

In May, June and July 1944, Lieutenant-Colonel László Ferenczy, the gendar-merie official charged with oversight of the concentration and deportation process, wrote regular situation reports to his superiors in the Interior Ministry in Budapest. Ferenczy – aged forty-six in 1944 – had been appointed Liaison Officer of the Royal Hungarian Gendarmerie to the German Security Police in the aftermath of the German occupation.[1] As the man on the ground, the Interior Minister instructed Ferenczy to submit daily reports on the clearing of areas of the country of Jews.[2] His first reports – sent on an almost daily basis – covered the process of gathering Jews into collection camps or 'assembly centres' (gyüjtőtáborokat)[3] in Northern Transylvania in early May.[4] From late May, less frequent reports outlined the deportations from this area (and the VIII Gendarmerie district in North-eastern Hungary), followed by occasional summary reports on deportations from other parts of the country in June and July.[5]

Ferenczy's movement across the country, from east to west, mirrored the implementation of deportations on a gendarmerie district by district basis, starting in the north east, moving south and westwards, before ending up in the suburbs of Budapest. This geography of deportations was, Braham suggests, 'established with an eye on a series of military, political, and psychological factors' and driven by a desire 'to prevent the Jews of Budapest, the most sophis-ticated and assimilated in the country, [and on the basis of Ferenczy's concerns, one might add, perceived to be the most wealthy] from fleeing the capital and hiding in the countryside.'[6]

The importance of these reports, covering as they do concentration and deportation from start to finish written by the man overseeing the process, has been widely recognized. For Braham, they 'are among the most important and authentic documents relating to the Final Solution in Hungary,'[7] and he drew on them both for statistical fact[8] as well as evidence of knowledge of the nature of deportations.[9] Although alive to the use by Ferenczy of what he described as 'the typical anti-Jewish tone in vogue at this time,'[10] reading these reports as narratives remains undeveloped.

Rather than simply describing historical reality, Ferenczy's reports also constructed historical realities. As Jews were being concentrated in Hungary and then deported from Hungary, Ferenczy's reports constructed – through statistics and prose – a narrative of this process for his intended audience of Interior Ministry officials in Budapest, hundreds of miles removed from where concentration and deportation was being implemented on the ground.[11] That these reports were written to be read by a superior is clear from the oneupmanship that comes through. They were not detached and objective reportage of the implementation of concentration and deportation. Rather, they tell us as much about Ferenczy's priorities and concerns – and his assumptions about the priorities of ministers in Budapest – as they do about the process he oversaw. Reading them this way suggests three main themes; first, Ferenczy's increasing use of statistical tables to narrate success to his superiors; second, his recounting of the failures of other institutions; and third, the centrality of asset-stripping to his reportage of ghettoization.

NARRATING SUCCESS THROUGH STATISTICS

Between 3 and 10 May, Ferenczy reported the concentration of Jews from Northern Transylvania into ten makeshift collection camps[12] and an urban ghetto[13] on a close to daily basis through a mixture of statistics and brief incident reports.[14] Over the course of the week, statistics assumed a growing importance within the paperwork he dispatched to Budapest. Initially, statistics were embedded within the text. On 3 May, Ferenczy reported that 1,664 Jews had been transported into the camp at Kolozsvár, making a total of 8,000 Jews in collection camps in Gendarmerie district IX, although he admitted that he had no figures for Gendarmerie district X yet.[15] This was remedied, at least in part, two days later when he wrote that 10,125 Jews were now in collection camps in Gendarmerie district IX and 8,215 in Gendarmerie district X, giving figures for a number of individual camps.[16] However, Ferenczy confessed that he did not have details from everywhere, and the provisionality of his numbers was made clear the following day when he revised his figures from the day before.[17] But by 7 May, Ferenczy had the confidence to provide headline figures of totals for the region, some details from one place or another *and* statistical tables with specific figures from each of the collection camps. At the bottom of the table was the grand total of 72,382 Jews transported into collection camps in this region within four days. This total was obviously based on either explicit (in the case of Kolozsvár with its question mark) or implicit (with the round numbers) estimates, but it was a headline figure offered proudly by Ferenczy as proof of a job well done.[18]

This highlighting of the sheer number of Jews successfully transported and concentrated can be seen in the placing of these statistics higher and higher up the reports as the days went by. On 3 and 5 May, the totals were reported at the very end of the report (points 10 of 10, and 15 of 15 respectively).[19] On 6 May they had marginally crept up the running order (point 15 of 16).[20] The next day they were more prominently displayed in tabular form on the second page of the report (point 3 of 7) and by 9 May, the table had made it to page one and point 2 of 6.[21] The following day, the statistics of Jews concentrated into these camps was the lead story – not only on the front page, but also point 1 of 6.[22] Tables of numbers continued to play a role in the reports sent by Ferenczy throughout the rest of the summer.[23] Rather than reading these statistics as the truth of how many Jews were gathered in each of these camps, as Braham tends to,[24] they can be seen as evidence of other truths. These figures, drawing on the visual power and claims to objective reality that statistical tables assert, were given as proof of the successful rapid implementation of a policy of concentration along the lines ordered by Baky. There was nothing like a declaration that after only one week 98,000 Jews were now concentrated in ten camps and one ghetto to reinforce that was a job being effectively done.[25] But they were also offered up as evidence of Ferenczy's expert oversight of this entire operation.

Both these aspects come through looking at the tables presented in the successive reports on 7 May, 9 May and 10 May. Across all three, the total numbers of Jews concentrated in the region increased, rising from 72,382 on 7 May to 94,800 on 9 May and 98,000 on 10 May.[26] These numbers were meant to speak for themselves (as statistics often are assumed to) of day-by-day successful implementation of ghettoization without major setbacks. But alongside this story of ever-greater success was another story of ever-greater claims to accuracy for the figures. On 10 May, as a footnote of sorts to the table, Ferenczy informed his readers in the Interior Ministry that 'in my previous report the number of persons at Szilágysomlyó was reported incorrectly because of erroneous reports. Please amend the figure of 8,500 to 7,200.'[27] This specific statement leant the raw figures in the table above an aura of accuracy. It told readers that Ferenczy's statistics were trustworthy (and by extension that he also was trustworthy). However, it would seem that in reality his statistics were increasingly approximations. While the table from 7 May contained some figures with at least a fiction of precision (2,852 from Szatmárnémeti, 4,252 from Beszterce, 1,426 from Szamosújvár, 5,502 from Dés), these figures were later rounded up (12,000 from Szatmárnémeti, 6,000 from Beszterce, 1,600 from Szamosújvár, 7,800 from Dés).[28] They were clearly estimates, despite Ferenczy's claims otherwise.

When Ferenczy shifted from reporting concentration to reporting deportation, he continued to deploy statistical tables to assert both successful implementation and his intimate grasp of the details of the operation. Rather than ever-increasing numbers of Jews being gathered together in camps and ghettos, Ferenczy now totalled up ever-larger numbers of Jews being deported out of the country by train. By the middle of May, the Jews concentrated in camps in Northern Transylvania were being readied for deportation out of the country. In his report on 9 May, Ferenczy noted, after listing the whereabouts of the 94, 800 Jews gathered in camps and ghettos in Northern Transylvania, that 'the plan for the deportation of the Jews has been prepared by the joint Hungarian–German committee. Transportation is to commence on 15 May and be finished by 11 June.'[29] Ferenczy then went on to announce a meeting with László Endre and Colonel Balázs Piri in Budapest 'in connection with the deportations' on 11 May, followed by a meeting in Munkács the day after, and the another in Kolozsvár on 17 May to discuss 'the security arrangements for the deportations'.[30] The minutes of the Munkács meeting survive.[31]

From the middle of May through to the first part of July, more than 430,000 Jews were deported from Hungary – a process reported through statistics by Ferenczy to the Interior Minister as he moved around the country overseeing mass deportations. On 21 May, he reported that 94,667 Jews were being deported in twenty-nine trains, between 21–24 May from VIII, IX and X gendarmerie district.[32] Just over a week later, he noted that this figure had almost doubled, with 184,049 Jews deported in fifty-eight trains by midday on 28 May, with another thirty-five trains 'ready to deport 110,000 of the remaining Jews' in the VIII, IX and X gendarmerie districts.[33] By 8 June, he proudly reported the successful deportation of 275,415 Jews in ninety-two trains, and that Jews in mixed marriages and their descendants aside, the VIII, IX and X gendarmerie districts were now *judenfrei*.[34] A further 67,000 Jews – from II and VII gendarmerie districts – were awaiting deportations in mid-June in twenty-one trains.[35] By the end of the month, following the deportation of 40,505 Jews from the V and VI gendarmerie districts in 14 trains, Ferenczy paused to reflect back on the entire process of the 'untroubled' deportation of 380,660 Jews from the country in the six-week period between 14 May and 28 June.[36]

In his final report on 9 July, Ferenczy reflected back on an operation successfully and speedily accomplished, informing the Interior Ministry that 'from 14 May 1944 until today, 434,351 persons of the Jewish race have left the country in 147 trains'.[37] The end result was that, 'with the exception of the capital city of Budapest, Jews have departed from the entire country. At this point in time, the only Jews who remain are the ones doing labour service for the armed forces, the Jews in Budapest, the ones working in armament factories, the ones in hiding, the ones who were baptized, and those who come from mixed-race families'.[38] The whole process of deportation from start to finish was implemented with extraordinary speed. In under two months, more than 400,000 Jews from across the country were deported, making use of just under 150 trains. It was an immense undertaking, and the speed with which it was accomplished continues to astonish historians. In reporting it to the Interior Ministry, Ferenczy – as had been the case in his earlier reporting of the concentration process – asserted his own role in the successful, rapid implementation of deportations.

While the statistical tables with their fiction of accuracy pointed to the successful implementation of a policy of concentration of large numbers of Jews, the accompanying prose told another story of problematic exceptions. Jews who were rounded up, subjected to a body search, concentrated in a collection camp and subsequently deported from the country without any hiccups were anonymous numbers within Ferenczy's statistics. However, alongside these tens of thousands of Jews who had been effectively processed were individual problem cases of those who had resisted transfer into collection camps or mass deportations. They were reported in some detail to the Interior Ministry, not in the anonymous general but the named particular. Thus Ferenczy reported that in Oláhlápos, Samu D. and Mozes D. had successfully escaped ghettoization with five children, that a further 40 Jews had been caught trying to escape – with German and Hungarian military help – across the Romanian border[39] and in Szatmárnémeti, a Jewish student, András W., had hidden at the Catholic Seminary 'dressed in a cassock'.[40] During the deportation process, he reported that a Jewish girl had been caught being smuggled out of the camp at Munkács,[41] a handful of Jews had been found with false papers,[42] an escaped Jew from Slovakia had been captured in Salgótarján, and Mrs Lajos N. had been shot in Szolnok attempting to escape.[43]

As well as reporting thwarted attempts at hiding and escape, Ferenczy recounted suicide attempts in considerable detail. During ghettoization in Marosvásárhely, Gyula Sz., Maria F., Antal S. and his wife, Mrs Mano T. and her daughter Ilona, and Maria M. were all reported as either successfully or unsuccessfully attempting suicide.[44] Further reports of attempted suicide came from Ditró, Vajdaszentivány and Szatmárnémeti.[45] In all cases, Ferenczy named not only individual victims, but also the method of suicide. Was there voyeurism, and not simply bureaucratic reporting, in detailing that Dr Oszkar Gy. poisoned himself and his mother with morphine and, upon regaining consciousness, ultimately suffocated himself with his pyjama top?[46] What is clear is that Jews were not supposed to be dying yet. Ferenczy reported what he saw as the untimely natural death (if there was such a thing during the Holocaust) of Mrs Zsigmond H. from Tőkés who had died 'during transportation' – 'according to the medical officer of old age'.[47] Descriptions of suicide and other untimely deaths continued to crop up in reports of the deportation process. Mrs Jozsef G. had committed suicide in Győr,[48] another 'unnamed Jew' had committed suicide at Szolnok where 'some deaths occurred in other ways',[49] with further individuals who had died of 'natural causes due to old age' also being seen as worth reporting in detail.[50]

Hiding, escape, untimely 'natural death' and successful or attempted suicide challenged the success of the concentration and deportation process, which had as their central logic the transfer of all Jews in the area into guarded camps, undergoing a thorough search for valuables in the process, and their subsequent deportation out of the country. While the bigger story told in statistical tables was of the successful implementation of concentration and deportation, Ferenczy pointed to localized and isolated mishaps, although as his statistical tables made clear, these had not – and did not – threaten to derail things. But it is striking that he chose to write setbacks into, rather than out of, his reportage to his superiors in Budapest. That he did so was in large part because of who it was who had reportedly failed and also because of what they had failed in.

Early on in his first report, after an introductory statement of sorts, Ferenczy informed the authorities in Budapest that the deputy chief of police in Kolozsvár, had 'issued orders contrary to previously issued regulations, that the Jews be transported to the collection camp without undergoing any house or body search or having their baggage examined, that the body search and examination of baggage be carried out at the camp and that the house search be carried out in the sealed-up dwellings after the Jews have been removed', which he saw providing 'a tremendous opportunity for the concealment of valuables'. When body searches were carried out at the camp, Ferenczy described these as 'inadequate since this was conducted on women by women civic employees without any expertise'.[51] A few days later, Ferenczy reported police failings at Nagyvárad, where 'house and body searches were done incompletely resulting in inadequate confiscation of valuables'.[52] The failure of the police in both guarding and searching Jews at Nagyvárad cropped up again and again in Ferenczy's reports.[53]

On the surface, these reported failings can be seen as evidence that concentrating Hungarian Jews, and stripping them of their valuables, was not an entirely straightforward task. It is clear that the rapid implementation of anti-Jewish measures in Hungary did not run entirely smoothly.[54] But there is more to these incidents reported by Ferenczy. They suggest his priorities and concerns, as well as those he assumed that the Interior Ministry shared, in May 1944. Two things stand out: first, the importance of searching, and not simply guarding, Jewish bodies in the concentration process, which suggests the centrality of asset-stripping to ghettoization, a theme I return to below; and second, these early reports introduce a recurring theme throughout subsequent reports. These regular reports provided an opportunity for Ferenczy to contrast the failings of another agency – the police – with the successes of his own. In short, here were multiple opportunities for him to blow his own trumpet.

INSTITUTIONAL RIVALRIES AND REPORTING THE FAILURE OF OTHERS

The relationship between the gendarmerie – responsible for policing rural areas – and the police – responsible for policing urban areas – in concentrating Jews had been left somewhat vague in the 7 April order issued by Baky. According to this, '[T]he rounding up of the Jews is to be carried out by the local police or by the Royal Hungarian Gendarmerie units concerned. If necessary, the gendarmerie will assist the Royal Hungarian Police in urban districts by providing armed help'.[55] As Ferenczy was keen to demonstrate, the involvement of the gendarmerie was absolutely necessary in a number of places because of failings by both the police and others that he reported in detail. In part the problem was the small numbers of police mobilized. But it was also the case, Ferenczy claimed in Nagyvárad, that 'those present performed their duties only lacsidasically',[56] 'committed repeated irregularities',[57] or lacked the necessary expertise.[58] In Kolozsvár, he pointed to a failure of leadership, writing that 'difficulties were encountered here at the start because the chief of the police station was ordered to report to Budapest and departed this morning' leaving 'his deputy ... completely uninformed'.[59]

In the midst of such failings, Ferenczy was quick to report the effective leadership that he – and his institution – offered. 'I put a stop to this immediately and ordered that it be carried out according to the previously issued regulations,' he informed the Interior Minister after describing the chaos in Kolozsvár. 'On my instructions, the body search on women will be conducted from now on by midwifes and nurses,' he added, before concluding with the reassuring words, 'I have now corrected these inadequacies.'[60] Throughout the reports, Ferenczy portrayed himself as personally active in correcting the mistakes of others and ensuring the thorough and effective implementation of a policy of concentration and expropriation. When he wasn't describing his own actions,[61] it was other members of the gendarmerie who he described as intervening similarly decisively. In Szilágysomlyó, the Zilah division commander, as Ferenczy phrased it, 'arrived at the scene and established order'[62] and in Nagyvárad it was the Nagyvárad training battalion that took over temporary guarding duties and conducted body searches (which provided these students with practice in 'the delicate and considerable circumspection required for house and body searches') and Colonel Paksy-Kiss who 'issued order on the scene'. [63] Ultimately in Nagyvárad, Ferenczy informed the Interior Minister on 9 May, that the entire operation had been taken over by the gendarmerie.[64] Everywhere, it seemed, the gendarmerie was quick to step in to correct the failings of the police.

In his self-portrayal as actively involved in solving the problems generated by others, Ferenczy was careful to represent himself as a loyal servant of ministerial regulations and orders. It was he who played things by the book, while others 'issued orders contrary to previously issued regulations' and 'deviated' from instructions coming from the Interior Ministry in Budapest.[65] Ferenczy offered himself to the Interior Minister as his man on the ground, who could be trusted to get the job done in the way that he wanted it doing. In some cases this meant intervening when the implementation of measures was judged to be overly lax. Thus in Sepsiszentgyörgy, when Izsó S. and his family were exempt from concentration by the chief of police, he reported that he had ordered the Jewish family sent to the camp.[66] But in other cases, Ferenczy portrayed himself limiting irregular or overly harsh anti-Jewish measures. On 3 May, Ferenczy reported that he had 'immediately put a stop' to 'the orders of the chief county constable and the local wing commander' that Jewish men pull the wagons loaded with baggage from Somkút 'to a collection place 5–20 km away'.[67] He offered himself as bringing a uniform approach to a policy being implemented rather differently from place to place.

Reflecting towards the end of his 5 May 1944 report on the implementation of the concentration (and expropriation) process thus far, Ferenczy drew a distinction between those areas where the police held sway – the cities – and those where the gendarmerie – rural areas – were in charge. It was 'in areas of the gendarmerie, where there were disproportionately fewer Jews in the territory' that 'there were no difficulties at all, and everywhere the rounding up and transportation of the Jews to the collection camps and the securing of their valuables proceeded in accordance with the regulations issued'.[68] In reporting (and crowing over) the successful and swift implementation of concentration and expropriation by members of the gendarmerie, in comparison to the mistakes committed in urban areas outside of gendarmerie jurisdiction, Ferenczy did pay regard to the somewhat different circumstances the gendarmerie and police faced in rural and urban areas, given the large numbers of concentrated Jewish populations in the latter.[69] But there was clearly jurisdictional friction between these two agencies, and the reports filed by Ferenczy offered a chance for empire building which he readily seized upon.

Conflict between different agencies during 1944 was something that Béla Zsolt, whose memoir I look at in the next chapter, noted, writing that 'the men in uniform were constantly competing with each other'.[70] Zsolt suggested that the police in Nagyvárad,

> had resented the gendarmes from the very first moment, on the one hand because they felt insulted by the authorities who hadn't trusted them and had brought in the 'reliable' gendarmes from Transdanubia, on the other hand because they were obliged to watch, grinding their teeth, how the gendarmes feathered their nests thanks to this 'Jewish business' without a soul calling them to account as they filled their kit-bags or fibre suitcases with 'Jewish loot'. The policemen were indignant because in their view the gendarmes had stolen it all from them.[71]

Competing over confiscated valuables from concentrated Jews extenuated longer-standing rivalries between the police and gendarmerie. Ferenczy's dismissal of the police as corrupt incompetents in his reporting built on a longer-standing sense of superiority. As Lajos Bajusz, a former Hungarian gendarme, told an interviewer in the late 1980s, 'If you [were] not good enough to be a gendarme, you could always be a policeman.'[72]

While it was the police that bore the brunt of Ferenczy's dismissal as incompetents or worse, the Hungarian army was not entirely spared Ferenczy's naming and shaming. 'In Marosvásárhely and Szászrégen,' wrote Ferenczy, 'the local special military administrative chiefs took over the direction of the operation on their own authority, and took steps that hindered the regular execution of the operation. Although the measures were taken in good faith, they created disorder because of a total lack of know-how.'[73] However, Ferenczy also claimed that the military was acting not simply 'in good faith'. He accused Hungarian and German soldiers of helping forty Jews to escape across the Romanian border on the night of 3–4 May.[74] In Naszód, the commander of the 22nd Border Guard was accused of giving 'a wealthy Jew', Simon V., a tip off which meant that he had 'started to hide and send away his valuables as early as 1 May'.[75]

On 10 May, Ferenczy reported for the first time an issue that became a recurring theme in later reports. His recounting of draft papers being 'delivered even in the collection camps' was, he asserted, evidence of 'two contradictory directives regarding the Jewish forced labourers', citing agreement between the German Security Police and Ministry of Defence that Jews could not be called up in areas where Jews were being concentrated into camps (Chapter 1). As a result he assured the Interior Ministry, 'I have stopped the delivery of draft notices to the camps until instructions are received from higher authorities.'[76] But this was a problem that did not go away. On 25 May, Ferenczy reported the continued delivery of call up notices to the camps, as well as the continued freedom of movement being enjoyed by Jewish labour battalion members who were still being granted leave.[77] Two weeks later, he reported 'new attempts to call Jews up for labour service' including, it turned out, a Jew who had escaped from Slovakia.[78] In addition, the earlier problem he had highlighted of Jewish men moving about freely during periods of leave was still an issue. Reporting the capture of four labour servicemen – Armin L., László S., László N. and Armin T. – with passes signed by first lieutenant in the Hungarian Army, by the German Security Police, Ferenczy did not identify this as an act of the disregard of Hungarian sovereignty on the part of the German authorities.[79] Far from it. It is clear that he sided with the Germany Security Police, rather than the Hungarian military, and encouraged the Interior Minister to do likewise.

This was another front in the institutional battles that Ferenczy fought through his report writing in 1944. Taken at face value, his reports suggest that the gendarmerie was the most zealous in implementing concentration – and later deportation – of Hungarian Jews, with the police and military plain incompetent. In part, there would seem to be something to this assertion of the zeal with which the gendarmerie enacted measures on the ground. But, as I have suggested, we need to be aware that this was the story that Ferenczy wanted his superiors in Budapest to believe.[80] We must read between the lines to see another story: the concentration and deportation of Hungarian Jews as an opportunity for oneupmanship and empire building which Ferenczy seized upon. Here was the careerism identified by Browning among Police Battalion 101 writ large in the paperwork of this desk killer.[81] Talk about the banality of evil, when genocide is an opportunity to play institutional power games.

Ferenczy's narrative of the effectiveness of the gendarmerie in comparison to the ineffectiveness of the police – and the military – makes it rather hard to uncover what lay beneath the teething problems that he assiduously reported. He had his own reasons to paint a picture of incompetence on the part of institutions and individuals other than the gendarmerie, but can we also see bureaucratic resistance or at least dragging of feet? Writing in his first report of the initial implementation of the concentration process, he hinted at some resistance on the ground, writing that the process was being undertaken, 'generally with the total support of the authorities everywhere'.[82] Who these authorities were was not made explicit, but was hinted at in places. On 6 May, Ferenczy reported that the deputy prefect of Szolnok-Doboka county – Dr János Schilling – had become ill on 2 May and therefore was not taking part in the action.[83] That there was more to Schilling's illness than simply coincidence is clear.[84] This was not the only case where specific local authorities were accused of being overly sympathetic towards Jews. In Szatmárnémeti, Ferenczy accused the mayor of exempting Sámuel E. and his family – nine Jews in total – from ghettoization on the grounds that they were 'raising 250 pigs for public consumption on his leased country estate', failing to assign the lease to a non-Jew who was ready to take it on.[85]

Once deportation got underway, Ferenczy pointed to sympathy for Jews on the part of the local authorities in the city of Békéscaba, where he claimed that the mayor – Dr Gyula Janossy – along with three policemen – Szokolai, Ladanyi and Sitkei, 'did not do their duty, but sank to the level of serving Jewish interests and vigorously supporting them'.[86] In Sajószentpéter, the chief constable was accused of transporting Jewish women from the ghetto there to the collection camp by car, justifying it on the grounds that they were 'genteel ladies'.[87] A camera and film were confiscated from someone working in the police station in Ungvár who photographed deportations.[88] More space was given to preferential treatment being given to some Jews by the local authorities at Ungvár where the city's deputy clerk was accused of arranging for some 'prominent and wealthy Jews' to leave the camp with the assistance of 'certain police officials'.[89] Here was a place where 'negligence' and 'reprehensible behaviour' on the part of some in the city were seen by Ferenczy as undermining the concentration and deportation process. His solution was to hand over 'the running of the camp and the handling of the affairs of the Jews' to the gendarmerie.[90] In part this was a familiar story, of the gendarmerie taking things over, but now it was not simply assuming control from incompetent officials. There were more straightforward suggestions of resistance and corruption on the part of the overly sympathetic and greedy authorities in this place.

It is difficult to work beneath the layers of institutional rivalries that characterize such incident-reporting; however, my sense is that there was at least a perception on the part of Ferenczy – which was more widely shared – that administrative and police leaders in urban centres were not wholly trustworthy when it came to the rigorous implementation of the deportation of Jews. It is striking that, 'for tactical considerations', Ferenczy noted, 'the desire of the German Security Police was to have the Interior Ministry alert the districts which are subject to a cleansing operation only a few days ahead of time, and to include only the narrowest circle in the communication, namely the Lord Lieutenants, the gendarme commanders of the particular areas, and the police chiefs only of the police forces in the countryside'. Mayors and police chiefs in the towns and cities were intentionally to be left in the dark and only alerted to plans 'two days prior to the operation'.[91] It may have been felt that local officials in urban centres were too closely connected to the largely urban Jewish population.

However, more widespread than suggestions of resistance underlying the actions of other agencies failings were more straightforward claims of corruption during the concentration and deportation process. Ferenczy informed the authorities of the arrest of 'a notary's assistant', András Lakatos, who had reportedly used the concentration process as an excuse for criminal behaviour – the attempted rape of Mrs Izrael R. and the theft of linen from her home.[92] At Marosvásárhely, members of the *Levente* paramilitary youth organization, who were supposed to be assisting in the concentration process, were found to have taken money from Jews to forward messages and letters for them.[93] In Beszterce, a special constable had reportedly pocketed 5,000 pengő from Jews in the camp 'and used most of the money for his own purposes'.[94] The head of one of the committees involved in confiscating Jewish valuables in Nagykároly had 'received a 12 place silver dinner service from a Jew',[95] and another committee member from Kolozsvár was caught with 'a gold fountain pen, leather, money and briefcase containing various jewellery taken from a Jew' and following a house search, 'money and valuables worth several thousand pengős'.[96] In Nagyvárad, the chief police councillor (*rendőrfőtanácsos*) Pál Krasznay was 'suspected of concealing Jewish valuables in his dwelling' and although nothing was found, Ferenczy reported that 'Krasznay requested retirement'.[97] In Gyergyószentmiklós, another member of the police (*rendőr tiszthelyettes*) was found to have concealed Jewish valuables in his home.[98]

Corruption in the locality continued to be reported as deportations commenced. A triumvirate of officials living on what was described as 'a Jewish farmstead in Ipolyság' were accused of taking 'four gold wristwatches, various pieces of jewellery, Persian carpets and an unknown amount of cash from the Jew living there for the purposes of safekeeping'.[99] It was a familiar story of Jewish wealth being hidden by sympathetic officials – including a superintendent of the Budapest police – or seized by anyone from members of the Hungarian military to ordinary non-Jewish neighbours such as Istvan M., described as an 'apprentice blacksmith from Balassagyarmat'.[100] However, Ferenczy also admitted to corruption within his own institution – the gendarmerie – informing the Interior Minister that Hajos Gy., 'a gendarme on guard duty at Sered' had been 'caught taking away valises full of clothing from area of displaced Jews'.[101] This low-ranking gendarme was not the only member of Ferenczy's own institution reported during the deportations. On 7 June, he outlined what he saw as the 'strange occurrence' of Gendarme Captain, Dr Endre N., who had concealed 'his clandestine fiancée [Baroness Alexandre H.], who is considered a Jew' and married her on 29 May without a licence. Ferenczy was quick to state that the woman had been arrested and 'punitive proceedings against the above named gendarme captain were begun without delay', thus preserving his own reputation, but the reputation of the gendarmerie did not emerge untainted.[102] Perhaps more strikingly, here was a high-ranking member of Ferenczy's own organization motivated it seemed, not by corruption, but love.

This long list meshes with what we know from elsewhere. Corruption and personal enrichment were widespread in the process of asset-stripping the victims.[103] Reporting these incidents provided Ferenczy with a chance to point the finger, in the majority of cases at least, at institutions other than the gendarmerie. But, it also reveals something else which dominated these early reports. Throughout, there was a repeated focus upon the confiscation process in the incident reporting. The successful confiscation of Jewish wealth was, in Ferenczy's eyes, threatened by incompetence and corruption on the part of some of the authorities *as well as* by Jewish attempts at hiding their valuables which he also regularly reported. On 3 May, writing of Kolozsvár where he was based, Ferenczy informed the Interior Ministry that, 'saving of Jewish wealth is widespread in this area also, and the necessary measures to prevent this have been taken'.[104] Two days later he offered detailed examples, reporting that Lorinc L. from Hidalmás, had given money and a 'valuable wall clock' to non-Jewish neighbours 'for safekeeping'. In Csucsa, Mrs Lajos S. had hidden clothing with neighbours. In Zsibó, Mrs Joseph G. and Mrs Ignác L. had sold clothing to neighbours. In Nagyilonda, a non-Jewish neighbour, Mrs Lászlo Cs. had 'received a large sum of money and clothing for safekeeping from several Jews'.[105] The following day, he reported that Simon V., 'a wealthy Jew' from Naszód, had been hiding his valuables since 1 May, after a tip-off.[106] At the end of this report, Ferenczy informed Interior Ministry officials that, 'In general, surprisingly few valuables were found on the Jews, which indicates that they have concealed their valuables. On request, several Christian families surrendered the Jewish valuables in their safekeeping, but investigations begun in such cases are continuing in very many localities.'[107]

His assumption of widespread hiding of valuables, in some cases with non-Jewish neighbours, was rooted in a widely shared perception of Jews as a wealthy elite. If valuables were not found, Ferenczy concluded that they must have been hidden away by scheming Jews. He did not entertain the possibility that the Jews being gathered into camps in Northern Transylvania may not have had valuables to hide. Rather, he adopted the prevailing antisemitic discourse of Jewish wealth, which underlay the opportunistic actions against Jews taken by the Hungarian state in the spring and summer of 1944. Every incident of hidden property, such as clothing to the value of 10,000 pengő which Mrs Mór F. reportedly attempted to hide in Terep,[108] can be read as evidence offered by Ferenczy of a widespread conspiracy on the part of Jews in the region who he assumed were all squirreling their valuables away. When he wrote that a Jewish student, András W., had reportedly hidden at the Catholic Seminary in Szatmárnémeti, Ferenczy could not resist throwing in the highly speculative assertion that, 'in all likelihood he had hidden his parents' valuables there'.[109] Here was a man who assumed that Jews were rich, that they were all busy hiding their valuables, and that the efforts of the gendarmerie needed to be redoubled to ensure that these were found. This logic led to intimate body searches as a central plank of concentration policy and practice.

THE CENTRALITY OF ASSET STRIPPING DURING GHETTOIZATION

That Ferenczy spent so much space outlining problems encountered in uncovering and collecting Jewish valuables pointed to the importance with which he approached the economic dimension of concentration, an importance he assumed to be shared by those reading his reports in Budapest. For Ferenczy, concentration equalled expropriation. This was clear from a reference in his 5 May report, to the process currently underway as 'the assembling of the Jews *and* the collection of their valuables'.[110] It can also be seen in the frequency of reporting the problems with expropriating Jewish wealth and the solutions being undertaken to remedy them.[111] That asset stripping was a central part of the planned concentration process was clear from the 7 April order.[112] That asset stripping remained central when concentration was enacted on the ground is clear from Ferenczy's reports. In this prioritizing of the material dimensions of ghettoization, Ferenczy was working not only with the 7 April order, but also with face to face communications with Baky, who had instructed him 'to have articles of clothing confiscated from the Jews distributed at a price [the suggestion was 35–40 pengő for a suit and 15–20 pengő for a pair of shoes] with priority given to working class people and tradesmen'.[113] This reflected a broader concern in governmental circles, highlighted by Kádár and Vági, that the implementation of anti-Jewish measures economically benefit the Hungarian non-Jewish population.[114] More broadly it fits with the picture painted across Europe by Martin Dean that, 'the seizure of Jewish property was not just a by-product of Nazi genocidal policies, but an integral part of the murder process'.[115]

However, there was competition over Jewish property, not only between Germans and Hungarians and different organs of the Hungarian State, but also between the State and the populace. According to Ferenczy, some members of the local population were not patient enough to wait for the sales of Jewish clothing. In Gyergyószentmiklós, two Hungarian soldiers stood accused of breaking into the sealed home of a Jew and stealing valuables.[116] In Felsőbudak, a neighbour had reportedly 'appeared at the home of Rudolf G., a Jew[,] on 2 May and took away a bicycle indicating that he would have no use for it any longer since the Jews were being rounded up and the bicycle would be confiscated by the State'.[117]

These specific incidents of non-Jews seizing goods – or the opposite story of non-Jews hiding goods – sat within a broader narrative of widespread passivity on the part of the local non-Jewish population. Writing in his report on deportations from the V and VI gendarmerie districts, Ferenczy noted in conclusion that 'among the population, the removal of the Jews was greeted with great satisfaction by the majority of the population. The minority keep their opinions to themselves.'[118] It was an echoing of words used in an earlier report, this time sent from Kolozsvár rather than Budapest. Then, Ferenczy had reported that 'the mood of the population is generally calm and in most localities the operation was welcomed. There have been sporadic occurrences in which people felt sorry for them, but these cases were found mainly among Romanian nationals.'[119] He painted the strongest picture of a content non-Jewish population relieved to be rid of the Jews in his report on 8 June, which portrayed a post-deportation Munkács in idealized terms. With the Jews gone, so were – Ferenczy asserted – gone a host of problems from high prices for black market goods to 'rumours and unrest' and crime.[120]

As with everything in these reports, it is hard to know what to make of such statements. They present a picture of view of passive bystanders welcoming the concentration, asset-stripping and later deportation out of the country of their Jewish neighbours. But, it is hard to know on what basis he made such claims. We should perhaps be somewhat cautious about drawing too much from his statement about 'the majority of the population' in his 29 June report, given that the paragraph ended with words which were something of a stock phrase for Ferenczy: 'In the course of gathering together Jews in collection camps and their subsequent removal by transportation there were no criminal actions, excesses and atrocities committed by the Hungarian organizations for public security.'[121]

But, while being cautious with reading too much into his statements on the local population, the silences within Ferenczy's reporting are perhaps significant. Ordinary non-Jewish neighbours are largely absent from his reporting of deportations. Named individuals do crop up more frequently in the earlier reports on concentration where non-Jewish neighbours hiding Jewish valuables or seizing property from vacated Jewish homes was seen as threatening to undermine the desire of the Hungarian state to get its hands on Jewish wealth which lay at the heart of the concentration process. But while non-Jews were portrayed as hiding Jewish goods, they were not portrayed hiding Jewish bodies once deportations got underway. There was of course less they could do at this stage, once Jews had already been gathered into collecting camps at entrainment sites and separated from their non-Jewish neighbours. It was a little too late to act on behalf of Jews, aside from writing with a complaint – as Géza Biro from Dés had reportedly done – 'on behalf of the Jewish infants, the sick and the old'.[122] But the relative lack of references to non-Jewish neighbours in these later reports is reflective of two things that characterized Ferenczy's reporting as May turned to June and concentration turned to deportation. Firstly, the German authorities became more present, and secondly, Ferenczy's reporting became ever briefer.

FINAL REPORTING

The German authorities are far more present in the later reports of deportations, than they were in the earlier reports of concentration. In his first reports, Ferenczy was not terribly complimentary of the German authorities he encountered. In Kolozsvár, Ferenczy reported that the deputy of police had 'issued orders contrary to previously issued regulations' '*after* consultation with the leader of the German advisory board'.[123] In his next report, he pointed the finger at German soldiers who had 'attempted to help 40 Jews escape across the Romanian border'.[124] There was at least some suggestion of friction on the ground between Hungarian and German officials. This had been seen, I think, as a potential source of conflict by Baky, who had noted in his 7 April concentration order that, 'the German security police will be on the spot as an advisory body. Special importance must be attached to achieving undisturbed cooperation with them.'[125] It would seem that cooperation was not always the case on the ground. As the infamous incident of the deal brokered by the SS with the four families who owned the Weiss-Manfréd works over the heads of Hungarian state officials shows, there was competition – and not simply collaboration – between Hungary and Germany over seizing Jewish wealth and property.[126] Given the centrality of expropriation to the phase of concentration reported on by Ferenczy in early May, it is perhaps not surprising that when mentioned, German officials tend to be shown in a poor light.

However, once concentration turned to deportations (and there was less emphasis on asset stripping in his reports) German officials crop up with much greater frequency, and in a more positive light. While concentration and expropriation were reported as largely actions undertaken by the Hungarian state apparatus, deportations were reported much more as a joint venture. Perhaps I am too cynical, but at this stage, all that was left were (gendered) Jewish bodies, rather than Jewish wealth, and the Hungarian state appeared to be more willing to share the former with the German authorities than the latter.

Once deportations got underway, it would appear from Ferenczy's reports, that German expertise, leadership and involvement was welcomed. Writing from Munkács on 29 May, Ferenczy reported that 'the German Security Police emphasized that according to their experience, it is only possible to hasten the deportation of Jews from the places where they are assembled if the Jews are brought together at the same time in a small, rather than a large area, from where with sufficient force, it will be possible in the smallest amount of time and with the greatest momentum to gather them together and set up camps'. Given their previous experience of mass deportations gathered over the preceding three years, 'the command of the camp and the technical arrangements for the loading is under the authority of the German officers group sent by the German Security Police'. Moreover, Ferenczy reported that the German Security Police were following 'established practice during the deportation of Jews from the camps' by sending 'the sick, the old, and their relatives first'.[127]

Reading through the reports sent by Ferenczy during May, June and July 1944, it is striking how what was reported initially as very much an operation dominated by organs of the Hungarian state became a much more shared activity with jointly drawn up plans,[128] as concentration and expropriation became deportation. Perhaps this in part explains why the reporting process became less thorough. The later reports on deportations were not daily reports, but rather a series of two reports from each place – a kind of before (reporting the planning for deportations) and after (reporting deportations). Moreover, by the end of the deportation process, the reports tended to be short, and included stock phrases. The lengthy daily reports of early May when concentration and expropriation were being implemented turned to more perfunctory, occasional reports by early July when the last batch of Hungarian Jews were dispatched to Auschwitz. You get a sense of a man (and the ministry he wrote to) for whom the novelty had worn off and the whole process had become increasingly normalized.

This sense of increasing boredom discernible in Ferenczy's reporting was also picked up on, by Béla Zsolt, on the ground. His memoir, postwar correspondence from his wife and the diary written by his stepdaughter form the basis for the next chapter, where I consider a rather different narrating – although with some overlapping themes – of ghettoization and deportation in Nagyvárad than that in Ferenczy's reportage. Zsolt, watching the successive deportations from Nagyvárad, noted,

> About the departure of the fourth transport there's nothing special to report. The gendarmes, who had mastered the tricks of the trade over the first two days, were working like old hands, quickly and efficiently. Perhaps the only difference between the first two days and the last two days was that their superiors were finding the mechanical nature of the deportation less and less interesting and were bringing less and less ceremony, energy and good humour to it.[129]

But I see something else behind the growing boredom of the process of deportation in Ferenczy's later reports than simply routinization. I get the sense of a man keen to get the job finished, and who appears to have cared less about mass deportations than he did about concentration and expropriation. This may well be because by the time that deportations took place, all there was left were (female, old and very young) Jewish bodies, rather than Jewish wealth.

8

Narrating Concentration and Deportation II: Diary, Memoir and Letters from Nagyvárad

On her thirteenth birthday, one of the presents that Éva Heyman received was a 'pretty little gold chain' from her aunt Lili. On the same day, she began writing in a diary that she had been given a few years earlier. 'Dear diary', Éva wrote on 13 February 1944, 'from now on I will carry on this chain the key with which I will lock you so that no one will ever know my secrets.'[1] Like many other teenage girls in nineteenth and twentieth century Europe, diary writing was an opportunity for self-exploration and self-reflection.[2] Éva's locked diary – referred to with the use of the affectionate diminutive 'my little diary' (kis Naplóm) – was a safe place to write of her ambivalent feelings towards her mother,[3] her fears over who her father might remarry,[4] her jealousy of an intelligent and popular friend of hers whose parents were not – unlike her own – divorced[5] and to admit that, 'something very odd has happened to me. I almost don't have the courage to confess it to you. I think I'm in love.'[6] Her encounters with Pista Vadas, the focus of her affections, were dissected and analysed in her 'little diary' that was a confidant and 'best friend' that she 'mustn't keep any secret from' as she negotiated adolescence.[7]

But for this Jewish teenager, living in the city of Nagyvárad in Northern Transylvania, the diary also became a place for negotiating and narrating the dramatic changes she experienced as the elements of the Holocaust were implemented in the spring and early summer of 1944. Writing from the newly established ghetto for the first time, she explained to her diary, 'now you aren't at 3 Istvan Gyöngyösi Street – that is, at home – any more, not even at Anikó's, nor at Tusnád, nor at Lake Balaton, nor in Budapest, places you've been with me too before, but in the Ghetto.'[8] In her diary entries from the ghetto, Éva not only reported changes in the families' (and the diary's) circumstances, but also sought to make sense of them in and through their narration. Diary writing offered a space for self-reflection. Describing hearing the bell of the ice-cream seller outside the ghetto, Éva reminded her diary that 'the Ghetto fence, as you know ... runs alongside our house, and when we were still allowed to look outside, before that became punishable by death, we could see what was happening in Várad. Isn't it that odd, I wrote: "In Várad," even though I'm also in Várad?!'[9] It was in the act of writing that she realized how quickly she felt removed from the city that she had grown up in.

Éva was not alone in diary writing during the ghettoization process in Hungary. For example, another diary written by a teenage girl in Budapest – Lilla Kánitz Ecséri – survives.[10] But my focus here is on Éva's diary for a number of reasons. First, Éva's is set in Nagyvárad, which is one of the cities that featured large in the reports of the concentration and deportation process sent by Ferenczy to his superiors in Budapest. Working with a victim's narrative of concentration and deportation in Northern Transylvania allows me to offer an alternative voice to that of the perpetrator's voice which forms the basis of the previous chapter. Second, Éva was not alone in her family in writing of ghettoization and deportation. Her mother – Ági – wrote about her wartime experiences between April and June 1945 in a series of letters to an old school friend.[11] Her stepfather Béla – an accomplished author – wrote one of the earliest Holocaust memoirs, which was originally published in weekly instalments in *Haladás* between 30 May 1946 and 27 February 1947, finally appearing in book form in 1980 in Hungarian as *Kilenc Coffer* (Nine Suitcases) followed by an English translation in 2004.[12] As well as setting Éva's voice against – and alongside – that of Ferenczy, I also set it alongside – and against – the voices of her mother and stepfather.

While the survival of a number of texts written by members of this literary family presents an opportunity for comparison of narratives of concentration, it also presents a problem. There are questions about the authenticity of Éva's diary given that the original is missing and it was 'in the possession of the Zsolts – Béla the writer, and Ági, an intellectual with a literary bent – for almost three years before it was first published', under the title *Éva lányom (My daughter Éva)* in 1948.[13] Although highlighting these concerns, Judah Marton, writing in the introduction to the English edition of the diary, assured readers of the 'authenticity' of Éva's voice in the diary on the grounds that it resonated with the Éva that family and friends remembered. However, Alexander Zapruder is more critical and dubs this diary 'perhaps the most controversial' of the 'quasi diaries', therefore excluding it from her edited collection of children's Holocaust diaries.[14]

The loss of the original diary is clearly problematic. Zapruder concludes that, '[T]hough there are most likely passages in Éva's diary that are authentic, written by a young Hungarian girl during the war, they are virtually impossible to extricate from what are very likely the postwar additions by her mother.'[15] It is likely that postwar editing took place.[16] However, Zapruder's focus upon inauthenticity reflects a rather unhelpful tendency to assert (and therefore judge on such terms) greater veracity to wartime diaries than postwar memoir accounts. This neat divide has been questioned by James Young, who suggests that, '[W]here the writing from within the whirlwind may be ontologically privileged insofar as it is empirically linked to events, it is not thereby more "real" or "authentic" if these terms denote factual veracity.'[17] Following Young's thinking, I work here with Éva's diary, whatever its precise status, Béla's postwar memoir with its literary flourishes, and Ági's letters asking for money, as all containing 'truths' about this family's narrating of Holocaust and post-Holocaust experiences.[18] Their narratives differ from the reporting of that same process by Ferenczy, but there are also times where they touch on themes of concern to Ferenczy, in particular the centrality of asset-stripping to concentration.

KEEPING HOLOCAUST SECRETS

Reading Éva's diary, I feel like an intruder. Diaries are often places for confiding secrets, and it is clear that Éva's functioned in this manner. In the weeks following her thirteenth birthday, the diary was a safe place to confess her feelings towards Pista, away from the gaze of her mother or grandparents. In the aftermath of the Nazi occupation when a whole series of anti-Jewish measures were implemented including ghettoization, the diary continued to function as a site of secrets. It was here that Éva confided that she felt 'so miserable',[19] and was afraid of being killed.[20] In April, she told her diary that 'Life is really hard'.[21] At the beginning of May, when the notices were issued that Jews were to be taken to the ghetto, Éva confided, 'I've never been so afraid'.[22] Her locked diary acted as a site for expressing emotions that she kept from the eyes of those around her, although an exception was occasionally granted to the all-seeing divine.[23] As well as a space for prayer of sorts, the diary was also a space for confession. In the ghetto, Éva confessed to her diary after she and a friend 'Marica ... hid in a corner of the garden and we gobbled up' all the food that her mother had brought which was intended to be shared out among all the family members.[24] A few days later, with this still on her conscience, she wrote, 'I'm so sorry about what hogs I and Marica were in eating up Grandpa's portion out in the corner of the garden'.[25]

The diary was a place for thinking out loud, but out of earshot of her family, and so a place to express the unthinkable. Twice, she wrote that if it came to it, she would choose the chance to live over sticking with other family members.[26] It was here that Éva could articulate in secret that her desire to live was stronger than her desire that her family stay together.[27] Éva used the diary to spare her family from painful knowledge. She told her diary alone, of seeing the removal of the neighbouring Waldmann family 'from the window of our children's room',[28] and later on of hearing that a gendarme had moved into their previous home.[29] After spending five days with her friend Anni, during which time Anni's father was called-up for labour battalion service, Éva told only her diary and grandfather about this tragedy.[30] The diary functioned as a hiding place – a repository of hidden knowledge, thoughts, emotions and confessions, safely kept under lock and key.

Keeping secrets was something that Éva was aware her parents were also trying to do, telling her to leave the room when her mother's cousin visited from Budapest and reported 'all kinds of horror stories'.[31] These attempts at protecting Éva from unwelcome knowledge continued in the ghetto, where the adults waited until they thought that the children were asleep before holding certain conversations. However, one night, Éva overheard one of these conversations intended only for the ears of grown-ups. This forbidden knowledge of the torture being meted out on those taken for interrogations at the *Dreher* brewery was both overheard and then carefully written down.[32] It would seem that the secretive whispering among adults that night had an impact on Éva. This was hidden knowledge that she knew she had to record.[33]

However, in reporting this late-night conversation apparently verbatim, there were things that she did not, and felt she could not, write down. 'Ági also told other things', Éva wrote, 'like what the gendarmes do to the women, because women are also taken there, things it would be better if I didn't write them down in you. Things that I am incapable of putting into words, even though you know, dear diary, that I haven't kept any secrets from your till now.'[34] She chose not to write down the details of intimate body searches of Jewish women. Sexual violence was something more problematic to describe than physical violence. This may in part have been due to embarrassment.[35] Vaginal searches were a sensitive subject for a middle class teenage girl to broach. Perhaps she wanted to save her own, and her diary's, blushes. At times Éva self-censored, it would seem in part at least to spare her friend – the diary – from the full horror of what was happening. Re-reading her diary in mid-March, she had expressed sorrow 'because I'm hardly writing anything in you that can give you some pleasure. Because things aren't all sad for me; I also have some happiness.'[36] Her relationship with her diary was such that she sought to spare it from too much grief. But in sparing the diary the details of gendered sexual violence she was also, in a sense, sparing herself the details of something which posed a threat to her own, and her mother's, bodies. There were secrets that Éva sought to keep from both the diary and herself.

There were clearly limits to diary writing. Writing back in the middle of March, Éva reported that, 'There are constant air raid alarms in Pest. Dear diary, I'm so afraid that here, too, there will be air raids. I can hardly write, because I kept thinking about what will happen if they bomb Várad, after all. I want to live at all costs.'[37] This sense of struggling to write, became more acute when Éva was taken to the ghetto in early May 1944. In her first entry in the ghetto, she expressed an inadequacy of conveying to her diary her emotions as the family waited to be taken from their home. 'Dear diary', she wrote, 'I'm still too little a girl to write down what I felt while we waited to be taken into the Ghetto.'[38] Five days later she confessed, 'I don't even know where to begin writing, because so many awful things have happened since I last wrote in you.'[39] This sense of paralysis is one that she had expressed earlier, writing that 'so many terrible things are happening, dear Diary, that I don't even feel like writing any more.'[40] In what was her final diary entry, she finished with the confession, 'I can't write anymore, dear Diary, the tears run from my eyes.'[41] And yet despite these confessions of the impossibility of writing, write she did, in 38 separate dated entries of varying lengths, between 13 February and 30 May 1944.

NARRATING THE HOLOCAUST AS STRANGE AND FAMILIAR

By its very nature, diary writing is episodic. The day-by-day reporting of events with the frequent use of the opening word 'today …' resulted in descriptions of the incremental worsening of experiences.[42] The German occupation was reported as 'terrible',[43] leaving a world where 'nothing is as it used to be',[44] but it was not until Jews were being removed from their homes in Nagyvárad (to make way for Germans) that Éva announced that, 'now the worst is only starting'.[45] With the transforming of the ghetto into a ghetto camp with further restrictions, Éva self-reflectively wrote, 'I have no idea how things are going to be now. Every time I think: This is the end, things couldn't possibly be worse, and then I find out that it's always possible for everything to get worse, and even much much worse.'[46] A week later, she felt justified in this feeling, noting, 'I did write in you some time ago, dear diary, didn't I, that every misfortune can be followed by something worse? You see how right I am? The interrogation has begun in the *Dreher* beer factory.'[47] By 29 May, she was sure that, 'now the end of everything has really come. The Ghetto has been divided up into blocks and we're all going to be taken away from here.'[48] This sense of incremental creep from bad, to worse, to even worse, is something that characterizes Holocaust diaries, lacking as they do the 'benefits' of hindsight.[49] It is a jarringly different rendering of the events of concentration and deportation than Ferenczy's statistical table-laden narrative of ever-increasing success.

Éva's apocalyptic rendering of the start of deportations as the coming of 'the end' was matched by her use of an alien word to describe an alien event: 'Now nobody says that we're being taken away, but that they deport us. I've never heard this word before …'[50] An example of experiencing and narrating a strange new world, came with the arrest of her father, who was held hostage in the elementary school. Éva, like other children, went to visit him during the day to take him lunch. 'When I left him', she wrote, 'it occurred to me that when I was going to elementary school, we children always used to be inside the gate and the parents would wait outside the fence to take us home after school. Now only adults, even old people, are inside the school fence, and we children are outside. There is no getting away from it: the world is topsy-turvy.'[51] The previous order being turned on its head was also something commented on when the ghetto became a 'ghetto camp' under new leadership (Gendarme Lieutenant-Colonel Péterffy) with a new set of rules. These horrified Éva, given the harshness of the threatened punishment:

> Actually, everything is forbidden, but the most awful thing of all is that the punishment for everything is death. There is no difference between things; no standing in the corner, no spankings, no taking away food, no writing down the declension of irregular verbs one hundred times the way it used to be in school. Not at all: the lightest and heaviest punishment – death. It doesn't actually say that this punishment also applies to children, but I think it does apply to us, too.[52]

As with the earlier entry about visiting her father to take him his lunch, school provided a reference point of her familiar world now turned upside down.

But alongside narrating the experiences of concentration as alien event in a 'world standing on its head',[53] Éva recounted and interpreted events through two stories from the past – of attacks on property (her maternal grandfather's pharmacy) and persons (her best friend Márta) in the early 1940s – that framed what was happening to the family in the spring and early summer of 1944. Both stories functioned as myths – in the sense of myth as defining story – that occupied dream-space, and were entrusted to the diary so that they could then be referred to again and again in shorthand. What is striking about the use of these stories from the past, is that Éva did not simply narrate the events around her as strangely new, but also as eerily familiar. In a very real sense, she saw history repeating itself.

In her first entry, Éva informed her diary of a shadowy figure who seemed to be waiting in the wings, ready to take over her grandfather's pharmacy again: Vitéz Szepesváry, 'who treated Grandpa so badly'.[54] The recounting of the 'Szepesváry affair' was the longest single entry in the diary, such was its significance in Éva's recent past that she sought to bring her diary up to date with.[55] Szepesváry had been given the pharmacy, so Éva told her diary, after the Hungarians had regained Nagyvárad from the Romanians as part of the wartime land settlement, on the grounds that he was more 'reliable' than her 'Rumanian-loving' Jewish grandfather.[56] The events of the next two months, when Szepesváry occupied the pharmacy, were ones that had left a traumatic impact on Éva. It was a period when she remembered how her beloved grandfather 'became sick because of that Szepesváry. He suffered so much that it was impossible to look at him.'[57] 'Thank God I've stopped thinking, except in my dreams', she wrote, 'about how much I suffered at that time.'[58] Ultimately, the story of the attempted confiscation of the pharmacy was one with a happy ending of sorts. After paying off the city's military commander 5,000 pengő ('Only Grandpa didn't have five thousand pengős, so we sold the piano'), the pharmacy returned to the family.[59] However, in Éva's telling, Szepesváry left 'raving mad' and threatening her grandfather that 'he would show him yet; Grandpa wouldn't die in bed, but in quite a different way altogether',[60] prompting in Éva a fear that 'Szepesváry will be brought back to the pharmacy',[61] and that her grandfather would not die a natural death.[62]

This story intersected with another dominant story in the diary: that of her childhood friend Márta, who 'they say … also didn't die in bed in Poland the Germans shot them'.[63] Like the story of Szepesváry, it was a story that the diary needed to be made of aware of. In her initial entry, Éva referred to when 'the Nazis took Márta away to Poland',[64] a story that she retold in more detail to her diary in the next entry, writing of 'that afternoon' just under three years ago when Márta and her family were among foreign-born Jews deported from Hungary to Kamenetz-Podolsk.[65] References to what happened to Márta were frequent throughout the diary.[66]

This sense of history repeating itself in 1944 was also central to the narrative strategy adopted by her stepfather, Béla Zsolt, in his postwar memoir *Nine Suitcases*. There he interwove the events of hiding in the ghetto hospital in Nagyvárad with his experiences of labour battalion service two years before.

The memoir is written imaginatively as if in real time, during the last week of the ghetto's existence. The artifice of the present in the memoir is not the day-to-day recent past of a diary narrative, but the moment-by-moment present of live reportage. In Béla's memoir, the narrator is there in the ghetto hospital, where 'the friendly gendarme now pushes the door open.'[67] We as readers are caught in the time and place of the ghetto, where 'it was Wednesday morning, and they would be taking people away on Saturday'.[68]

But alongside this real-time reportage in an imaginary present, Béla introduces flashbacks from his time spent in labour service in the occupied Soviet Union. There, as he tells the man sitting on his hospital mattress who had been digging graves for those who committed suicide in the ghetto, he dug graves after a German retaliation massacre of villagers near Minsk.[69] It is a scene as seemingly unbelievable as that in the ghetto on the eve of mass deportations.[70] Béla saw the past being replayed in the present, and portrayed a world where history was repeating itself. Thus he described his first two journeys by cattle wagon during the First World War and on his way to Ukraine for labour battalion service, wryly describing himself as 'an an expert cattle-wagon traveller. All my other journeys were merely a shuttle service between two cattle wagons.'[71] 'And now', Béla wrote, 'I'm about to be taken away from my homeland for the third time in a cattle wagon. The wheel comes full circle ...'[72] The year 1944 was not an aberration – although there was something alien about mass deportations[73] – but the terrible culmination of a personal and societal trajectory begun years before, most markedly in the minefields of the Ukraine.[74]

Alongside this personal trajectory, Béla painted a broader picture of ghettoization as the continuation of 'envy and greed' directed against Jews more widely, 'first by the laws they had designed to deprive us of our money and our civilized pleasures, then informers and detectives they sent after us, and the loud-mouthed, mechanically rowdy press campaigns they conducted against us; then in Russia with cables and lashes'.[75] His personal story of historical continuity was one that he saw shared by Hungarian Jews *en masse*.

It is striking that, in both the postwar memoir written by Béla and the wartime diary written by Éva, such strong connections were drawn between 1941–2 (and before) and 1944. The German occupation was clearly a traumatic moment. For Éva, 19 March 1944 was a time when there were advantages to being, like her diary was, an inanimate object: 'You're the luckiest one in the world', she told her diary, 'because you cannot feel, you cannot know what a terrible thing has happened to us. The Germans have come!'[76] But 19 March 1944 was not a radical turning point in narrative terms for either Éva or Béla. Rather, there were stories from before this point in time that were seen as repeating themselves or coming to fruition in the aftermath of the German occupation.[77] The events of the spring and summer of 1944 that we dub the Holocaust were frighteningly new (as Éva's fears made clear) but also (equally) frighteningly familiar.

NARRATING THE LIMITS OF VICTIMS' AGENCY

In the midst of this old/new world where external forces (variously 'the Hungarians', 'the Nazis' the 'Fascists') took away people and property,[78] Éva described her family's attempts to counter these through a combination of contacts and money. Her grandfather had tried to pay a waiter to marry their governess so that she could remain with the family.[79] The idea was mooted that Éva might go into hiding at the Poroszlay estate, but 'Uncle Poroszlay said that it was out of the question', putting an end to this plan.[80] According to Éva, 'Grandpa is trying everything': attempting to secure forged papers and hide her Grandmother's jewellery.[81] Conversion was discussed, but ultimately rejected.[82] A friend of their parents who was director of the Archives was unable 'to get forged documents for us … Unfortunately, in the Archives, you can get all kinds of forged grandfathers and grandmothers, whereas Uncle Béla needs forged army papers and a forged registration card and all sorts of other papers which can't be found in Zoltán Nadányi's archives.'[83]

But these thwarted attempts at fixing things, were not simply narrated by Éva as failing as a result of impersonal external forces. Rather, she pinned the blame on her grandmother, who was portrayed as hell-bent on keeping the whole family together, and opposed any and every plan that one or more family member escape or go into hiding on their own.[84] When her mother's non-Jewish cousin arrived from Budapest with 'forged documents which he stole from the hotel', in order to smuggle Ági, Béla and Éva to Budapest, Éva wrote, '[W]hen Grandma heard what was going on, she threw herself on the floor and literally screeched. She said that Ági is a murderer, because if Ági and Uncle Béla run away they will kill her in their place.'[85] Her grandmother responded similarly when the family's seamstress, Mrs Jakobi, offered to take Éva into hiding.[86]

Recalling both the arrival of Mrs Jakobi and the earlier arrival of a cousin from Budapest with forged papers, Béla also painted a picture of crazed resistance from his mother-in-law.[87] But, unlike Éva, he also placed some of the blame on his wife, who 'adored her father to an almost neurotic degree'.[88] More strikingly, when he narrated earlier discussions of escape, Béla did not portray the resistant grandmother so dominant in Éva's narrative. Rather he wrote that, 'from the very first moment, these unfortunate people, my wife's parents and even my wife, had been asking, almost begging, me to flee. They kept saying that I was in greater danger than they.'[89] It was not only his father-in-law who was 'trying to persuade me',[90] but also 'my mother-in-law also kept telling me to go, and I must admit I would have liked to.'[91]

Rather than being held back by a dominant mother-in-law, Béla asserted far greater agency on his part, explaining the rejection of early plans for escape as a personal choice rooted in both a certain weariness on his part,[92] as well as the more sacrificial and heroic decisions taken by a loyal family man.[93] Béla's masculine self-identity was one where 'a man doesn't, and can't, leave his wife in danger, particularly if she's ill'.[94] His masculine scruples were illustrated perfectly in a dramatic story he proudly recounted of when, 'my father-in-law ran across to the apartment where I was hiding, waving the card, and demanding that I let the lieutenant take me to a safe place in the evening ... My wife had even packed the basic necessities for me – but I wouldn't go. "No," I said to the old man. "Who do you think I am? I'm not going to leave my wife and family *now*."' [95]

Although Béla and Éva tell rather different stories – in the former it is Béla rather than his mother-in-law who is active agent – they tell parallel stories of the overwhelming desire to keep this extended family together hindering plans to escape or go into hiding. As Béla suggested, it was common knowledge in the ghetto that, 'the only way to make a successful escape was on one's own. Whoever wasn't a Jew nowadays was a detective, and people fleeing in groups, with families, were conspicuous and inevitably gave themselves away. The children and mothers forgot themselves – and that was that!' [96] Yet while both Béla and Éva were prepared to entertain the thought of hiding or escaping in secret, [97] the pressures to remain together as a family were too strong. Or were they?

DISCREPANT ENDINGS

Éva's diary and Béla's memoir offer rather different endings. These divergent endings may simply reflect the slightly different end-dates of the two accounts. Éva's final diary entry is dated 30 May, just before the diary was entrusted to the family's former maid Mariska, and prior to the onset of deportations. In contrast, Béla's memoir is set in the ghetto hospital a few days later on the eve of deportations. But what is particularly striking reading these accounts alongside each other is that while Éva's diary portrayed a family still together at the very end, Béla's memoir showed a family split apart. In her penultimate entry, Éva wrote that 'when we found out that everybody is going to be taken away from here', her mother 'hurried right over to the hospital for Uncle Béla and brought him home, *because she wants us all to be together*'. [98] In her final diary entry on 30 May, Éva reported that, 'Ági and Uncle Béla are whispering something to each other about our staying here in some kind of typhoid hospital, because they plan to say that Uncle Béla has typhoid fever. It's possible, because he had it when he was in the Ukraine.' [99] This final diary entry is one of a girl at her wits end, but of a family together where there was still hope as long as her mother was trying to fix things. In contrast, Béla's memoir portrays a more lonely scene of his failed attempt to arrange for Éva and her grandparents to be moved to another section of the ghetto, while his wife lies in another part of the hospital blissfully unaware of what was happening as a result of the false reports he was making sure she was being fed, [100] a 'calm' that turned to anguish when 'she discovered that she had been misled, and her parents and her child had been deported', and she attempted suicide. [101] If the family were really together at the end of May as Éva's diary has it, then this was clearly not seen as important enough to warrant a mention.

Ági's account in a letter to an old school fried in April 1945, at a time when she still did not know whether her daughter and parents were still alive, gives relatively little away about the family's last days (together or apart) in the ghetto. She explained, 'I stayed behind, unfortunately only alone with my husband, my little daughter along with my parents were transported together' before going on to recount the separation of her husband accompanied by herself as nurse into a house on the last day of the deportations because he had previously had typhus.[102] It is impossible to reconstruct this family's last few days and say with any degree of certainty which – if any – of the narratives penned by the members of this family contains the 'truth' of the final days of this family prior to deportation. My concern is not to note discrepancies between accounts in order to falsify these victims' accounts, or state which is the more 'true'.[103] Rather, I am interested in the two competing stories that emerge in the final pages of these accounts.

In Éva's diary it is striking how, in the circumscribed space of the ghetto camp where misdemeanours were punished with death, the later entries portrayed Ági fixing things for Éva and Béla. Rather than being taken for labour, 'somehow a cane was found for Uncle Béla, who suddenly pretended to be crippled, and Ági and Grandpa took him to the hospital',[104] although then she managed to get him home again in order to spend the last few hours together as a family. Ági managed to get hold of canned food from the hospital,[105] 'a pass for Papa because I had begun to miss my father very much', which meant that Éva could now see him again,[106] and even strawberries for her daughter.[107] 'She always brings something back', wrote Éva, 'even Grandma says that Ági is very efficient', clever or crafty.[108] Her mother was presented as not only active agent but akin to wonder worker. It may be that these final words were written by an admiring Éva who trusted her mothers' ability to fix things, but it may also have been that they were the result of postwar editing by a guilt-ridden Ági who regretted that she had not been able to prevent the deportations, and so rewrote the story in such a way that she was seen doing what she could and – *post-facto* – bring the family together on the eve of deportations.

In contrast, in Béla's account of a family separated, he reflects on his own impotence despite his best efforts to try 'to arrange for the child at least to be deported in the same wagon as her mother'.[109] In a striking exchange, Béla portrays himself torn over whether to leave and in the process save himself or remain in the hospital as an act of heroic solidarity. Ultimately, in Béla's telling, it was the doctor who insisted that he leave with the words,

> Stop fussing! If anybody gets a chance to stay behind, he should. Nobody's going to think you're a traitor or a coward if you stay. At least there'll be more air and water for the others in the wagon. The quarantine lasts three weeks. In that time something may happen. Or not. I'm glad you're staying. Perhaps you'll be able to report what was done to them. You'll write about it.[110]

It is a fascinating piece of reported speech, particularly given the injunction to survive in order to write about 'what was done to *them*' within the pages of a survivor's memoir. Here is an authority figure – whether 'real' or imagined – who not only assures Béla that he has not failed as a masculine protector in leaving others (his wife's child and parents) behind, but gives him a reason for his sole survival: to bear witness through the solitary task of writing.

The discrepancies between Éva and Béla's endings bear a striking resemblance to that uncovered by Mark Roseman when writing of one woman's experience of hiding in Germany during the Second World War. He discovered that Marianne's claim to have gone to visit her fiancé in the barracks where Essen's Jews were interned the night before their deportation was not 'true'. Rather, it seemed that Marianne had adopted someone else's story and made it into her own. He saw in this, an attempt 'to impose control on memory' and bring a traumatic past under control.[111] Roseman writes that, '[T]he small changes in her testimony show, I would argue, how Marianne had struggled to cope with these feelings of loss and guilt. Thus, in her testimony, she borrowed Hanna Aron's story (and sincerely believed it to be her own memory, I am sure) of accompanying her fiancé into the barracks before departure. In her account she went a little further distance with him than she had actually gone in reality.'[112] In the case of Marianne, and also it seems the Zsolt family, it was the moment of familial separation prior to deportation which was a trauma demanding rewriting in order to assert control and offer the closure of a final farewell at the very last moment. The separation of the family was something that could not be entertained either in 1944, *or* retrospectively in the immediate postwar years prior to the publication of both Éva's diary and Béla's memoir. It was only once the family had been separated by someone else through the act of deportation, that Béla could recount escape from the isolation hospital and the journey to Budapest,[113] where, in Éva's words, 'it will be possible to find some Aryan Socialist or Communist who will be willing to hide Ági and her husband'.[114] Ultimately, both Ági and Béla later left Budapest as part of the group of prominent Jews taken to Bergen-Belsen through the controversial negotiations of Rezső Kasztner.[115]

In their description of escaping from the isolation hospital in Nagyvárad, Béla and Ági signalled the importance of the shift in oversight of the ghetto from the gendarmes to the city's police.[116] As Béla explained,

> The main reason why the police were less frightening was that we all knew how corrupt they were at all levels, from top to bottom … they preferred being bribed rather than going in for robbery. This had been an ingrained professional custom with them for decades … It was above all their traditional corruption that made them more humane.[117]

Writing to an old school friend, Ági offered a similar story: 'After clearing the ghetto, the gendarmerie left and the police took over. They were luckily a great deal more corrupt …'[118] According to Ági, a 'hidden cigarette lighter and fountain pen' was the bribe necessary to get a message out of the isolation hospital to Budapest, followed by a sum of 1,000 pengő to ensure that the police turned a blind eye while they made their escape.[119] They were not the only Jews to escape from the isolation hospital by bribing the police. Béla recalled other escapes, although the amount of money changing hands he saw as reaching 3,000 pengő per head,[120] or in their own case 10,000 pengő.[121] It seems, as László Karsai suggests, that 10,000 pengő was how much a Jewish life was worth in 1944.[122]

The corruptibility of the police, which for Ferenczy was both problem and cause for institutional oneupmanship, was an opportunity for Ági and Béla. In their accounts, as well as Éva's diary, the division drawn up by Ferenczy between the job undertaken by police and gendarmes in Nagyvárad (and beyond) is one paralleled in this rather different reporting of gendarmes and police. Both Ferenczy and the Zsolt family were in agreement about the corruptibility of the police. Where they differed was in their description of the gendarmes. Ferenczy's glowing descriptions of efficient and effective implementation of the concentration process by the gendarmerie was radically different from more impassioned descriptions of the gendarmes as a feared, brutal force, rendered by Béla in animalistic terms.[123] They were 'rabid'[124] and 'the prehistoric beast'.[125] Given such descriptions it is unsurprising that, according to Éva, her mother 'was more afraid of the gendarmes than of wild animals'.[126] The one 'friendly gendarme' drew the attention of both Éva and Béla, given that he was the exception to the rule.[127] However, Béla was dismissive of this seemingly 'friendly gendarme', seeing behind his apparent desire to help the very same thing that he sees behind the entire operation: greed and opportunism: a desire to get hold of 'enough to buy a cow for the old people at home or a motor-bike for himself'.[128] It was this battle over Jewish property which Béla saw underlying the conflict between gendarmes and police.[129]

THE CENTRALITY OF ASSET STRIPPING DURING GHETTOIZATION

At the heart of Béla's memoir is the story of concentration as an experience of ever increasing asset stripping, something also noted by Éva. Even prior to ghettoization, the family had experienced a series of one-off confiscations. Initially, it was bed linen, requisitioned by the Jewish community for the German authorities.[130] Then, on 7 April, 'Éva wrote, '[T]oday they came for my bicycle. I almost caused a big drama.'[131] Her big red bicycle, nicknamed 'Friday' for its loyalty, was her most beloved possession. Friday's confiscation by the police was a traumatic event.[132] But after this, it seems that Éva became strangely used to the confiscations that followed. She no longer recorded them as single entries. Rather she wrote in the third person, reporting that, 'Every day they keep issuing new laws against the Jews', before illustrating this,

Today, for example, they took all our appliances away from us: the sewing machine, the radio, the telephone, the vacuum cleaner, the electric fryer and my camera. I don't care about the camera any more, even though they didn't leave a receipt for it, like when they took the bicycle. They also took Uncle Béla's typewriter, but he didn't care either. When the war ends we'll get everything back.[133]

In the diary, confiscations became normalized. By the second half of April, Éva was writing, '[U]ntil now she [grandma] constantly fussed about polishing the silverware, but today all our silverware was taken away from us. I've stopped giving you an account, dear diary, or exactly what is taken away from us on which day, because in the end everything will be taken away.'[134] It was as if she were bored by a process no longer deemed newsworthy. The end result of weeks of confiscations though was that, prior to relocation to the ghetto, their home had been steadily stripped of anything of value. 'The apartment was still so lovely in March when Ági and Uncle Béla came', recalled Éva just over six weeks later, but 'now the apartment isn't pretty any more. All the beautiful things in it have been taken away. The silverware, the rugs, the painting, the Venetian mirror. They left a receipt for the rugs, but even Grandpa says that we will never get them back.'[135]

During the journey to the ghetto, another set of confiscations took place, of apartment and furniture, extra bedding and clothing, and foodstuffs in the pantry.[136] Her grandfather's valise was confiscated, because it was made out of leather, as was her red purse.[137] The wedding rings on her mother and grandmother's fingers were removed by the policemen who escorted them to the ghetto, along with the chain around Éva's neck on which the key to her diary hung.[138] The confiscation of this birthday present was recounted at length by Éva in her diary entry on 5 May 1944, given its intimate connection to the diary itself.[139]

In the ghetto there were further confiscations. Gendarmes 'took everything away from us', wrote Éva, including the food the police had allowed them to bring with them, along with 'the logs out of the basement, the cigarettes they found, and even the thirty pengős each person had been allowed to take into the Ghetto'.[140] The confiscation of cigarettes – described in great detail – had a similar impact on her mother that the confiscation of the red bicycle had had on Éva.[141] But the confiscations were not finished yet. This process of stripping the Jews of everything they possessed continued, with the feared interrogations and body searches conducted in the *Dreher* brewery.[142]

In contrast to this day-by-day summary reporting of confiscations in her diary, Béla's postwar memoir (with its benefits of hindsight) centres asset stripping – the materiality of the Holocaust – at the heart of the experience. 'They ['these gendarmes'] have taken everything away from me', wrote Béla. 'They looted our apartment, gobbled up everything in our kitchen, and slung on to their truck the nine suitcases that held all my possessions, my clothes and my wife's clothes and all the necessities and small luxuries we had collected in our lives: the objects, the fetishes.'[143] These nine suitcases – which give the memoir its title – are seen by Béla as at least in part responsible for bringing him and his wife back from Paris to Budapest, and thus in a sense responsible for both his years in Russia and his ending up in the ghetto hospital from where he imaginatively writes.[144] He sees in his wife's obsession with these nine suitcases (she 'had a mania for having more suitcases than necessary') and the objects they contain, a broader obsession with objects that he is so critical of in the Jewish bourgeoisie, and had characterized his interwar writing.[145] But this obsession with material objects is seen as being shared by the perpetrators. Thorough-going theft lies at the heart of the Holocaust that Béla narrates. His experience of the spring of 1944, was of the rapid confiscation of all his personal property – including these nine suitcases.[146]

After stealing everything – 'the furniture, the clothes, the children's toys, the family pictures, the laundry tub, the bicycle, the shop, in a word, the objects'[147] – the nadir of this operation of theft was found in the brutality of body searches and torture meted out in the brewery in Nagyvárad, where, 'this gang, the government and its knackers, are after "loot". They want money and jewellery, these primitive natives, they want glittering objects.'[148] For Béla, the Holocaust in Hungary was an event motivated by greed: 'They pretend to hate us as a pretext for taking our objects away.'[149]

As I have argued in the previous chapter, something that comes through as a prime concern for Ferenczy (and, he also assumed, for his recipients) was the centrality of asset-stripping Jews to both concentration policy and practice. This concern is mirrored in the very different narratives of the Zsolt family. Reading them, it is clear that asset-stripping was far more brutally achieved than Ferenczy reported, in particular in the (gendered) violence meted out in the *Dreher* brewery in Nagyvárad.[150] Robbing the Jews lay at the heart of not only national policy as well as policy on the ground, but was also at the heart of the victims' experiences. For Béla, 'they are killing us for the sake of objects',[151] although he argued that this remained unrealized by Jews at the time.[152] This was, for him, the tragedy of Hungary in 1944: that Jews 'were unable to realise that this state had become a rabid dog, this homeland the free range of bandits'.[153]

Epilogue
Counter Journeys, Counter Stories

György András M. was on vacation in the village of Csehimindszent in western Hungary in the early summer of 1944. He had left his parents behind in Budapest and was spending the summer with the village tobacconist. In the middle of May 1944, György András was taken along with other Jews from the village to the ghetto established in the nearby city of Vasvár.[1] Somehow, his father found out about this and wrote to the town authorities with the request that György András be allowed home. On 23 May 1944, the chief constable of Vasvár agreed to his request.[2] He was, to use Holocaust parlance, a native collaborator, given his role in initiating and overseeing ghettoization in the locality, but he was also the man who agreed to the request for György András to be returned to Budapest. Was he a bureaucrat troubled by a minor in the wrong place and put this right – the Pesti was returned to Pest – or was there more to his decision than simply a bureaucratic crossing of the 'ts' and dotting of the 'is'? Given the boy's age – he was eleven or twelve years old at the time – a local lawyer was to be entrusted with accompanying György András on his journey out of the Vasvár ghetto and back to the capital, at a time when Jews were forbidden from travelling around the country.

When I came across the chief constable's decision, it was one of those moments, so familiar to historians, of chancing upon a fragment of someone's story. As Carolyn Steedman describes this experience, 'You find nothing in the Archive but stories caught half way through: the middle of things; discontinuities.'[3] In the case of this particular story that I had come across in the middle, what I wanted to know was how it ended. Did György András really leave the Vasvár ghetto and take the train to Budapest, and if so, did he survive the Holocaust?

It seems that György András did leave Vasvár in May 1944. His name does not appear on the list of Jews concentrated in the Vasvár ghetto. There is a section on this list of names which includes the handful of Jews brought into the ghetto from Csehimindszent, but György András is not among them.[4] But his name does appear on another list of names recorded in Budapest. In 1946, a city-wide survey of Jews living in the capital was undertaken. It is a book I have on the shelf in my office, and when I first read discovered György András' story, I turned to it and began scanning the pages of survivors with surnames starting with the letter M. In that list I found György András M., living with his mother Margit Magdolna Sz. and his maternal grandmother, Lujza on Dohány utca just a few doors down from the main synagogue in the capital.[5] However, his father, János M., who wrote the letter that set the whole chain of events into action, is missing, presumably having died at some point between May 1944 and 1946.[6]

György András is a boy, like so many of the other men, women and children whose stories I have told in this book, who enters and then rapidly disappear from the historical record.[7] We never hear György András, like so many ordinary people in the past, tell his own story. But we do have fragments of his story, told by others, because of what Michel Foucault, describes as 'an encounter with power'. 'Without this collision,' writes Foucault of countless people like György András in the past,

> doubtless there would no longer be a single word to recall their fleeting passage. The power which lay in wait for these lives, which spied on them, which pursued them, which turned its attention, even if only for a moment, to their complaints and to their small tumults, which marked them by a blow of its claws, is also the power which instigated the few words which are left for us of those lives: whether because someone wished to address themselves to power in order to denounce, to complain, to solicit, to beg, or because power decided to intervene, and then judged and sentenced in a few words. All these lives, which were destined to pass beneath all discourse and to disappear without ever being spoken, have only been able to leave behind traces – brief, incisive, and often enigmatic – at the point of their instantaneous contact with power.[8]

In the case of György András, traces of his life during the war are left by the chief constable of Vasvár, keen to ensure that a minor was returned to his parents, and by the Statistical and Search Department set up by the Hungarian Section of the World Jewish Congress, the American Joint Distribution Committee and the Jewish Agency for Palestine, eager to ensure that as full a list (as possible) of survivors was available in Budapest for those searching for family members and friends. Those traces allow us to piece together, in a very fragmentary way, the story of his journeying from Vasvár to Budapest towards the end of May 1944: a journey that saved his life.

It would seem that György András was not the only one journeying to Budapest (and therefore away from Auschwitz) in May 1944. In the daily reports submitted by the Jewish Councils in provincial ghettos to the Jewish Council in Budapest, plans for the return of minors to the capital were occasionally noted. On 3 May, it was reported from Kassa that the camp commander was prepared to send back minors – children under the age of sixteen from Budapest – if a request was submitted from the Jewish Council in Budapest and the child's birth certificate and registration form were sent.[9] On 4 May, a similar report came from Nyíregyháza.[10] Karsai describes the story of another Jewish boy, Manfréd Szilárd, who was denounced in July 1944, but the police refused to take the boy because he was a minor, and he ended up in Budapest.[11] Not only do these references suggest that there were other Jewish children spending the early summer of 1944 outside the capital, but also that the return of György András to Budapest was not as exceptional as it might at first seem.

Also making his way to Budapest was another eleven-year-old Jewish boy, the well-know author György Konrád, who lived in Berettyóújfalu in south-east

Hungary. After his parents' arrest, he describes in his postwar memoir visiting a local non-Jewish lawyer with 30,000 pengő, which his father had hidden in his shop. A deal was made with the local authorities and György Konrád was allowed to travel to Budapest with his fourteen-year-old sister and two cousins, where all four survived the war.[12] This was not, as it was in György András' case, the return of a Pesti to Pest. Rather it would appear to be a more maverick decision on the local authorities' part, motivated by money. Reflecting on Konrád's story, István Deák suggests that, 'the deal made with the lawyer, and through him, with the local authorities proved the astuteness and the foresight of the little boy. It also proved that … money in Hungary could often buy security.'[13]

But the traffic between the provinces and the capital was not only one way.[14] Later on that summer, another eleven-year-old – Judit Brody – journeyed from Pest to the countryside near Debrecen in south-eastern Hungary. Judit, along with the rest of her family – father, mother and fourteen-year-old sister – had remained living in their Pest apartment when a highly dispersed form of ghettoization was implemented in June 1944.[15] Because of the compromise solution reached in Budapest, as a result of non-Jewish pressure parallel to that I have described in Szeged, non-Jews were permitted to remain in their apartments in the just under two thousand apartment buildings that were marked with the large yellow star and formed the ghetto spread across the capital.[16] In Judit's apartment building, their non-Jewish next-door neighbour remained living in the yellow-star house – in effect the ghetto – in the summer of 1944. He arranged someone who would 'for payment of course' take Judit to the countryside with forged papers 'in order to avoid the bombing in Budapest'. Judit – but not her older sister who was already an adolescent and therefore, so Judit later reflected, harder to pass as a non-Jewish child evacuee from the capital – spent a month in the countryside as a 'hidden child' now named Edit Varga, and supposedly the daughter of the caretaker of the apartment building where she lived. Her 'guardian' came to collect her in Budapest, and the two of them travelled by train to Debrecen in July 1944. There, she spent a 'wonderful' summer. 'Edit' wrote letters home via the next-door neighbour relaying the experiences of a Pesti spending the summer in a rural Hungary – a place of fruit orchards where families kept pigs.[17]

Both at the time, and as she reflected later in her memoir, her rural sojourn was purportedly about escaping Allied bombing, rather than ghettoization.[18] However, with news of the Soviet advance, her parents decided in late summer that she should return to Budapest for what was expected to be the final stages of the war. 'My parents thought it was better to die together than separately', wrote Judit in an unpublished memoir, adding 'although it was even better to live together'. Ultimately the family did survive the final bloody months of the war, sheltering in a Swedish house in the so-called International ghetto in Pest.

The stories of György András, György and Judit point to shifting perceptions of sites of safety and danger across the turbulent year of 1944. In the late

Judit with her guardian and the fiancée of her guardian's sister in Debrecen in the summer of 1944. Photos courtesy of Judit Brody.

spring and early summer, it seems that György András' parents assumed that the village of Csehimindszent was a safer place for an eleven-year-old than the capital now under Allied bombing attack.[19] However, in May it is clear that György András' parents changed their mind and decided that it would be safer for him to be with them in the capital than in the countryside. By the time that ghettoization was implemented, anti-Jewish measures were of more concern than allied bombing. This perception of Budapest as a site of safety in May as deportations got underway was more widely shared. It drove György Konrád's decision to head for the capital with his sister and cousins, as well as Béla Zsolt's choice of destination in early June. He left a provincial city that he described as a place 'where every Tom, Dick and Harry knew her [Ági] – in short, the most dangerous place in the whole world'[20] to hide in the greater anonymity of a big city. He was not alone in such thinking. According to Margit Jarovitz, inter-viewed in the late 1980s, 'A lot of them escaped to Budapest from the cities or the countryside, from all over they came to Budapest, because you could hide in a big city, but you cannot hide in a city where you live because everybody knows each other.'[21] However, by July 1944, Judit Brody's parents had decided that the Hungarian countryside was a safer place for a child than living in the ghetto in a capital still suffering Allied bombing. After only a month, they changed their minds, and Judit was brought back to Budapest, where the family survived the war intact.

The Brody family's experience of survival in the capital was far from exceptional. Rather than being deported, Budapest's Jews were spared deportation after the intervention of the Regent, Miklós Horthy, who came under pressure from the neutral powers. In late summer and autumn of 1944, Jews in Budapest continued to live in yellow-star houses, at a time when rural Jews – the labour battalion members aside – had long been deported from the country. In the winter of 1944–5, they were moved to two ghettos in the city – the International ghetto protected by the neutral legations and the closed Pest ghetto around the Dohány utca synagogue. In both, food was hard to get in a city under siege, and Budapest Jews were subject to deportation on foot to build fortifications on the Austrian–Hungarian border, and round-ups by Arrow Cross gangs shooting Jews into the Danube.[22] Although far from safe in the second half of 1944, Budapest Jews – like the Jewish men removed from provincial ghettos in May and June 1944 – were spared deportations to Auschwitz. As Ivan Gabor, a child in 1944, reflected on the family's relocation following his father's loss of his job as an accountant in a carpet factory in Nagybánya, 'We moved to Budapest and this is what saved our life.'[23] Being in Budapest, rather than Vasvár, at the end of May 1944 was what also saved György András' life. You could not get a clearer picture of place mattering during the Holocaust.

But as I hope I have shown in this book, place mattered during the Holocaust in smaller ways than the dramatic differences in experience between the capital and the Hungarian provinces. Even one element of the process that we dub the Holocaust – ghettoization – could and did vary from place to place. There were certain common elements – segregation, concentration and control – but ghettos differed from place to place in important ways, with implications for the degree and nature of segregation, concentration and control. As I examine in Chapter 5, in Körmend it seems that a uniquely porous form of segregation was adopted for at least some Jews and non-Jews to allow for a variety of forms of economic exchange to continue in this place despite ghettoization. As I have explored in Chapter 4, because of the adoption of dispersed forms of ghettoization in some places, micro ghettos were established in some towns and cities in Hungary. For the D family in Tolna, ghettoization meant moving into one room in their house which was now occupied by eighteen Jews. Here, they were separated not only from non-Jews, but also other ghetto Jews in the town. Theirs was a very different ghetto experience from say, Szabolcs county Jews living in makeshift ghetto camps in farmsteads on the outskirts of Nyíregyháza, or Veszprém Jews living in buildings around the synagogue. All were ghettos, but to use the blanket term, threatens to erase what were significant differences. Throughout I have been interested in laying bear, rather than erasing, differences, both in the nature of the events themselves and the surviving traces of those events.

However, whatever the ghetto – whether micro or macro in scale or located in the centre or on the periphery – Jews from towns and cities like Körmend, Tolna,

Nyíregyháza and Veszprém were deported from these ghetto to Auschwitz-Birkenau in the summer of 1944. I am reminded of Judit Molnár's memorable phrase 'two cities, two policies, one outcome' in her comparative study of Pécs and Szeged.[24] In some senses the differences that I identify between the ghettos in these places meant little once deportations had commenced. György András' journcy from Vasvár to Budapest was not only a counter journey to the journeys of other Jews in the village of Csehimindszent, but most Hungarian Jews period. For most Hungarian Jews in 1944, ghettoization was a beginning not an end. After their initial journey to the ghetto, there were further journeys: first, in many cases to a still larger entrainment point – in the case of Vasvár this was Szombathely – and from there out of the country, and in most cases, on to Auschwitz – a place where the life expectancy of eleven-year-old-Jewish boys in 1944 was very, very short. It is these histories and geographies of rapid concentration and deportation (and murder) that form the big story in Hungary in the spring and summer of 1944, when over 400,000 Jews were placed into ghettos and then deported from these short-lived ghettos within a matter of months if not weeks. The speed and lateness of ghettoization, deportation and killing continues to astound.

But counter journeys were taken not only by György András M. and a handful of other eleven-year-old Hungarian Jewish children. There is bigger story of counter-journeys that I have examined in this book: counter journeys taken by Hungarian Jewish men from their upper teens to upper forties out of ghettos such as those in Veszprém in May and June 1944. Here – and this place was not alone – there was a gendered inflow into the city's ghettos of rural Jews, and a gendered outflow from the city's ghettos of labour battalion conscripts in the summer of 1944. The danger in attempting to tell *the* story is to downplay or erase important counter stories such as these.

That danger was something that Joan Ringelheim drew attention to over twenty-five years ago. Speaking on the opening day of the first academic conference devoted to studying women and the Holocaust, Ringelheim provocatively asserted, 'I would like to suggest that there is no such thing as "The Holocaust"'. As her subsequent words revealed, Ringelheim saw the problem with the term 'The Holocaust' to be that it hid more than it revealed, giving an artificial coherence to the events of second-world-war Europe and erasing the variety of experiences of the victims. For Ringelheim,

What men, women and children experienced was not one event, but a myriad of events which we've tied into an analytical knot so we can speak about it with ease and with single breaths. The Holocaust is made up of individual experiences. They may have been momentous experiences for some, but it seems to me that the momentousness often occurs after we've identified what the event is. There was no such language for those experiences when people were going through them. It also seems to me important to say that not everyone experienced this event in the same way. One of the things we're exploring here is not just the commonalities, but the differences between

Reliefs on Synagogue Wall, Újpest. Photo: Tim Cole.

men and women's experiences and the differences in experience among women. We need to be able to listen to those who experienced the Holocaust, to understand the differences in those experiences and to hear the silences ...[25]

Given the context when these words were first spoken, it is clear that Ringelheim's challenging of 'The Holocaust' as monolithic event, was primarily intended to highlight the different experiences of Jewish men and women. As I have shown, this is particularly striking in the Hungarian case. The history of labour battalion service that pre-dated 1944 and was significantly extended in scope during 1944 is central to Hungarian Jewish experiences. In particular, familial separation was something that had already taken place in Hungary, prior to the selection ramps at Auschwitz-Birkenau.

This reality was one that was recognized in early postwar literature and memorials. Perhaps the most striking example of this visually, are a series of memorial reliefs, designed by Edith Kiss, which were placed on the exterior wall of the synagogue in Újpest, a suburb of Budapest, in July 1948. This early rendering of the events of 1944–5 chose to tell the story in four acts. In the first relief, a Hungarian gendarme escorts Jews to waiting cattle cars, for deportation from Hungary. In the second, an Arrow-Cross guard watches over a group of men in a labour battalion. In the third, a Nazi soldier herds Jews into the gas chambers. In the fourth, liberating Red Army soldiers are welcomed by joyful Budapest Jews.

Most obviously, here is an ideologically driven story of destruction of Jews by fascism, and liberation by communism. But here is also a story of destruction and liberation (by male agents) taking rather different forms for Jewish men and women in different places. Deportation is shown as primarily the experience of women, the elderly and children from provincial Hungary. The young men missing from this relief are shown in the next, labouring under the watchful eye of an armed Arrow-Cross soldier. The scene before the gas chambers is much more mixed – made up of a family group, men and women, the young and old. In the final relief, the liberating Red Army is greeted by a group of Jewish women, plus a couple of older men in the capital. In this early postwar memorial plaque the experiences of Jews within Hungary are clearly represented as gendered.[26] However, I wonder if that early postwar sensitivity to differences in experiences was subsumed by a more monolithic (and non-gendered) memory of the Holocaust, that arguably emerged from the 1960s onwards.[27]

Ringelheim's call for sensitivity to multiple Holocaust events and experiences, rather than a singular, monolithic 'Holocaust' event and experience, has broader implications than simply integrating gender into Holocaust historiography. Her cautioning against creating an overly unified 'Holocaust' event and 'Holocaust' experience is echoed in Martin Jay's reminder that the Holocaust is 'a *post facto* conceptual entity not in use at the time, which no one individual ever witnessed'.[28] Not only was the Holocaust a series of events that 'no one individual ever witnessed' and multiple victims experienced in various ways in different places, but also an event that no single individual or state implemented in its entirety. The Holocaust was a dispersed event, involving a large number of actors.

How to write difference into, rather than out of, history remains a challenge. Here I have sought to do this through a fragmented approach focused around particular traces. Working from the traces back, I hope that I have been sensitive to the wide range of genres that traces of the past include – each of which demands a different reading – as well as to the exceptionality of traces. Throughout I have sought to explore differences between people and places, as well as commonalities. The end result is that there is so much I haven't said. I have examined only a handful of the places where the policies of ghettoization and deportation were enacted, and a few of the people who initiated, facilitated, watched, resisted, experienced and narrated those journeys into and out of Hungarian ghettos in 1944. But in telling these few stories, I hope that I have pointed to the complex nature of the events of the Holocaust on the ground as well as redistributed power more broadly than tends to be the case in more centralized, top-down renderings of this event. As I show, it was not only regional and local officials who were active agents in 1944, but also newspaper editors, non-Jewish city dwellers, non-Jewish rural farmworkers, as well as Jewish leaders and ordinary Jews themselves.

It is striking I think that the three counter journeys taken by eleven year olds in 1944 all suggest some limited room for manoeuvre. Writing the Holocaust, the tendency is to see agency lying largely, if not solely, with the perpetrators. This is something that Debórah Dwork has suggested is particularly the case when writing of the death camps, where, 'we lose our ability to see the distinguishing characteristics, to hold on to the particulars of their different lives, to remember that each was a separate entity. The German view prevails. The Jewish inmates become an undifferentiated mass'[29] – an undifferentiated mass devoid of agency. While not wishing to suggest that there were not real differentials in power between perpetrators and victims, János M's and György Konrád's approaches to local officials, Judit Brody's parents' negotiations through their non-Jewish next-door neighbour as well as Béla Zsolt's bribing of the police in Nagyvárad all challenge a view of agency in simply top-down terms. It is perhaps telling that Roseman's story of Marianne Ellenbogen's wartime hiding in Nazi Germany has 'little of the passivity and isolation we associate with being hidden', but rather revealed a woman who was able to maintain contact with her fiancé in a Polish ghetto for six months, thus painting a complex picture of victim agency during hiding.[30] Micro histories of the Holocaust reveal the ways in which individuals sought to adapt (both successfully and unsuccessfully) to the rapidly changing circumstances in which they found themselves.

But alongside revealing agency among the victims, the stories of these three eleven-year-olds, and Béla Zsolt's story, point once more to the importance of money in 1944. It would be crass to reduce the Holocaust to economics. As

I suggest, financial gain is not sufficient to explain the mass participation of rural cart owners in undertaking the hundreds and hundreds of journeys to and from the ghettos around Nyíregyháza. Compulsion – while not total – appears to have played a part here. But, economics did play a major role in the concentration process in particular. It was a central concern of Ferenczy's, and ghettoization was experienced as an ongoing process of asset-stripping by Béla and Éva in the Nagyvárad ghetto. Newspaper editors in Szeged and the wider urban population there also had an eye on economic concerns as ghettoization was enacted in this city. But, the economics of the Holocaust could – and did – work both ways. It was also a potential means to escape the destruction. In the case of György Konrád and Judit, it is clear that money changed hands. This was also the case with Béla Zsolt. Whether this was the case with György András is not clear. The only hint of the exchange of money in securing György András' return is a line in the chief constable's memorandum that notes that the issue of expenses is left as a matter between the father and the lawyer who would accompany the child back to Budapest. But we can assume, I think, that he was paid handsomely for his services.

Writing social histories of the Holocaust with people like György András M., György Konrád and Judit Brody in view – not to mention the host of others whose stories I have told – points to the complexity of this event. Alongside the waft of mass ghettoization and deportation is the weft of counter-journeys made by those who used money to try to make a difference, or whose gendered bodies were deemed of greater value to the Hungarian state. What the Hungarian Holocaust brings to the fore – and perhaps here it reflects the tragedy of genocide writ large – is what happens when a state makes decisions about the value and lack of value of citizens. When humans are reduced to their differential value to the state, trouble is never far off.

Notes

PROLOGUE

1   Lanzmann, C., *Shoah. An Oral History of the Holocaust. The Complete Text of the Film* (New York: Pantheon Books, 1985), 141–2. For more on *Fahrplananordnung*, see Hilberg, R., *The Destruction of the European Jews* (New Haven: Yale University Press, 2003), 433.
2   Rabinowitz, P., 'Wreckage upon Wreckage: History, Documentary and the Ruins of Memory', *History and Theory* 32, 2 (1993), 134, writes of the paperwork in this scene that it is, 'the trace of 10,000 dead Jews ... this piece of paper represents all that is left of more than ten thousand men, women, and children whose lives were lost and whose accumulated wealth, seized by the Nazis, paid for their final journey to death'.
3   In previous work I have used quotation marks around the word 'Jew' to emphasize the constructed nature of this category in wartime Europe. For more on my thinking in this regard see, Cole, T., 'Constructing the "Jew," Writing the Holocaust: Hungary 1920–45', *Patterns of Prejudice* 33, 3 (1999), 19–27; and Cole, T., *Holocaust City. The Making of a Jewish Ghetto* (New York: Routledge, 2003), 44–48. I do not use quotation marks round every reference to 'Jew' in this book, but ask the reader to consider the category as far from unproblematic.
4   See the central exhibiting of a single typewriter in the Holocaust permanent exhibit at the Imperial War Museum in London.
5   Browning, C., *Ordinary Men. Reserve Police Battalion 101 and the Final Solution in Poland* (New York: HarperCollins, 1992).
6   With the opening up of archives in the former Soviet Union, there has been a greater emphasis on the importance of face-to-face killings in the East in 1941–2 within the historiography.
7   Burke, P., *Eyewitnessing. The Use of Images in Historical Writing* (London: Reaktion, 1991), 98.
8   Renier, G., *History. Its Purpose and Method* (London: George Allen & Unwin Ltd., 1950), 96.
9   Burke, *Eyewitnessing*, 13.
10 Burke, *Eyewitnessing*, 97 and 104 where Burke gives by way of an example, 'The lecture notes of a professor were produced in the course of transacting academic business. Of what are they a trace? Not of what the professor said in his lecture: to believe this would be placing time on its head: how can Monday's trace inform us of Tuesday's event? No, the lecture notes are the trace of what the professor intends to say in his lecture. They are also the traces of his knowledge and of his ignorance, of his opinion and prejudices; they may be the trace of the state of accepted history in his day, as reflected by his mind. The students' lecture notes are a trace – how faint! – of what the professor actually said. The question: of what, or for what, are the professor's notes a "source", could not have been so fruitful in results, unless a deliberate effort had been made to forget the metaphor it embodies, and that would have meant thinking, however inarticulately, in terms of traces. It is better to be frank and to clear up our vocabulary. Sources are a source of confusion.'
11 Burke, *Eyewitnessing*, 99.
12 Burke, *Eyewitnessing*, 97–8.
13 For more on this see Braham, R., *Politics of Genocide. The Holocaust in Hungary* (New York: Columbia University Press, 1981), 230–62.
14 Kádár, G. and Vági, Z., 'Rationality or Irrationality? The Annihilation of Hungarian Jews', *The Hungarian Quarterly* 45, 174 (2004), 39; Braham, *Politics of Genocide*, 572–805. While

the German Ambassador Edmund Vessenmayer gave a figure of 437,402, Lieutenant Colonel László Ferenczy of the Hungarian gendarmerie put the number at 434,351.

15 Gerlach, C. and Aly, G., *Das letze kapital. Realpolitik, Ideologie und der Mord an den ungarischen Juden 1944/1945* (Stuttgart München: Deutsche Verlags-Anstalt, 2002); Braham, *Politics of Genocide*. For, an extensive and highly critical review of Aly and Gerlach, see Karsai, L., 'The Last Chapter of the Holocaust', *Yad Vashem Studies* 34 (2006), 293–329.

16 Wiesel, E., 'Introduction' in Braham, R. and Vágo, B. (eds), *The Holocaust in Hungary: Forty Years Later* (New York: Columbia University Press, 1985), xv.

17 On the spatiality of the Holocaust see the nascent literature on Holocaust geographies: Charlesworth, A., 'The Topography of Genocide' in Stone, D. (ed.), *The Historiography of the Holocaust* (Houndmills: Palgrave Macmillan, 2004), 216–52; Cole, T., *Holocaust City*; Beorn, W., Cole, T., Gigliotti, S., Giordano, A., Holian, A., Jaskot, P., Knowles, A., Marurovsky, M. and Steiner, E., 'Geographical Record: Geographies of the Holocaust', *The Geographical Review* 99, 4 (2009), 563–74.

18 Hilberg, R., *Perpetrators, Victims, Bystanders. The Jewish Catastrophe 1933–1945* (London: Secker and Warburg 1993); Ehrenreich R. and Cole, T., 'The Perpetrator-Bystander-Victim Constellation: Rethinking Genocidal Relationships', *Human Organization* 64, 3 (2005), 213–24.

19 Dean, M., *Robbing the Jews. The Confiscation of Jewish Property in the Holocaust, 1933–1945* (New York: Cambridge University Press, 2008).

20 Cole, *Holocaust City*; Molnár, J., *Zsidósors 1944–ben az V. (szegedi) Csendőrkerületben* (Budapest: Cserépfalvi Kiadó, 1995); Gergely, A., *A Székesfehérvári és Fejér Megyei Zsidóság Tragédiája 1938–1944* (Budapest: Vince Kiadó, 2003).

21 Braham, *Politics of Genocide*; Braham R. (ed.), *A Magyarországi Holokauszt. Földrajzi Enciklopédiája* (Budapest: Park Kiadó 2007).

22 The so-called 'I collection' is a valuable, if problematic, series of microfilms from national and regional archives across Hungary. The main problem, as with any microfilmed collection, is that of editing by the individual archivists who made decisions about what to microfilm and what not to microfilm. However, an advantage is that reading through the entire run of microfilm reels provides a more manageable overview of sources from local and regional archives than trekking from individual archive to archive would. Hungary is a relatively small country, but still such an undertaking would require a team of scholars working with one, two or a handful of counties each, rather than a single scholar working their way round each county archive. The model of teamwork is one fruitfully used in Braham, *Magyarországi Holokauszt*. The 41 individual county chapters that make up this massive undertaking were authored by 24 separate individuals.

23 United States Holocaust Memorial Museum archives (USHMM), RG 52.001M, reel 99 (hereafter I adopt the more commonly used short form I 99, etc. which is the original designation at the Hungarian National Archive), 2502/1944. For an article drawing on these ghetto passes in a rather different way from my use of them as the basis for Chapter 5, see Cole, T., 'Building and Breaching the Ghetto Boundary: A Brief History of the Ghetto Fence in Körmend, Hungary 1944', *Holocaust and Genocide Studies* 23, 1 (2009), 54–75.

24 Braham, *Magyarországi Holokauszt*, 208, 219, 235, 377, 403, 501, 926, 930, 1017, 1275, 1311.

25 I am cautious of an overly teleological reading of the events of 1944, and question the 'inevitability' of mass deportations once ghettoization was underway. See Cole, *Holocaust City*, ch. 3; Cole, T., 'Budapest 1944: Changing the Shape of the Ghetto' in Roth J. (ed.), *Remembering for the Future. The Holocaust in an Age of Genocide. Volume 1. History* (Houndmills: Palgrave, 2001), 198–210.

26 Lorimer, H., 'Telling Small Stories: Spaces of Knowledge and the Practice of Geography', *Transactions of the Institute of British Geographers* 28, 2 (2003), 197–217.

27 Roth, J., 'Equality, Neutrality, Particularity: Perspectives on Women and the Holocaust' in Baer, E. and Goldenberg, M. (eds), *Experience and Expression. Women, the Nazis, and the Holocaust* (Detroit: Wayne State University Press, 2003), 14.

28 See especially, White, H., *Metahistory. The Historical Imagination in Nineteenth-Century Europe* (Baltimore: The Johns Hopkins University Press, 1973); White, H., *Tropics of Discourse. Essays in Cultural Criticism* (Baltimore: The Johns Hopkins University Press, 1978).

29 See e.g. Rosenstone, R., *Mirror in the Shrine. American Encounters with Meiji Japan* (Cambridge, Mass.: Harvard University Press, 1988); Schama, S., *Dead Certainties (Unwarranted Speculations)* (New York: Knopf, 1991); Spence, J., *The Gate of Heavenly Peace: The Chinese and their Revolution, 1895–1980* (New York: Viking, 1981); Hampson, N., *The Life and Opinions of Maximilian Robespierre* (London: Duckworth, 1974).
30 Price, R., *Alabi's World* (Baltimore: The John Hopkins University Press, 1990).
31 Price, R., 'Invitation to Historians: Practices of Historical Narrative', *Rethinking History* 5, 3 (2001), 359.
32 Stone, D., *Constructing the Holocaust* (London: Vallentine Mitchell, 1973), 212, 224.
33 Braham, *Politics of Genocide*, chapter titles for Chapters 1, 11, 16, 17, 22, 32 and 33.
34 Braham, *Magyarországi Holokauszt*.
35 Spielberg, S., 'Preface' in Spielberg S. and Survivors of the Shoah Visual History Foundation, *The Last Days* (London: Weidenfeld & Nicolson, 1999), 7.
36 Cf. the centrality of differences such as these in Palosuo, L., *Yellow Stars and Trouser Inspections. Jewish Testimonies from Hungary, 1920–1945* (Uppsala: Uppsala Universitet Department of History and The Uppsala Programme for Holocaust and Genocide Studies, 2008). For my own critical review of this work see Cole, T., 'Multiple Experiences of the Holocaust in Budapest', *Historisk Tidskrift* 4 (2008), 707–13.
37 For some reflections on this see Cole, T., 'The Return of György András M.: Writing Exceptional Stories of the Holocaust', *Journal of Jewish Identities* 1, 2 (2008), 29–48.
38 Cole, 'Building and Breaching the Ghetto Boundary', 54–5; 59–60.
39 See Peltonen, P., 'Clues, Margins, and Monads: The Micro-Macro Link in Historical Research', *History and Theory* 40 (2001), 349, who suggests that, 'The unifying principle of all micro-historical research is the belief that microscopic observation will reveal factors previously unobserved ... Phenomena previously considered to be sufficiently described and understood assume completely new meanings by altering the scale of observation. It is then possible to use these results to draw far wider generalizations although the initial observations were made within relatively narrow dimensions and as experiments rather than examples.'
40 Ginzburg, C., *The Cheese and the Worms: The Cosmos of a Sixteenth-century Miller* (Baltimore: The John Hopkins University Press, 1997).
41 Zemon Davis, N., *The Return of Martin Guerre* (Cambridge, Mass.: Harvard University Press, 1983), 4.
42 Ginzburg, C. and Poni, C., 'The Name and the Game: Unequal Exchange and the Historiographic Marketplace' in Muir, E. and Ruggiero, G. (eds), *Microhistory and the Lost Peoples of Europe* (Baltimore: The Johns Hopkins University Press, 1991), 7.
43 Wisse, R., 'Introduction' in Shapiro, R. (ed.), *Holocaust Chronicles: Individualizing the Holocaust through Diaries and Other Contemporaneous Personal Accounts* (Hoboken, N.J.: KTAV Publishing House, 1999), xviii.
44 Waxman, Z., *Writing the Holocaust. Identity, Testimony, Representation* (Oxford: Oxford University Press, 2006), 33.
45 Waxman, *Writing the Holocaust*, 33. See also Appelfeld, A., 'Individualization of the Holocaust' in Shapiro (ed.), *Holocaust Chronicles*, 4–5, who describes Holocaust era journals as, 'the last effort to preserve the self before it was taken. One of the horrors of the Holocaust is the eradication of the self. First you lose your house, your personal belongings, you are pressed into a crowded ghetto, you are separated from your parents, your brothers and sisters, and finally, if you are left alive, you remain deprived of your self, a famished body that moves from place to place, without the divine image. The dread of the Holocaust is embodied, among other things, in the large numbers, the horrors that have no limit or boundary, whose darkness is never-ending. There the individual is rubbed out. These journals are the final effort to preserve a shred of one's self before it is rubbed out. Naked anonymity was the gateway to death.'
46 Browning, *Ordinary Men*; Browning, C., 'German Memory, Judicial Interrogation, and Historical Reconstruction: Writing Perpetrator History from Postwar Testimony' in Friedlander. S. (ed.) *Probing the Limits of Representation. Nazism and the 'Final Solution'* (Cambridge, Mass.: Harvard University Press, 1992), 35.
47 See Braham, *Politics of Genocide*, and also e.g. Molnár, J., 'Two Cities, Two Policies, One

Outcome: The De-Judaization of Pécs and Szeged in 1944', *Yad Vashem Studies* 32 (2004), 97–129 who refers throughout to named national, regional and local officials, as well as the chairman of the Jewish Council in Szeged.

48   On the importance of names within Holocaust memorialization, see e.g. the Yad Vashem names project <http://names.yadvashem.org/wps/portal/IY_HON_Entrance> and the Beate Klarsfeld foundation books of names <http://www.klarsfeldfoundation.org/>.

49   Hilberg, R., *Sources of Holocaust Research. An Analysis* (Chicago: Ivan R. Dee, 2001), 149.

50   Haidu, P., 'The Dialectics of Unspeakability: Language, Silence, and the Narrative of Desubjectification' in Friedlander (ed.), *Probing the Limits*, 280.

51   I use abbreviations of surnames in the interests of personal privacy.

52   See the subtitle of Muir and Ruggiero, *Microhistory*.

53   Reay, B., *Microhistories: Demography, Society and Culture in Rural England, 1800–1930* (Cambridge: Cambridge University Press, 1996), 258, writes that, 'the advantage of placing a small community under the microscope is that it becomes possible to see and explore the complexity of social interaction and social and economic processes'. Dave Rollison suggests that micro histories of early modern England have revealed a past that is 'more anarchic, various and eccentric than authorized styles and versions have had us believe' in Rollison, D., 'Microhistory and Epic History', conference paper given at the University of East Anglia (24 April 2002) cited in Spicksley, J., 'Conference Report: The social and cultural history of early modern England: new approaches and interpretations'. University of East Anglia, 24 April 2002', *Social History* 28, 1 (2003), 84.

54   Levi, G., 'The Origins of the Modern State and the Microhistorical Perspective' in Schlumbohm, J. (ed.), *Mikrogeschichte, Makrogeschichte: komplementär oder inkommensurabel?* (Göttingen: Wallstein Verlag, 1998), 61–2.

55   Levi, G., 'On Microhistory' in Burke, P. (ed.), *New Perspectives on Historical Writing* (Cambridge: Polity Press, 1991), 106. See the notion of the 'exceptional normal' coined by Edoardo Grendi as a way of understanding the relationship between the micro with the macro, briefly discussed in Peltonen, 'Clues', 348, 356–57, who notes, the emphasis of Ginzburg and Levi on 'clues' – 'starting an investigation from something that does not quite fit, something odd that needs to be explained. This peculiar event or phenomenon is taken as a sign of a larger, but hidden or unknown, structure' (p. 349). For Petonen, 'Micro historians are actually trying to discover very big things with their microscope and magnifying lenses' (p. 350). For more on the relationship between micro and macro see Schlumbohm, *Mikrogeschichte, Makrogeschichte*.

56   Roseman, M., *A Past in Hiding. Memory and Survival in Nazi Germany* (New York: Henry Holt, 2000), 11. Roseman describes (p. 8), the correspondence between Marianne and her fiancé Ernst as 'unique'.

57   Roseman, *Past in Hiding*, 13, emphasis mine.

58   Roth, 'Equality, Neutrality, Particularity', 14.

1 ENTERING AND EXITING THE GHETTO: NAME LISTS FROM VESZPRÉM

1   Braham, *Politics of Genocide*, 578.

2   Braham, *Politics of Genocide*, 551, 579–80.

3   I 116, 74/1944, Rabbi Kun to Veszprém mayoral office (3 May 1944).

4   Braham, *Politics of Genocide*, 551.

5   Braham, *Politics of Genocide*, 578.

6   Braham, *Politics of Genocide*, 579, 551.

7   Varga, L., Soós, L. and Gecsényi, L., 'Report on the work of the committee investigating the fate of the so-called Jaross Lists drawn up in 1944 in Hungary' (Budapest, 24 February 2004). I am grateful to Ferenc Katona for drawing my attention to this report.

8   Varga, Soós and Gecsényi, 'Report'.

9   Alongside a number of name lists in regional archives, there is a rich collection in the Budapest Jewish Museum.

10   I 116, Name lists of Jews in Veszprém (2 May 1944); I 171, Jewish synagogue ghetto name list (15 June 1944); I 171, Undated Komakuti Jewish Camp Name List; I 171, lists of men mobilized by Hungarian III Army (20 May 1944, 4 June 1944, 12 June); Máthé, É. (ed.), *Töredék. Fejezetek a Veszprémi Zsidó Közösség Történetéből* (Budapest: MAZSIHISZ, 2001) partially reproduces these lists, which also feature on the walls of a memorial in the Jewish cemetery in the city; Matyikó, J., *Zsidók Siófokon* (Budapest: ETHNICA, 2002), 44–51, reproduces those sections including Jews from Siófok; see also references to these lists in Braham, *Magyaroszági Holokauszt*, 1311.

11   For earlier reflections on this see, Cole, T., 'A Gendered Holocaust? The Experiences of "Jewish" Men and Women in Hungary, 1944' in Braham, R. and Chamberlin, B. (eds), *The Holocaust in Hungary: Sixty Years Later* (New York: Columbia University Press, 2006), 43–61.

12   For more reflections on this see Cole, 'Constructing the "Jew"'.

13   I 116, Name lists of Jews in Veszprém (2 May 1944).

14   For more on the divided nature of Hungarian Jewish communities, see Braham, *Politics of Genocide*, ch. 3; Frojimovics, K., 'Who Were They? Characteristics of the Religious Streams within Hungarian Jewry on the Eve of the Community's Extermination', *Yad Vashem Studies* 35, 1 (2007), 143–77.

15   Braham, *Politics of Genocide*, 30.

16   Gonda, L., *A Zsidóság Magyarországon 1526–1945* (Budapest 1992), 271–2; Katzburg, N., *Hungary and the Jews. Policy and Legislation, 1920–1943* (Ramat Gan: Bar-Ilan University Press, 1981), 61, 76–7; Spira, T., 'Hungary's Numerus Clausus, the Jewish Minority, and the League of Nations', *Ungarn Jahrbuch* 4 (1972), 117–9. When asked to explain how the 'Jew' was defined in practice, Klebelsberg – the Hungarian representative to the Council – answered that it was 'not necessarily based on the present religion of a person, but on his religious status as revealed by extracts from State registries. If a person changed his religion to avoid the law, he would still be considered Jewish. If his conversion was sincere, the law would not apply to him.' The Law was repealed in Law No. XIV (1928).

17   Gonda, *A Zsidóság Magyarországon*, 276–9.

18   Gonda, *A Zsidóság Magyarországon*, 279–92.

19   Braham, *Politics of Genocide*, 200.

20   Gonda, *A Zsidóság Magyarországon*, 292–4.

21   See e.g. Beneschofsky, I. and Karsai, E., *Vádirat a Nácizmus Ellen I* (Budapest: A Magyar Izraeliták Országos Képviselete Kidása, 1958), 56, 72, 78.

22   Gonda, *A Zsidóság Magyarországon*, 276–9; Katzburg, *Hungary and the Jews*, 103–4; Hanebrink, P., *In Defense of Christian Hungary. Religion, Nationalism and Antisemitism, 1890–1944* (Ithaca: Cornell University Press, 2006), 161–2; 164–91 points to the status of converts being a particular concern of senior church leaders discussing this law and subsequent anti-Jewish laws in the Upper House.

23   Katzburg, *Hungary and the Jews*, 140–1; Schmidl, E., 'Jews in the Austro–Hungarian armed forces, 1867–1918' in Mendelsohn, E. (ed.), *Studies in Contemporary Jewry: Jews and other Ethnic Groups in a Multi–Ethnic World Volume III* (Oxford: Oxford University Press, 1987), 138, writes that, 'the reserve officer's uniform hanging in the wardrobe was the final, and much-coveted, symbol of Jewish emancipation and acceptance into Gentile society'.

24   Gonda, *A Zsidóság Magyarországon*, 279–92.

25   Cited in Braham, *Politics of Genocide*, 158.

26   Gonda, *A Zsidóság Magyarországon*, 292–4; Katzburg, *Hungary and the Jews*, 178.

27   See the issuing of a list of exemptions related to the measure ordering Jews to wear a yellow star in Beneschofsky and Karsai, *Vádirat I*, 108–9.

28   Beneschofsky and Karsai, *Vádirat I*, 250; Braham, *Politics of Genocide*, 901.

29   1.730/1944 M.E. (10 May 1944); see Braham, *Politics of Genocide*, 782 for a translation. See also 108.500/1944 K.M. (27 April 1944) and 1240/1944 M.E. (5 April 1944).

30   I 116, 2 May list cf. I 171, 15 June list. The 'Jewish persons of Christian faith' separately listed by Kun's did end up in the ghetto (see below).

31 I 116, 2 May list cf. I 171, 15 June list.
32 1.730/1944 M.E. (10 May 1944).
33 Veszprémi Megyei Levélatara (VML), V. 173/b 2532/1944, letter from Mrs Lázár S. to mayor (25 April 1944).
34 VML, V. 173/b 2532/1944, letter from mayor to clerk at welfare organization for disabled servicemen and their relatives (5 May 1944).
35 VML, V. 173/b 2532/1944, report from clerk at welfare organization for disabled servicemen and their relatives to mayor (8 May 1944).
36 VML, V. 173/b 2532/1944, handwritten decision signed by deputy mayor (17 May 1944). See also Beneschofsky and Karsai, *Vádirat I*, 250–3.
37 See e.g. Karsai, E., *Vádirat a Nácizmus Ellen III* (Budapest: A Magyar Izraeliták Országos Képviselete Kiadása, 1967), 18–19, which reproduces a letter sent to the prefect of Borsod County on 30 June requesting information about those exempt persons who had 'possibly' been deported.
38 On the labour service system, see Braham, R., *The Hungarian Labor Service System, 1939–1945* (New York: Columbia University Press, 1977); and Braham, *Politics of Genocide*, 294–380.
39 Kramer, T., *From Emancipation to Catastrophe. The Rise and Holocaust of Hungarian Jews* (Lanham MD: University Press of America, 2000), 120.
40 1.730/1944 M.E. (10 May 1944).
41 Shaked, G. (ed.), *Nevek. Munkaszázadok Veszteségei a Keleti Magyar Hadműveleti Területeken* (New York: Beate Klarsfeld Foundation, 1992) vol. 2, 592.
42 I 171, 15 June list.
43 Shaked (ed.), *Nevek. Munkaszázadok* vol. 2, 580; I 116, 2 May list.
44 Shaked (ed.), *Nevek. Munkaszázadok* vol. 2, 334; I 116, 2 May list.
45 Shaked (ed.), *Nevek. Munkaszázadok* vol. 1, 158, 321; volume 2, 18, 389; I 116, 2 May list.
46 Pihurik, J., 'Hungarian Soldiers and Jews on the Eastern Front, 1941–1943', *Yad Vashem Studies* 35, 2 (2007), 86.
47 Shaked (ed.), *Nevek. Munkaszázadok* vol. 1, 321.
48 Shaked (ed.), *Nevek. Munkaszázadok* vol. 2, 389.
49 Shaked (ed.), *Nevek. Munkaszázadok* vol. 1, 158.
50 Rosen, I., *Hungarian Jewish Women Survivors Remember the Holocaust: An Anthology of Life Histories* (Lanham, MD: University Press of America, 2004), 47–8.
51 I 116, 2 May list. The figures were 401 female (59.5 per cent) and 273 male (40.5 per cent) cf. in 1930 the Jewish population in Hungary as a whole was 52.08 per cent female. This proportion roughly matched the proportions in other national communities: Poland – 52.08 per cent in 1931; Germany – 52.24 per cent in 1933; Czechoslovakia – 50.81 per cent in 1930; Lithuania – 52.08 per cent in 1923; Latvia – 53.68 per cent in 1930; Ukraine – 53.70 per cent in 1939; Byelorussia – 53.25 per cent in 1939. See Hilberg, *Perpetrators, Victims, Bystanders*, 127.
52 There were 119 women aged between eighteen and forty-two on 2 May list (72 per cent) compared to forty-seven men (28 per cent).
53 The exception to this general rule was the expulsion – and subsequent execution – of between 16,000–18,000 Jews from Kamenets-Podolsk in 1941. On this, see Braham, *Politics of Genocide*, 207–14.
54 Hilberg, *Perpetrators, Victims, Bystanders*, 127.
55 1.610/1944. M.E. (28 April 1944), paragraph 8, no. 4.
56 I 171, list of men mobilized by Hungarian III Army (20 May 1944). The date on the original is hard to read. Máthé, *Töredék*, 91, gives the date as 30 May, rather than 20 May.
57 I 171, list of men mobilized by Hungarian III Army (4 June 1944).
58 I 171, list of men mobilized by Hungarian III Army (12 June 1944).
59 Letter from Veszprém Jewish Community (23 May 1944) reproduced in Králl, Cs. (ed.), *Holocaust Emlékkönyv. A vidéki zsidóság deportálásának 50 évfordulója alkalmából* (Budapest: TEDISZ, 1994), 388.
60 USHMM, RG–52.009.04/2, Ferenczy report to Interior Ministry (29 May 1944), para. 7. See also para. 12.
61 USHMM, RG–52.009.04/1, Ferenczy report to Interior Ministry (12 June 1944), para. 5.

NOTES

62 I 171, list of men mobilized by Hungarian III Army (12 June).

63 I 99, 2767/1944, letter from chief constable to Jewish Council in Körmend (9 June 1944).

64 Szita, Sz., *Trading in Lives? Operations of the Jewish Relief and Rescue Committee in Budapest, 1944–1945* (Budapest: Central European University Press, 2005), 27; Szita, Sz., 'A Zsidó Munkaszolgálat' in Braham, R. and Pók, A. (eds), *The Holocaust in Hungary Fifty Years Later* (New York: Columbia University Press, 1997), 340, notes in the case of the Miskolc gendarmerie district that Jewish men aged between eighteen and forty-eight years old were being called up out of ghettos 'from Losonc to Gyöngyos'.

65 Braham, *Magyarországi Holokauszt*, 362, 429,.467, 506, 850, 853, 858, 1284, 1334; *Szegedi Új Nemzedék* (2 June, 1944), 5.

66 Braham, *Politics of Genocide*, 349–65, 969–71, 1368–70; Pihurik, 'Hungarian Soldiers and Jews', 100.

67 Braham, *Politics of Genocide*, 352 and 1122, where Braham notes that, 'the institutional approach ... was more effective in saving Jewish lives. Among the agencies of the government that contributed toward this end were the Ministry of Defense, which recruited able-bodied Jewish males into the labor service system ...'. See also Braham, *The Wartime System of Labor Service*, vii–viii, where Braham notes the irony that, 'when the Final Solution program was launched ... the labor service system became refuge for many thousands of Jewish men. While the newly established quisling government of Döme Sztójay virtually surrendered control over the Jews to the SS, the labor service system continued to remain under the jurisdiction of the Hungarian Ministry of Defense. As a result the labor servicemen were not subjected to the ghettoization and deportation that took place during April–July 1944.'

68 Braham, *Politics of Genocide*, 352 and 356, where Braham notes that, 'on June 7, the Minister of Defense issued a secret decree under which the labor servicemen were to be treated like POWs. On the surface, the decree was punitive in character (and it was so implemented in many companies), but in fact it was most probably designed to protect the Jews from the danger of arrest by the SS and their Hungarian hirelings and from subsequent deportation. The decree stipulated, among other things, that the new labor servicemen as well as the mobilized skilled workers, engineers, and technicians were to be placed in special POW-like camps in the vicinity of the plants or factories in which they were to be employed. The camps were to be surrounded by barbed-wire or planks and guarded on a permanent basis. The Jews were not allowed to leave the camps except in the company of Christian escorts, and they were even forced to spend their leaves within the confines of the camps.' Szita, 'Zsidó', 340, notes the problem of a lack of sources to determine exactly what lay behind Ministry of Defence mobilizing of Jews in the aftermath of the Nazi German occupation. On the contemporary politics of this debate, see Karsai, L., 'The Hungarian Holocaust as Reflected in the People's Court Trials in Budapest', *Yad Vashem Studies* 32 (2004), 65.

69 Braham, *Politics of Genocide*, 352–3.

70 Ungváry, K., 'Robbing the Dead: The Hungarian Contribution to the Holocaust' in Kosmala, B. and Tych, F. (eds), *Facing the Nazi Genocide: Non-Jews and Jews in Europe* (Berlin: Metropol, 2004), 254–5.

71 Anders, E. and Dubrovski, J., 'Research Note. Who Died in the Holocaust? Recovering Names from Official Records' in *Holocaust and Genocide Studies* 17, 1 (2003), 131–2.

72 Hilberg, *Perpetrators, Victims, Bystanders*, 128–9.

73 Braham, *Politics*, 357–8, Jewish men between the ages of sixteen and sixty and Jewish women between the ages of sixteen and forty were called up 'for national defense service' on October 26, 1944. Jewish women aged sixteen to fifty who knew how to sew were called up on 2 November. Although see also Karsai, *Vádirat III*, 53–4, which refers to the call-up of eighteen- to thirty-year-old Jewish and non-Jewish women in Budapest in July 1944.

74 I 116, 2 May list. Mrs Adolf N., born in 1871, was recorded living at Völgyikut utca 3.

75 I 171, list of men mobilized by Hungarian III Army (20 May 1944).

76 I 171, 15 June list.

77 Shaked, G. (ed.), *Nevek. Magyar zsidó nők a stutthofi koncentrációs táborban* (New York & Paris: Beate Klarsfeld Foundation, 1995), 474.

78 *Hirek az Elhurcoltakról* 3 (14 August 1945), 11.

79   See their presence on the Yad Vashem central database of Shoah Victims' Names, which gives
      their place and date of death as Auschwitz in July 1944. Strangely, György's name also appears
      on this list as having died in Auschwitz in July 1944. This may have been a mistake, or it may
      be that while he was on the labour service list, he was never mobilized.

80   I 171, list of men mobilized by Hungarian III Army (12 June 1944).

81   I 116, 2 May list.

82   Shaked, *Nevek. Magyar zsidó nők*, 106; *Hirek* 3, 10.

83   Yad Vashem central database of Shoah Victims' Names.

84   Palosuo, *Yellow Stars*, 10–12.

85   Hilberg, *Perpetrators, Victims, Bystanders*, 3.
      I 171, list of men mobilized by Hungarian III Army (20 May 1944)

86   See e.g. copies of *Hirek az Elhurcoltakról* 1 (5 July 1945); 2 (17 July 1945); 3 (14 August 1945);
      4 (1 September 1945); 5 (20 October 1945).

87   Yad Vashem, The Central Database of Shoah Victims' Names, see 'page of testimony' of Oszkár
      F.'s death submitted by his cousin in 1956.

88   Veress, Cs., 'Adatok a Zsidósag Veszprém Megyében a II Világháború Idején Lejátszódott
      Tragédiájához' in Máthé (ed.), *Töredék*, 29.

89   Gerlach and Aly, *Das letze kapitel*, 285–98.

90   The figures are 434 women (69.2 per cent) cf. 193 men (30.8 per cent). A similar picture existed
      in the other ghetto in the former Komakuti barracks which contained 316 women (70.75) cf.
      131 men (29.3 per cent).

91   In the Komakuti ghetto, women accounted for 96.7 per cent of twenty- to twenty-nine-year-
      olds and 97.4 per cent of thirty- to thirty-nine-year-olds – there were 129 women aged between
      eighteen and forty-nine but only eight men of the same age.

92   The figures are 187 women from the Horthy Miklós utca ghetto cf. thirteen men and 129
      women from the Komakuti ghetto cf. eight men. The proportions of men and women were
      roughly similar in the case of Körmend.

93   Veress, 'Adatok', 24.

94   I 171, undated list of Jews brought in from countryside into the Horthy Miklós utca ghetto.

95   I 171, undated Komakuti Jewish Camp name list.

96   Braham, *Politics of Genocide*, ch. 14; Molnár, J., 'The Foundation and Activities of the
      Hungarian Jewish Council, March 20 to July 7, 1944', *Yad Vashem Studies* 30.

97   Braham, *Politics of Genocide*, 447.

98   I 116, 2 May list cf. I 171, 15 June list.

99   Veres, 'Adatok', 22.

100   On Lódz, see Unger, M., 'The Status and Plight of Women in the Lódz Ghetto' in Ofer, D.
      and Weitzman, L. (eds), *Women in the Holocaust* (New Haven: Yale University Press, 1998),
      123–7. In the Lódz ghetto, women made up 57.7 per cent of those Jews aged between twenty
      and forty-five in June 1940. This predominance became more marked over time, with women
      forming an increasing majority of twenty- thirty-four-year-olds in 1941 (151 per 100 men) and
      1944 (196 per 100 men). On Warsaw see Ofer, D., 'Gender Issues in Diaries and Testimonies of
      the Ghetto: The Case of Warsaw' in Ofer and Weitzman, *Women*, 145. On Theresienstadt see
      Bondy, R., 'Women in Theresienstadt and the Family Camp in Birkenau' in Ofer and Weitzman,
      Women, 313, who notes that, 'from May 1942, when the transports of old people started to pour
      in from Germany and Austria, until the liberation, the number of women in the ghetto always
      exceeded the number of men ...' In January 1944, the ghetto population was 60 per cent female,
      and 'after seventeen thousand people left with the transports of autumn 1944, Theresienstadt
      was a city of women. The only men remaining were most of the prominents, all the Danish
      Jews, and others privileged in German eyes.'

2 JOURNEYING TO AND FROM THE GHETTO: RECEIPTS FROM NYÍREGYHÁZA

1 Hilberg, *Destruction*, see esp. 424–33, 483–7; Lanzmann, *Shoah* (1985); on the postwar centrality of railcars see especially Stier, O., 'Different Trains: Holocaust Artifacts and the Ideologies of Remembrance', *Holocaust and Genocide Studies* 19, 1 (2005), 81–106; for a recent study of victim experiences of train travel during the Holocaust, see Gigliotti, S., *The Train Journey: Transit, Captivity, and Witnessing in the Holocaust* (New York: Berghahn Books, 2009). In more recent historiography the modernity of train transport to death camps has been replaced with greater focus on face-to-face killings in the East in 1941–2. In many ways, popular renderings of the Holocaust are yet to catch up with these historiographical developments.
2 See photographs reproduced in Braham, *Politics of Genocide*, 676–7.
3 My translation of 6163/1944 B.M. in Beneschofsky and Karsai, *Vádirat I*, 126. Braham, *Politics of Genocide*, 575, translates this sentence as 'Jews are to be transported as prisoners, by train or if necessary by relay coaches to be ordered by the municipal authorities.'
4 See photograph of horse drawn transports from Bezdán in Braham, *Magyarországi Holokauszt*, 124. See also photograph reproduced in fig. 17.1 in Braham, *Politics of Genocide*, 588, and the recollections of Jimmy Elephant and Bill Vegh in Friedman, S. (ed.), *Amcha: An Oral Testament of the Holocaust* (Washington: University Press of America, 1979), 286, 349.
5 Siegal, A., *Upon the Head of a Goat. A Childhood in Hungary 1939–1944* (London: J. M. Dent & Sons Ltd., 1982), 139–40.
6 Siegal, *Upon the Head of a Goat*, 152–3.
7 I 155, 246/1944, Nyíregyháza mayoral office decision for drafting of horses (2–31 May 1944); I 155, 10.000/1944, Nyíregyháza mayor, Outlay of transport expenses incurred in transport of Jews (3 August 1944).
8 Extracts from one of the accounts are reproduced in Ságvári, Á. (ed.), *Dokumentumok a zsidóság üldöztetésének történetéhez. Iratok a Szabolcs-Szatmár-Bereg megyei levéltárból* (Budapest: Magyar Auschwitz Alapítvány, 1994), 59–61 with more reproduced in Nagy, F. (ed.), *A Nyíregyházi Zsidóság Pusztulása. Forrásközlés* (Nyiregyháza: Szabolcs-Szatmár-Bereg Megyei Önkormányzat Levéltára, 2004), 101, 107, 119–20. These are also referenced by István Néző in his entry on Nyíregyháza in Braham, *Magyarországi Holokauszt*, 973. Ságvári, Á., *Studies on the History of Hungarian Holocaust* (Budapest: Napvilág Kiadó, 2002), 23–4, writes that, 'In Szabolcs County alone haulage from villages to the ghettos and from the ghettos to the trains were carried out by 80 haulers. Horse-drawn carriages were used to complete 190 runs. The fees were between 6.40–20 Hungarian Pengős, according to distance.' As I go on to suggest, she massively underestimates the number of drivers and journeys, and payment was by fixed daily rate per cart.
9 Braham, *Magyarországi Holokauszt*, 938.
10 Braham, *Magyarországi Holokauszt*, 935.
11 1610/1944 M.E. (28 April 1944).
12 6163/1944 res. B.M. See Beneschofsky and Karsai, *Vádirat I*, 124–7; Braham, *Politics of Genocide*, 572–8.
13 Braham, *Politics of Genocide*, 590.
14 I 154, K 10.000/1944, Order from Nyíregyháza mayor (14 April 1944).
15 I 154, K. 10.000/1944, Order from Nyíregyháza mayor (21 April 1944); Braham, *Magyarországi Holokauszt*, 969–74.
16 Braham, *Politics of Genocide*, 602, gives the early date of 14 April for the beginning of this process. Braham, *Magyarországi Holokauszt*, 936 gives the date of 16 April.
17 Braham, *Magyarországi Holokauszt*, 969–74.
18 Lévai, J., *Zsidósors Magyarországon* (Budapest: Magyar Téka, 1948), 114.
19 Braham, *Politics of Genocide*, 602; Harsányi, L., 'A nyíregyházi zsidók történetéhez' in Scheiber, S. (ed.), *Évkönyv 1973/74* (Budapest: Magyar Izraeliták Országos, 1974), 84; Nagy, *Nyíregyházi Zsidóság*, 23.

20   I 153, 11692 K, Szabolcs county prefect correspondence with Ministry of Food Supplies (5 May 1944).
21   I 153, 11984, Szabolcs county prefect correspondence with Minister of Food Supplies (9 May 1944).
22   Braham, *Magyarországi Holokauszt*, 936.
23   Braham, *Magyarországi Holokauszt*, 938.
24   According to the 1941 census statistics, 36.2 per cent of Jews in the county lived in these two cities.
25   Braham, *Magyarországi Holokauszt*, 971 which gives a figure of 67 per cent of the population of the area of the city designated as the ghetto being Jewish. See also Nagy, *A Nyíregyházi Zsidóság*, 22, 71, 93, who notes that between 130 and 150 buildings in the ghetto were owned by Jews.
26   Interview with Judit Brody (Oxford, 26 November 2009).
27   Gabor, E., *The Blood Tattoo* (Dallas: Monument Press, 1987), 46.
28   Gottlieb, E., *Becoming my Mother's Daughter: A Story of Survival and Renewal* (Waterloo, Ontario: Wilfred Laurier University Press, 2008), 102.
29   See Braham, *Magyarországi Holokauszt*, 942–4, 959, 961–90, 992–4.
30   Rivka, B., *15 éves voltam … A nácik poklában* (Bné-Brák, Israel: Lipe-Friedman Nyomda, 1990), 67–73.
31   Rivka, *15 éves*, 92–3; Nagy, *A Nyíregyházi Zsidók*, 113, reproducing V.B. 186.XI.700.1944.
32   Rivka, *15 éves*, 92–3.
33   Gabor, *Blood Tattoo*, 33.
34   I 155, 10.000/1944, Nyíregyháza mayor, Outlay of transport expenses incurred in transport of Jews (3 August 1944). My estimate is a figure of 2,534 between 23 April and 4 June.
35   I 155, 10.000/1944, Nyíregyháza mayor, Outlay of transport expenses incurred in transport of Jews (3 August 1944). I estimate 1,149 between 23 April and 11 May.
36   I 155, 10.000/1944, Nyíregyháza mayor, Outlay of transport expenses incurred in transport of Jews (3 August 1944). I estimate 152 on 3 May, 139 on 4 May.
37   I 155, 10.000/1944, Nyíregyháza mayor, Outlay of transport expenses incurred in transport of Jews (3 August 1944).I estimate ninety-eight on 6 May, 94 on 7 May, 243 on 10 May, 238 on 11 May.
38   I 155, 10.000/1944, Nyíregyháza mayor, Outlay of transport expenses incurred in transport of Jews (3 August 1944). I estimate fifty-nine on 14 May.
39   I 155, 10.000/1944, Nyíregyháza mayor, Outlay of transport expenses incurred in transport of Jews (3 August 1944). I estimate 185 on 15 May, 183 on 16 May.
40   I 155, 10.000/1944, Nyíregyháza mayor, Outlay of transport expenses incurred in transport of Jews (3 August 1944). I estimate 139 on 20 May, forty-three on 21 May, 147 on 22 May.
41   I 155, 10.000/1944, Nyíregyháza mayor, Outlay of transport expenses incurred in transport of Jews (3 August 1944). I estimate eighty-nine on 24 May, sixty-eight on 25 May, 117 on 26 May.
42   I 155, 10.000/1944, Nyíregyháza mayor, Outlay of transport expenses incurred in transport of Jews (3 August 1944). I estimate 104 on 30 May, 98 on 31 May, 153 on 4 June.
43   I 155, Kv. 246/1944 (16 May 1944).
44   Karsai, 'Hungarian Holocaust', 81.
45   Kádár, G. and Vági, Z., *Self-financing Genocide. The Gold Train, the Becher Case and the Wealth of Hungarian Jews* (Budapest: Central European University Press, 2004).
46   I 154, K14127, Letter from Jewish Council to mayor (12 May 1944).
47   *Szegedi Új Nemzedék* (20 June 1944), 4.
48   *Szegedi Új Nemzedék* (20 May 1944), 6.
49   I 155, 246/1944, Nyíregyháza mayoral office decision for drafting of horses (19 May 1944).
50   I 155, 246/1944, Nyíregyháza mayoral office decision for drafting of horses (19 May 1944).
51   I 155, 246/1944, Nyíregyháza mayoral office decision for drafting of horses (19 May 1944).
52   I 155, 246/1944, Nyíregyháza mayoral office decision for drafting of horses (23 May 1944).
53   I 155, 10.000/1944, Nyíregyháza mayor, Outlay of transport expenses incurred in transport of Jews (3 August 1944).
54   I 155, 246/1944, Nyíregyháza mayoral office decision for drafting of horses (2 May 1944).
55   I 155, 246/1944, Nyíregyháza mayoral office decision for drafting of horses (13 May 1944).

56 I 155, 246/1944, Nyíregyháza mayoral office decision for drafting of horses (23, 24, 31 May 1944).

57 I 155, 246/1944, Nyíregyháza mayoral office decision for drafting of horses (19 May 1944).

58 I 155, 246/1944, Nyíregyháza mayoral office decision for drafting of horses (13 May 1944), cf. I 155, 10.000/1944, Nyíregyháza mayor, Outlay of transport expenses incurred in transport of Jews (3 August 1944).

59 I 155, 246/1944, Nyíregyháza mayoral office decision for drafting of horses (19 May 1944), cf. I 155, 10.000/1944, Nyíregyháza mayor, Outlay of transport expenses incurred in transport of Jews (3 August 1944).

60 I 155, 246/1944, Nyíregyháza mayoral office decision for drafting of horses (19, 23 May 1944), cf. I 155, 10.000/1944, Nyíregyháza mayor, Outlay of transport expenses incurred in transport of Jews (3 August 1944). The exceptions were Alsópazsit and Alsósima.

61 I 155, 246/1944, Nyíregyháza mayoral office decision for drafting of horses (24, 31 May 1944), cf. I 155, 10.000/1944, Nyíregyháza mayor, Outlay of transport expenses incurred in transport of Jews (3 August 1944).

62 Lakatos had provided twelve of the fifteen carts ordered on 2 May, but only eight of fifteen on 20 May. On 4 June they provided fourteen carts. A similar picture of some improvement in the number of carts being delivered in early June can be seen in the case of I Manda 2nd district, which provided twelve of the fifteen carts ordered on 2 May, twelve of the fifteen on 20 May and fourteen of fifteen on 4 June. II Manda provided nine of the ten requested carts on both 2 May and 20 May. Marko provided eleven of fifteen on 2 May, all ten carts ordered on 22 May and then only eight of the ten ordered on 4 June.

63 I 155, 246/1944, Nyíregyháza mayoral office decision for drafting of horses (2 May 1944), cf. I 155, 10.000/1944, Nyíregyháza mayor, Outlay of transport expenses incurred in transport of Jews (3 August 1944).

64 I 155, 246/1944, Nyíregyháza mayoral office decision for drafting of horses (19 May 1944), cf. I 155, 10.000/1944, Nyíregyháza mayor, Outlay of transport expenses incurred in transport of Jews (3 August 1944).

65 See parallels in Browning, *Ordinary Men*, 63, who tells how 'a driver assigned to take Jews to the forest made only one trip before he asked to be relieved. "Presumably his nerves were not strong enough to drive more Jews to the shooting site," commented one man who took over his truck and his duties of chauffeuring Jews to their deaths.'

66 I 155, 246/1944, Nyíregyháza mayoral office decision for drafting of horses (2–31 May 1944), cf. I 155, 10.000/1944, Nyíregyháza mayor, Outlay of transport expenses incurred in transport of Jews (3 August 1944).

67 I 155, 246/1944, Nyíregyháza mayoral office decision for drafting of horses (2–31 May 1944), cf. I 155, 10.000/1944, Nyíregyháza mayor, Outlay of transport expenses incurred in transport of Jews (3 August 1944).

68 I 155, 246/1944, Nyíregyháza mayoral office decision for drafting of horses (2–31 May 1944), cf. I 155, 10.000/1944, Nyíregyháza mayor, Outlay of transport expenses incurred in transport of Jews (3 August 1944).

69 Kenez, P., *Hungary from the Nazis to the Soviets. The Establishment of the Communist Regime in Hungary, 1944–1948* (Cambridge: Cambridge University Press, 2006), 107–8.

70 I 155, 10.000/1944, Nyíregyháza mayor, Outlay of transport expenses incurred in transport of Jews (3 August 1944), where there appears to be 969 separate named individuals.

71 I 155, 10.000/1944, Nyíregyháza mayor, Outlay of transport expenses incurred in transport of Jews (3 August 1944).

72 I 155, 246/1944, Nyíregyháza mayoral office decision for drafting of horses (2–31 May 1944), cf. I 155, 10.000/1944, Nyíregyháza mayor, Outlay of transport expenses incurred in transport of Jews (3 August 1944).

73 I 155, 10.000/1944, Nyíregyháza mayor, Outlay of transport expenses incurred in transport of Jews (3 August 1944).

74 I 154, K10.000/1944, letter from Nyíregyháza mayor (22 April 1944).

75 I 155, 10.000/1944, Nyíregyháza mayor, Outlay of transport expenses incurred in transport of Jews (3 August 1944); 60 per cent of the farmsteads did not provide women.

76   I 155, 10.000/1944, Nyíregyháza mayor, Outlay of transport expenses incurred in transport of
     Jews (3 August 1944).

77   I 155, 10.000/1944, Nyíregyháza mayor, Outlay of transport expenses incurred in transport of
     Jews (3 August 1944).

78   I 155, 10.000/1944, Nyíregyháza mayor, Outlay of transport expenses incurred in transport of
     Jews (3 August 1944).

79   I 155, 246/1944 Nyíregyháza mayoral office decision for drafting of horses (24 May 1944).

80   I 155, 10.000/1944, Nyíregyháza mayor, Outlay of transport expenses incurred in transport of
     Jews (3 August 1944) detail payments to cart owners, and therefore do not necessarily provide
     a full picture of who physically undertook the work of driving cartloads of Jews around central
     Szabolcs county on any given day. An owner was not necessarily driving the cart laden with
     Jews, but was sending their cart to the place identified by Dr Gönczy at the required time. It
     is clear from reading through the extant accounts that in at least some cases cart owners and
     cart drivers were separate. In a very small number of cases, more than one cart was provided
     by the same owner. Most of these cases concerned the various members of the aristocratic D.
     family. Not only is it hard to imagine Count Gyula D., Count Aurel D. or Count Tivadar D.
     turning up with their carts in person, but it was also physically impossible for any of these
     men to drive anything from two to six carts on the same day. In another case, a business was
     paid as the owner of a cart used for transporting Jews. However in the vast majority of cases,
     it was named individuals who were paid for the use of one cart. The carts being delivered to
     Jewish ghetto camps in the vicinity of Nyíregyháza were, in the main, not delivered there by
     companies or aristocratic families, but by individuals for whom, presumably, this cart was their
     main personal means of transport. They were not haulage businesses, but individual country
     folk who used carts to get to market, and in 1944 used those same carts to transport Jews. But
     this still raises the question of whether women carters were in effect hidden beneath the names
     of their husbands as owners on the accounts I work with. It does not seem that this was the
     case – e.g. see the separate entries on the lists of payments to carters in Bundás for Mrs Mihály
     Cs., who transported Jews on 10–11 May, and then her husband, Mihály Cs. (living at the same
     address) who transported Jews a few days later on 15–16 May. It may have been the same cart,
     but presumably it was not the same carter who appeared on these different occasions. Instead,
     it would appear that it was first the wife, and then the husband who carted Jews in the middle
     of May 1944, and were duly paid for their duties. The separate rendering of the husband and
     wife suggests that there is not a hidden layer of women carters in the accounts.

81   I 155, 10.000/1944, Nyíregyháza mayor, Outlay of transport expenses incurred in transport of
     Jews (3 August 1944). On 6–7 May, József M. transported Jews. On 22 May it was his wife who
     provided the cart. On 4 June, József M. returned. Similarly, while Mihály B. had transported
     Jews on 6–7 May, it was his wife who took over from him on 4 June.

82   I 154, 1203/45.1944, letter from police captain to Nyíregyháza mayor (24 April 1944).

83   USHMM, RG52.007.04, 43275/944, letter from Nyíregyháza mayor to Interior Minister sent
     through the prefect (9 August 1944).

84   USHMM, RG52.007.04, 43275/944, letter from Nyíregyháza mayor to Interior Minister sent
     through the prefect (9 August 1944).

85   Desbois, P., *The Holocaust by Bullets: A Priest's Journey to Uncover the Truth behind the Murder
     of 1.5 Million Jews* (Houndmills: Palgrave Macmillan, 2009), 134.

86   Braham, *Magyarországi Holokauszt*, 961–2.

87   I 156, 2410/1944 (23 September 1944).

88   V.B. 186.XI.700.1944, Letter from József R. to Nyíregyháza mayor (12 May 1944) reproduced
     in Nagy, *A Nyíregyházi Zsidóság*, 113.

89   On this in Budapest see Cole, *Holocaust City*, esp. ch. 6.

3 DEBATING THE GHETTO: NEWSPAPERS FROM SZEGED

1   USHMM, RG52.006.0204, letter from deputy mayor to editors of *Szegedi Friss Újság*, *Szegedi Új Nemzedék* and *Tanyai Hiradó* (7 June 1944).
2   See e.g. the publishing of lists of house making up the ghetto in *Szegedi Új Nemzedék* (16 May 1944), 3.
3   O.L. K27, box 260 (1 June 1944); see also Beneschofsky and Karsai, *Vádirat II*, 125.
4   USHMM, RG52.006.0204, 7671/944, letter from deputy clerk to mayor (7 June 1944) flagging 1.990/1944 M.E.
5   Molnár, *Zsidósors*, 55 sees this as 'evidence of Buócz's zeal'. See also Molnár, J., 'Two Cities', 117.
6   *NépÚjság* (9 May 1944), 2, which also reported that a night-time curfew was implemented in Szeged, with Jews not permitted to leave their apartments between 7 pm and 7 am.
7   *Szegedi Új Nemzedék* (23 May 1944), 7.
8   It would seem that shopping hours were restricted for Jews in Makó, Győr, Pécs and Kőszeg prior to the issuing of national legislation. See Molnar, *Zsidósors*, 55; Domán, I., *A Győri Izraelita Hitközség Története 1930–47* (Budapest: A Magyar Izraeliták Országos Képviseletének Kiadása, 1979), 54; Schweitzer, J., *A Pécsi Izraelita Hitközség Története* (Budapest: A Magyar Izraeliták Országos Képviseletének Kiadása, 1966), 143; Harsányi, L., *A Kőszegi Zsidók* (Budapest: A Magyar Izraeliták Országos Képviseletének Kiadása, 1974), 203–4.
9   *Szegedi Új Nemzedék* (3 May 1944), 3.
10 Vágo, B., 'The Hungarians and the Destruction of the Hungarian Jews' in Braham, R. and Vágo, B. (eds), *The Holocaust in Hungary. Forty Years Later* (New York: Columbia University Press, 1985); Karsai, E., 'Deportation and Administration in Hungary' in Braham and Vágo, *The Holocaust in Hungary. Forty Years Later*; Kádár and Vági, *Self-financing Genocide*; Kádár, G. and Vági, Z., 'Rationality or Irrationality? The Annihilation of Hungarian Jews', *The Hungarian Quarterly* XLV, 174 (2004), 32–54; Kádár, G. and Vági, Z., 'Plunder and Collaboration in Hungary: Financial Aspects of a Genocide' in Kosmala and Tych (eds), *Facing the Nazi Genocide*, 263–88.
11 On the longer history of this see Bodo, B., 'The Hungarian Press and the Evolution of Antisemitism after World War One', *Yad Vashem Studies* 34 (2006), 45–86, who goes as far as suggesting (p. 86) that the dynamic role played by the rightist press in popularizing antisemitism in the interwar period means that the press bears 'indirect responsibility for the Holocaust'. On the press in 1944 see Berkes, T., 'Napilapok a Zsidókérdésröl. 1944 Március-Július' *Világosság* 34, 6 (1993); Róbert, P., 'A Holokauszt a Magyar Sajtóban' in Braham, R. (ed.), *Tanulmányok a Holokausztról I* (Budapest: Balassi Kiadó, 2001).
12 Bodo, 'White Terror', 57; Lackó, M., 'Budapest during the Interwar Years' in Gerő, A. and Poór, J. (eds), *Budapest. A History from its Beginnings to 1998* (New York: Columbia University Press, 1997), 168; although see the Church's distancing from the paper in 1944: USHMM, RG52.006.0109, 1603/1945, letter from Szeged bishop's secretary to *Szegedi Népszava* (17 August 1945).
13 *Szegedi Új Nemzedék* (30 April 1944).
14 Molnár, J., 'Two Cities', notes the reportage by the paper in footnote 29, 105.
15 1.240/1944 M.E. See Beneschofsky and Karsai, *Vádirat I*, 163.
16 Braham, *Politics of Genocide*, 527.
17 *Szegedi Új Nemzedék* (6 April), 4.
18 *Szegedi Új Nemzedék* (13 April 1944), 4.
19 *Szegedi Új Nemzedék* (13 April 1944), 4.
20 *Szegedi Új Nemzedék* (13 April 1944), 4.
21 *Szegedi Új Nemzedék* (16 April 1944), 9.
22 *Szegedi Új Nemzedék* (30 April 1944), 3.
23 *Szegedi Új Nemzedék* (30 April 1944), 3.
24 *Szegedi Új Nemzedék* (2 May 1944), 3.
25 *Szegedi Új Nemzedék* (3 May 1944), 3.
26 *Szegedi Új Nemzedék* (5 May 1944), 4.
27 *Szegedi Új Nemzedék* (3 May 1944), 3.

28 *NépÚjság* (8 May 1944), 3.
29 *Szegedi Új Nemzedék* (7 May 1944), 6.
30 *Szegedi Új Nemzedék* (7 May 1944), 6.
31 For more on the Party of Hungarian Renewal see Braham, *Politics of Genocide*, 178–9, 423–4; Sipos, P., *Imrédy Béla és a Magyar Megújlás Pártja* (Budapest: Akadémiai Kiadó, 1970).
32 *Szegedi Új Nemzedék* (7 May 1944), 6.
33 *Szegedi Új Nemzedék* (3 May 1944), 3.
34 *Szegedi Új Nemzedék* (7 May 1944), 6.
35 *Szegedi Új Nemzedék* (7 May 1944), 6.
36 *Szegedi Új Nemzedék* (11 May 1944), 4.
37 *NépÚjság* (8 May 1944), 3.
38 *NépÚjság* (8 May 1944), 3.
39 *Szegedi Új Nemzedék* (7 May 1944), 6; (10 May 1944), 4.
40 *Szegedi Új Nemzedék* (7 May 1944), 6.
41 *Szegedi Új Nemzedék* (10 May 1944), 4.
42 *Szegedi Új Nemzedék* (10 May 1944), 4.
43 Lukács, J., *Budapest 1900. A Historical Profile of a City and its Culture* (New York: Weidenfeld & Nicolson, 1988), 56.
44 *Szegedi Új Nemzedék* (3 May 1944), 3.
45 For an alternative interpretation of the debates over ghettoization in the city by a survivor from Szeged see USHMM, RG52.006.03, Report 3618 recorded in Szeged on 18 November 1945.
46 *NépÚjság* (1 June 1944), 2.
47 *Szegedi Új Nemzedék* (10 May 1944), 4; *NépÚjság* (11 May 1944), 3.
48 *NépÚjság* (1 June 1944), 2.
49 Molnár, 'Two Cities', 105.
50 *Szegedi Új Nemzedék* (11 May 1944), 5.
51 *Szegedi Új Nemzedék* (5 May 1944), 4.
52 USHMM, RG52.007.04, 2872, memo from Endre to all police stations and gendarme commands (11 May 1944).
53 *NépÚjság* (20 May 1944), 1.
54 *NépÚjság* (1 June 1944), 2.
55 USHMM, RG52.007.06, 29237/1944, report sheet from mayor to Szeged District Police HQ (4 June 1944).
56 *Szegedi Új Nemzedék* (3 May 1944), 3.
57 USHMM, RG52.007.01, 23356/1944, mayoral decision on the establishment of the Szeged ghetto (17 May 1944).
58 On this, see Cole, T., 'Contesting and Compromising Ghettoization, Hungary 1944' in Jonathan Petropoulos, J., Rapaport, L. and Roth, J. (eds), *Lessons and Legacies VIII* (Evanston: Northwestern University Press, 2010), 152–66.
59 Braham, *Magyarországi Holokauszt*, 412, 418.
60 *Szegedi Új Nemzedék* (12 May 1944), 3.
61 *Szegedi Új Nemzedék* (14 May 1944), 3.
62 *Szegedi Új Nemzedék* (14 May 1944), 3.
63 *Szegedi Új Nemzedék* (14 May 1944), 3.
64 *Szegedi Új Nemzedék* (16 May 1944), 3 .
65 *Szegedi Új Nemzedék* (14 May 1944), 3.
66 *NépÚjság* (27 May 1944), 8.
67 *Szegedi Új Nemzedék* (14 May 1944), 3.
68 Nagy-Talavera, N., 'The Second World War as Mirrored in the Hungarian Fascist Press', *East European Quarterly* 4, No. 2 (1971), 201; Robért, 'A Holokauszt a Magyar Sajtóban' 54; Cole, *Holocaust City*, 115–25.
69 *Szegedi Új Nemzedék* (16 May 1944), 3.
70 *Szegedi Új Nemzedék* (14 May 1944), 3.
71 *Szegedi Új Nemzedék* (16 May 1944), 3.
72 *Szegedi Új Nemzedék* (16 May 1944), 3.

73 *Szegedi Új Nemzedék* (20 May 1944), 6.
74 *Szegedi Új Nemzedék* (16 May 1944), 3; *NépÚjság* (27 May 1944), 8.
75 *Szegedi Új Nemzedék* (25 May 1944), 2; *Szegedi Új Nemzedék* (11 June 1944), 9; Braham, *Politics of Genocide*, 725.
76 *Szegedi Új Nemzedék* (15 June 1944), 4.
77 *Szegedi Új Nemzedék* (14 June 1944) 5. See also *Szegedi Új Nemzedék* (20 June 1944), 4, which gave more examples of the inflated charges of some day labourers who were described as 'hyenas'.
78 *Szegedi Új Nemzedék* (14 June 1944), 5.
79 *Szegedi Új Nemzedék* (14 June 1944), 5.
80 *Szegedi Új Nemzedék* (14 June 1944), 7; USHMM, RG52.006.0109, 32766/1944, mayoral resolution (14 July 1944).
81 *Szegedi Új Nemzedék* (15 June 1944), 4.
82 *Szegedi Új Nemzedék* (15 June 1944), 4.
83 Molnár, 'Two Cities', 127.
84 *Szegedi Új Nemzedék* (21 June 1944), 6.
85 *Szegedi Új Nemzedék* (11 May 1944), 4.
86 *Szegedi Új Nemzedék* (21 June 1944), 6.
87 Braham, *Politics of Genocide*, 729.
88 Braham, *Politics of Genocide*, 731.
89 Cole, *Holocaust City*; Cole, 'Writing Bystanders'; Cole, 'Compromising'.
90 Csősz, L., '"Keresztény Polgári Érdekek Sérelme Nélkül …" Gettósítás Szolnokon 1944-ben' in Braham, R. (ed.), *Tanulmányok a Holokausztról II* (Budapest: Balassi, 2002), 203–55.

4 PLACING THE GHETTO: MAPS FROM TOLNA COUNTY

1 I 133, Untitled ghetto map from Tolna.
2 Black, J., *Maps and Politics* (London: Reaktion Books, 1997), 13.
3 For copies of all eight, see I 133. These are reproduced in Balog, J. (ed.), *Évszázadókon át. Tolna Megye Történetének Olvasókönyve III* (Tolna: A Tolna Megyei Levéltár, 1990); Braham, *Politics of Genocide*, 796 refers to these maps in a footnote.
4 I 133, 8.100/1944, Tolna county deputy prefect (11 May 1944); 8.101/1944, Tolna county deputy prefect (11 May 1944).
5 I 133, 8.101/1944 Tolna county deputy prefect (11 May 1944).
6 Wood, D., *The Power of Maps* (London: Routledge 1993), 1.
7 I 133, Map of Number One and Two ghettos in Bonyhád (15 May 1944).
8 On the interplay between these two in Budapest see Cole T. and Smith, G., 'Ghettoization and the Holocaust: Budapest 1944', *Journal of Historical Geography* 21, 3 (1995), 300–16.
9 For more on this see Cole, *Holocaust City*, esp. 36–9; Cole, T., 'Ghettoization' in Stone, *Historiography of the Holocaust*, 65–87.
10 1.610/1944. M.E. (28 April 1944); I 133, 8.100/1944 Tolna county deputy prefect (11 May 1944).
11 The population figures are from the 1941 census.
12 The population figures are from the 1941 census.
13 Toronyi, Zs., 'Tolna Vármegye' in Braham, *Magyarországi Holokauszt*, 1122.
14 'Szekszárdról elköltöztették a sárgacsillagos zsidókat', *Tolnamegyei Ujság* (3 June 1944), 1–2, reproduced in Blau, L., *Bonyhád: A Destroyed Community. The Jews of Bonyhád, Hungary* (New York: Shengold Publishers, 1994), 157. The precise figures of dispersal from Szekszárd are hard to determine. While the newspaper article reproduced by Blau gives figures of 117 Jews taken to Bonyhád by cart, with the remainder – 62 to Dombóvár, 69 to Paks, 40 to Pincehely and 40 to Tamási – transported by train, making a total of 328 Jews, Braham, *Magyarországi Holokauszt*, 1141, gives a higher figure of 380: 131 to Bonyhád, 62 to Dombóvár, 80 to Paks, 57 to Pincehely and 50 to Tamási – see Braham, *Magyarországi Holokauszt*, 1141. These higher figures may be too high given that a list of Jews brought into the Tamási ghetto gives the names of 40 Jews

from Szekszárd brought into the ghetto on, or just before 5 June – see I 149, handwritten correspondence from the Jewish Council in Tamási to the chief constable (5 June 1944).

15 Jews living in Dombóvári district were to move into the ghetto in Dombóvár and those in Tamási district to the ghetto in Tamási. However, it was not always this straightforward. Jews living in Völgységi district were joined in the ghetto in the district seat, Bonyhád, by Jews from the town of Bátaszék in the neighbouring central (*központi*) district. The Jews living in központi district were planned as being concentrated in three places. Those from Bátaszék were to be sent to Bonyhád, those living in the county and district seat were to be concentrated in Szekszárd, with the rest of the district sent to Tolna. As was the case in központi district, Dunaföldvári district was to have more than one ghetto. Jews from the towns of Dunaföldvár and Nagydorog were to be concentrated in Dunaföldvár. Jews from the remainder of the district were to relocate to Paks.

16 1.610/1944. M.E. (28 April 1944), emphasis mine.

17 Not only in Hungary, but also in, e.g., Poland. See Browning, C., 'Nazi Ghettoization Policy in Poland: 1939–1941', *Central European History* 19, 4 (1986), 343–63.

18 1.610/1944. M.E. (28 April 1944), emphasis mine. Three weeks earlier, the secret ghetto order issued by Baky had specified that Jews living in towns or large villages were to be housed in 'Jewish buildings or ghettos'. See Braham, *Politics of Genocide*, 574 for translation: 'In every town or large village where the number of Jews necessitates the assignment of separate buildings for them, the police authorities are to take the necessary steps on their own initiative, since only the Jews dangerous form the point of view of state security are to be detained in concentration camps, whereas the others are to be accommodated in Jewish buildings. Buildings where Jews have dwelt in large numbers are to be turned into Jewish buildings. People of non-Jewish origin living in such Jewish buildings are to be assigned residences of a similar value and similar rent within thirty days of the purge in the district concerned.'

19 I 133, 8.100/1944, Tolna county deputy prefect (11 May 1944).

20 I 133, 8.101/1944, Tolna county deputy prefect (11 May 1944).

21 I 133, Map of Number One and Two ghettos in Bonyhád (15 May 1944); Untitled ghetto map from Dombóvár; Tamási ghetto map.

22 I 133, Untitled ghetto map from Dunaföldvár.

23 I 133, Pincehely collective Jewish settlement (ghetto) map (21 May 1944).

24 I 133, Map of central Hőgyész; Untitled ghetto map from Tolna.

25 I 133, Undated hand written notes. This is reproduced in Ságvári, Á. (ed.), *Dokumentumok a zsidóság üldöztetésének történetéhez. Iratok a Tolna megyei levéltárból* (Budapest: Magyar Auschwitz Alapítvány, 1994), 30–1.

26 I 147, 2.368/1944, Tolna chief constable (30 May, 1944).

27 I 133, Map of Number One and Two ghettos in Bonyhád (15 May 1944).

28 1.610/1944. M.E. (28 April 1944); I 133, 8.100/1944, Tolna county deputy prefect (11 May 1944); 8.101/1944, Tolna county deputy prefect (11 May 1944).

29 Csősz, 'Keresztény Polgári Érdekek'.

30 I 147, 2.368/1944, Tolna chief constable (30 May, 1944); I 149, 9060/1944, undated handwritten name lists.

31 I 147, Tolna name list.

32 I 147, 2.368/1944, Tolna chief constable (30 May, 1944).

33 I 133, 8.100/1944, Tolna county deputy prefect (11 May 1944).

34 Kádár and Vági, *Self-financing Genocide*.

35 I 147, 8.880/1944, Tolna county deputy prefect (30 May 1944).

36 Braham, *Magyarországi Holokauszt*, 1122.

37 Lavi, T. (ed.), *Pinkas Hakehillot Hungary* (Jerusalem: Yad Vashem, 1975) cited in Spector, S. and Wigoder, G., *The Encyclopedia of Jewish Life Before and During the Holocaust* (New York: New York University Press, 2001), 1279.

38 'Szekszárdról elköltöztették a sárgacsillagos zsidókat', *Tolnamegyei Ujság* (3 June 1944) in Blau, *Bonyhád*, 157.

39 Cole, 'Contesting and Compromising Ghettoization', 155–6.

40 I 133, 8.100/1944, Tolna county deputy prefect (11 May 1944), paragraph 9.

41 "Szekszárdról elköltöztették a sárgacsillagos zsidókat," *Tolnamegyei Ujság* (3 June 1944) in Blau, *Bonyhád*, 157.
42 I 133, 8.101/1944, Tolna county deputy prefect (11 May 1944).
43 I 133, 8.101/1944, Tolna county deputy prefect (11 May 1944).
44 Joyce, P., 'Maps, Blood and the City. The Governance of the Social in Nineteenth century Britain' in Joyce, P. (ed.), *The Social in Question. New Bearings in History and the Social Sciences* (London: Routledge, 2002), 99.
45 Harley, J., 'Deconstructing the Map', *Cartographica* 26, 2 (1989), 12.
46 I 149, 9060/1944, undated handwritten list.
47 I 149, 9060/1944, undated handwritten list.
48 I 149, 9060/1944, undated handwritten list.
49 I 149, 9060/1944, undated handwritten list.
50 I 147 name list; I 149, 9060/1944, undated handwritten list.
51 Rosen, *Hungarian Jewish Women*, 100.
52 Gabor, *Blood Tattoo*, 46.
53 I 149, 9060/1944, undated handwritten list.
54 I 133, 8.101/1944, Tolna county deputy prefect (11 May 1944).
55 I 149, 9060/1944, undated handwritten list.
56 I 147 name list; I 149, 9060/1944, undated handwritten list.
57 I 147 name list; I 149, 9060/1944, undated handwritten list.
58 I 133, 8.101/1944, Tolna county deputy prefect (11 May 1944).
59 I 149, 9060/1944, undated handwritten list.
60 I 147 name list; I 149, 9060/1944, undated handwritten list.
61 Although it shares some similarities with the dispersed ghetto adopted in Budapest in June 1944, which was in reality enacted at the scale of the individual apartment. See Cole, *Holocaust City*, esp. chs. 5 and 6.
62 Rosen, *Hungarian Jewish Women*, 15.
63 I 149, undated handwritten list.
64 I 149, 9060/1944 (30 May 1944).
65 Subsequent censuses recorded Jewish populations of 1209 (1870), 1154 (1880), 1274 (1890), 1143 (1900), 1153 (1910), 1058 (1920), 1022 (1930) and 1159 (1941).
66 Braham, *Magyarországi Holokauszt*, 1125–6.
67 Dr George Vidor cited in Blau, *Bonyhád*, 129.
68 Braham, *Politics of Genocide*, 755–6.
69 I 133, Untitled ghetto map from Dunaföldvár, Tamási ghetto map.
70 I 133, Untitled ghetto map from Dombóvár; Untitled ghetto map from Dunaföldvár; Paks street map; Untitled ghetto map from Tolna.
71 Library of Congress, Map Library, Dombóvár street map.
72 I 133, Map of Number One and Two ghettos in Bonyhád (15 May 1944); Pincehely collective Jewish settlement (ghetto) map (21 May 1944); Tamási ghetto map. I assume that these places had such maps – certainly a town the size of Bonyhád would have.
73 I 133, Tamási ghetto map.
74 I 133, Pincehely collective Jewish settlement (ghetto) map (21 May 1944).
75 I 133, Untitled ghetto map from Dunaföldvár.
76 I 133, Undated handwritten notes.
77 I 133, Pincehely collective Jewish settlement (ghetto) map (21 May 1944).
78 I 133, Map of central Hőgyész.

5 EXITING AND ENTERING THE GHETTO: PASSES FROM KÖRMEND

1   I 99, 7431/1944, letter from Vas county deputy prefect to chief constables and mayors (6 May 1944); Braham, *Magyarországi Holokauszt,* 1260.
2   I 99, 2245/1944, ruling by Körmend chief constable (9 May 1944).
3   I 99, 2245/1944, ruling by Körmend chief constable (16 May 1944).
4   I 99, handwritten letter from Körmend Jewish Council to chief constable (19 May 1944).
5   I 99, 2502/1944, letter from Körmend Jewish Council to chief constable (20 May 1944). This included one individual listed on the earlier list for whom additional permission was requested.
6   I 99, 2502/1944, passes 1, 2, 3, 4, 5, 6, 14, 15, 16, 17, 18, 19, 20, 21, 23, 24, 30, 31, 36, 37, 38 (23 May 1944).
7   I 99, 2245/1944, ruling by Körmend chief constable (8 May 1944), which also restricted Jewish access to the market (8 am–9 am), shops (9 am–10 am) and the baths (Friday mornings).
8   I 99, handwritten letter from Körmend Jewish Council to chief constable (19 May 1944); I 99, 2502/1944, letter from Körmend Jewish Council to chief constable (20 May 1944), cf. I 99, 2502/1944, passes 1, 2, 3, 4, 5, 6, 7, 8, 9, 10, 11, 12, 13 [although made out to a different person], 14, 15, 16, 17, 18, 19, 20, 21, 22, 23, 24, 25, 26, 27, 28, 29, 30 (23 May 1944).
9   Hilberg, R., 'The Ghetto as a Form of Government', *Annals of the American Academy of Political and Social Science* 450 (July 1980), 100–101.
10 I 99, 2502/1944, passes 1, 2, 3, 4, 5, 6, 7, 8, 9, 10, 11, 12, 13, 14, 15, 16, 17, 18, 19, 20, 21, 22, 23, 24, 25, 26, 27, 28, 29, 30 (23 May 1944); Braham, *Magyarországi Holokauszt,* 1262.
11 I 99, 2502/1944, template pass (23 May 1944).
12 Hilberg, *Sources of Holocaust Research,* 26.
13 Hilberg, *Destruction,* 228.
14 I 99, 2502/1944, template pass (23 May 1944), cf. I 99, handwritten letter from Körmend Jewish Council to chief constable (19 May 1944); I 99, 2502/1944, letter from Körmend Jewish Council to chief constable (20 May 1944).
15 I 99, handwritten letter from Körmend Jewish Council to chief constable (19 May 1944); I 99, 2502/1944, letter from Körmend Jewish Council to chief constable (20 May 1944), cf. I 99, 2502/1944, passes 1, 2, 3, 4, 5, 6, 7, 8, 9, 10, 11, 12, 13, 14, 15, 16, 17, 18, 19, 20, 21, 22, 23, 24, 25, 26, 27, 28, 29, 30, 31, 36, 37, 38 (23 May 1944).
16 I 99, 2502/1944, pass 1 (23 May 1944).
17 I 100,2989/1944, Körmend ghetto list (16 June 1944).
18 I 99, 2245/1944, letter from Körmend chief constable to village authorities re. implementation of 1610/1944: Designation of Jewish dwellings (9 May 1944).
19 I 100,2989/1944, Körmend ghetto list (16 June 1944).
20 I 99, 2502, pass 48 (2 June 1944).
21 Braham, *Politics of Genocide,* 76, estimates that 55.2 per cent of doctors were Jews; Ungváry, K., 'Robbing the Dead', 239, notes that the proportion of Jewish doctors in Budapest was 38 per cent compared to the national average of 55.2 per cent; Stark, T., *Hungary's Human Losses in World War II* (Uppsala: Center for Multiethnic Research, Uppsala University, 1995), 9, estimates that 60 per cent of doctors were Jewish in 1920.
22 Kádár and Vági, 'Rationality or Irrationality?', 45. See also Kovács, M., *Liberalizmus, Radikalizmus, Antiszemitizmus. A Magyar Orvosi, Ügyédi és Mérnöki Kar Politikája 1867 és 1945 között* (Budapest: Helikon, 2001).
23 Kádár and Vági, 'Rationality or Irrationality?', 47–8.
24 Kádár and Vági, 'Rationality or Irrationality?', 46–8, who see this as evidence of 'those in power' giving preference to 'the solution of the Jewish question' over the 'interests of production'.
25 I 100,2989/1944, Körmend ghetto list (16 June 1944).
26 I 100,2989/1944, Körmend ghetto list (16 June 1944), gives his wife's age as fifty-seven.
27 I 99, 2502/1944, passes 1–65 (23 May–18 June 1944).
28 I 99, 2502/1944, passes 1, 2, 3, 4, 5, 6, 14, 15, 16, 17, 18, 19, 20, 21, 23, 24, 30, 31, 36, 27, 38 (23 May 1944), pass 35 (25 May 1944), pass 55 (10 June 1944), pass 59 (12 June 1944).

29   I 99, 2502/1944, pass 39 (26 May 1944), pass 45 (31 May 1944), pass 46 (1 June 1944), pass 48
     (2 June 1944), pass 50 (7 June 1944), pass 51 (9 June 1944), pass 54 (10 June 1944), passes 62,
     63 (14 June 1944).
30   Trunk, I., *Judenrat. The Jewish Councils in Eastern Europe under Nazi Occupation* (New York:
     Macmillan, 1972), 71.
31   Don, Y., 'Economic Implications of the Anti–Jewish Legislation in Hungary' in Cesarani, D.,
     Genocide and Rescue. The Holocaust in Hungary 1944 (Oxford: Berg, 1997), 75.
32   Braham, *Politics of Genocide*, 243,
33   Cited in Kádár and Vági, 'Plunder and Collaboration', 278. See also Csõsz, L., 'Õrségváltás? Az
     1944–es deportálások közvetlen gazdasági-társadalmi hatásai' in Karsai, L. and Molnár, J. (eds),
     Küzdelem az igazságért. Tanulmányok Randolph L. Braham 80. születésnapjára (Budapest:
     MAZSIHISZ, 2002), 75–98.
34   I 99, 2502/1944, pass 24 (23 May 1944).
35   I 99, 2502/1944, pass 45 (31 May 1944).
36   I 99, 2502/1944, pass 39 (26 May 1944), pass 46 (1 June 1944).
37   I 99, 2502/1944, passes 50 (7 June 1944), 51 (9 June 1944), 54 (10 June 1944), 62 (14 June 1944),
     63 (14 June 1944).
38   I 99, handwritten letter from Körmend Jewish Council to chief constable (19 May 1944); I 99,
     2502/1944, letter from Körmend Jewish Council to chief constable (20 May 1944).
39   I 99, 2502/1944, pass 2 (23 May 1944).
40   I 99, 2502/1944, pass 3 (23 May 1944).
41   I 99, 2502/1944, pass 5 (23 May 1944).
42   I 99, 2502/1944, pass 6 (23 May 1944).
43   I 99, 2502/1944, pass 30 (23 May 1944).
44   I 99, 2502/1944, pass (23 May 1944).
45   I 99, 1966/1.1944, request to Körmend chief constable (31 May 1944); I 99, 2502/1944, pass 47
     (2 June 1944).
46   Ungvary, 'Robbing the Dead', 253, notes that 'All Jewish businesses had to close on April 21,
     such that the owners could not sell their good illegally: by that point, Jewish assets had been
     declared property of the state. There was concern that Jews would hide their fortunes with
     Christian acquaintances. Jews' trade and work permits were rescinded. If a business was
     "indispensable," managers were instated and the enterprise resumed. Even with the companies
     closed, Christians employed by Jews still had a right to their wages, which the Jewish owners –
     not the state – had to pay.'
47   I 99, 2502/1944, pass 29 (23 May 1944).
48   I 99, 2502/1944, pass 32 (24 May 1944); pass 41 (27 May 1944); pass 42 (28 May 1944); pass 44
     (31 May 1944); pass 49 (2 June 1944); pass 52 (9 June 1944); pass 53 (9 June 1944).
49   I 99, 2502/1944, unnumbered pass (10 June 1944).
50   I 99, 2502/1944, pass 56 (10 June 1944).
51   I 99, 2502/1944, pass 58 (12 June 1944).
52   Kádár and Vági, 'Plunder and Collaboration', 270.
53   Cited in Kádár and Vági, 'Plunder and Collaboration', 271–2.
54   Ungváry, 'Robbing the Dead', 253.
55   I 99, 2502/1944, pass 6 (23 May 1944).
56   I 99, 2502/1944, pass 6 (23 May 1944), cf. pass 2 and pass 3 (23 May 1944). Pass 5 (23 May 1944)
     had an end date of 30 June.
57   I 99, undated letter from *Levente* headquarters.
58   I 99, 2502/1944, pass 33 (24 May 1944).
59   I 99, 2502/1944, pass 64 (15 June 1944).
60   I 99, 2502/1944, pass 33 (24 May 1944) specified that the boys would leave the ghetto from
     7–12 in the morning and 1–7 in the afternoon/evening. The pass was extended on 10 June in
     order to extend the hours in the afternoon/evening from 1–7, to 1–8. The pass issued on 15
     June specified the hours as 7–12 in the morning and 2–8 in the afternoon/evening.
61   I 99, 2502/1944, pass 34 (25 May 1944).
62   I 99, 2571/1944, telegrams to Körmend chief constable (25 May 1944, 26 May 1944).

63   I 99, 2502/1944, pass 40 (27 May 1944).
64   I 99, 2502/1944, pass 57 (10 June 1944).
65   I 99, 2502/1944, pass 61 (12 June 1944).
66   I 99, 2502/1944, pass 60 (12 June 1944).
67   USC Shoah Foundation Institute for Visual History and Education Archive, interview 42429
     with Margaret B.
68   Braham, *Magyarországi Holokauszt*, 235, 926, 930.
69   I 99, 2767/1944, letter from Körmend chief constable to Jewish Council, Körmend borough
     council, Körmend community doctor, Gendarmerie HQ re. draft of Jews (9 June 1944).
70   I 99, 2502/1944, pass 43 (30 May 1944).
71   I 100, 2989/1944, Körmend ghetto list (16 June 1944); I 99, 2502/1944, pass 64 (15 June 1944).
72   I 100, 2989/1944, Körmend ghetto list (16 June 1944).
73   I 99, letter from Körmend chief constable (12 June 1944).
74   I 100, 2989/1944, Körmend ghetto list (16 June 1944).
75   I 100, 2989/1944, Körmend ghetto list (16 June 1944).
76   I 99, 2502/1944, pass 58 (12 June 1944).
77   I 99, 2502/1944, pass 65 (18 June 1944).
78   Ungvary, 'Robbing the Dead', 252.

6 VIEWING DEPORTATIONS: PHOTOGRAPHS FROM KÖRMEND, KŐSZEG AND BALATONFÜRED

1   USHMM Photo Archives, Designation number 300.4525, Worksheet number 98990 and
    98990A.
2   Hirsch, M., 'Surviving Images: Holocaust Photographs and the Work of Postmemory' in
    Zelizer, B. (ed.), *Visual Culture and the Holocaust* (New Brunswick: Rutgers University Press,
    2001), 217.
3   Harsányi, *Kőszegi Zsidók*, 204 suggested that of all the photographs taken of deportations only
    four survived from Soltvadkert, three from Sopron and seven from Kőszeg, although in reality
    larger numbers of photographs survived but most were only single images.
4   Milton, S., 'Images of the Holocaust – Part II', *Holocaust and Genocide Studies* 1, 2 (1986), 194,
    where she refers to Stuttgart, Nuremberg and Würzburg.
5   As the controversy surrounding the Wehrmacht war crimes exhibition in Hamburg in 1995
    showed, perpetrator photographs were objects of popular and not simply academic interest. The
    exhibition catalogue was later published by the Hamburger Institut für Sozialforschung (ed.),
    Vernichtungskrieg. Verbrechen der Wehrmacht 1941 bis 1944: Ausstellungskatalog (Hamburg:
    1996).
6   Goldhagen, D., *Hitler's Willing Executioners: Ordinary Germans and the Holocaust* (New York:
    1996), 246, 559; Levin, J. and Uziel, D., 'Ordinary Men, Extraordinary Photos', *Yad Vashem
    Studies* 26 (1998), 270.
7   Rossino, A., 'Eastern Europe through German Eyes. Soldiers' Photographs 1939–42', *History of
    Photography* 23, 4 (Winter 1999), 315, 319–20.
8   See Hirsch, 'Surviving Images', 217; Rossino, 'Eastern Europe', 313–14; Zelizer, B., *Remembering
    to Forget: Holocaust Memory through the Camera's Eye* (Chicago: University of Chicago Press,
    1998).
9   Braham, *Politics of Genocide*, 760, although here they are misattributed with one of the photo-
    graphs included in a sequence (fig. 22.1) captioned 'Ghettoization and Deportation of the Jews
    of Kőszeg'. Braham, *Magyarországi Holokauszt*, 1267.
10 Harsányi, *Kőszegi Zsidók* end plates, although note that Harsányi, 204, does make specific
    reference to the surviving images which he notes form the largest collection of depor-
    tation photographs in Hungary; see also the use and references to the photographs in the
    documentary film *Once they were Neighbours* (2005) directed by Zsuzsanna Varga.
11 Harsányi, *Kőszegi Zsidók*, 208, identifies some of the individuals that can be seen on the

photographs. This is also something that one of the 'bystanders' from the town does in *Once they were Neighbours*.

12 Milton, 'Images of the Holocaust', 194.
13 Trachtenberg, A., *Reading American Photographs: Images as History, Matthew Brady to Walker Evans* (New York: Hill and Wang, 1989), 251.
14 Tagg, J., *The Burden of Representation. Essays on Photographies and Histories* (London: Macmillan, 1988), 65. Although note that Tagg goes further, arguing that, '[P]hotographs are never "evidence" of history; they are themselves the historical.' Responding to this sentiment, attributed to Michael Griffin rather than John Tagg, Burke, *Eyewitnessing*, 23, argues that, 'This is surely too negative a judgement: like other forms of evidence, photographs are both.'
15 Lutz, C. and Collins, J., 'The photograph as an intersection of gazes. The example of National Geographic' in Taylor, L. (ed.), *Visualizing Theory: Selected Essays from V.A.R. 1990–1994* (New York: Routledge, 1994), 363.
16 Burke, *Eyewitnessing* 14.
17 Burke, *Eyewitnessing*, 30–1.
18 Burke, *Eyewitnessing*, 30; see also Brothers, C., *War and Photography. A Cultural History* (London: Routledge, 1997), esp. 27–8.
19 Sontag, S., *On Photography* (London: Penguin Books, 2002), 88.
20 Hirsch, 'Surviving Images', 223, argues that photographs represent, 'more or less visibly or readably, the context of its production and a very specific embodied gaze of a photographer'.
21 Marrus, M., *The Holocaust in History* (London: Penguin, 1993), 156.
22 Novick, P., *The Holocaust in American Life* (Boston: Houghton Mifflin, 1999), 245; Barnett, V., *Bystanders. Conscience and Complicity during the Holocaust* (Westport, Conn.: Greenwood, 1999), xiv.
23 Marrus, *Holocaust in History*, 157; Bauer, Y., *The Holocaust in Historical Perspective* (Seattle: University of Washington Press, 1978), 18.
24 Interview with Father John S., Fortunoff Video Archive for Holocaust Testimonies, Yale University, T216, cited in Stier, O., *Committed to Memory. Cultural Mediations of the Holocaust* (Amherst, Ma: University of Massachusetts Press, 2003), 72–3.
25 Cole, 'Writing bystanders'.
26 Sontag, *On Photography*, 109–110, where she writes that 'cameras … transform history into spectacle'.
27 Sontag, *On Photography*, 10–11, 28, 174–5, who writes that 'to photograph is to confer importance'.
28 Sontag, *On Photography*, 10–11. I wonder if Kádar and Vági, 'Plunder and Collaboration' 265, go too far in normalizing ghettoization and deportation. My sense is that these photographs (and see also Chapter 8) point to deportation being seen as not simply the 'normal'.
29 Westerbeck, C. and Meyerowitz, J., *Bystander: A History of Street Photography* (London: Thames & Hudson, 1994), 335.
30 Galassi, P. (ed.), *Lee Friedlander* (New York: Museum of Modern Art, 2005) cited by Campany, D., 'A few remarks on the lens, the shutter, and the light–sensitive surface' in Elkins, J. (ed.), *Photography Theory* (London: Routledge, 2007), 311, where the contemporary American photographer Lee Friedlander recounted: 'I only wanted Uncle Vern standing by his new car (a Hudson) on a clear day. I got him and the car. I also got a bit of Aunt Mary's laundry, and Beau Jack, the dog, peeing on a fence, and a row of potted tuberous begonias on the porch and 78 trees and a million pebbles in the driveway and more. It's a generous medium, photography.'
31 Sontag, *On Photography*, 10.
32 Sontag, *On Photography*, 12.
33 Sontag, *On Photography*, 11.
34 Sontag, *On Photography*, 12.
35 Sontag, *On Photography*, 55.
36 Harsányi, *Kőszegi Zsidók*, 204.
37 USHMM photo archives, Designation number 300.4530, Worksheet number 06306, 06305, 68627, 68622, 68623, 68624 and 68628; Harsányi, *Kőszegi Zsidók*, 204, noted that there were seven photographs in total, reproducing four of them in his memorial volume.

38 See e.g. the deportation photograph from Szombathey in USHMM photo archives, Designation number 300.4555, Worksheet number 79109.
39 See e.g. the railway station photographs from Soltvadkert in USHMM photo archives, Designation number 300.4550, Worksheet number 27195 and 27196; Braham, *Politics of Genocide*, 676–7.
40 Harsányi, *Kőszegi Zsidók*, 204.
41 Ferenczy report (8 June 1944).
42 USHMM photo archives, Designation number 300.4510, Worksheet number 77642.
43 USHMM photo archives, Designation number 300.4505, Worksheet number 15512; Braham, *Magyarországi Holokauszt*, 1322.
44 Westerbeck and Meyerowitz, *Bystander*, 171–9.

7 NARRATING CONCENTRATION AND DEPORTATION I: LÁSZLÓ FERENCZY'S REPORTS

1 For more on Ferenczy, including his apparent *volte face* in the August 1944 and his postwar trial and execution in 1946, see Braham, *Politics of Genocide*, 436–7, 582–3, 906–10, 1321; copies of the reports I work with here are included in Karsai, L. and Molnár, J., *Az Endre-Baky-Jaross per* (Budapest: Cserépfalvi, 1994), 497–525.
2 Braham, *Politics of Genocide*, 573; Karsai, 'Last Chapter', 309.
3 'Assembly centres' was used in the translation of Lévai, J., *Black Book on the Martyrdom of Hungarian Jewry* (Zurich: The Central European Times Publishing Company, 1948). In Lévai, J., *Eichmann in Hungary* (Budapest: Pannonia Press, 1961) the term 'concentration camps' was used, adopted by Braham in his writings. On this history of these terms see Cole, *Holocaust City*, 77–8.
4 Ferenczy reported from Kolozsvár on 3, 5, 6, 7, 9 and 10 May.
5 Ferenczy reported from Munkács on 21 and 29 May, from Hatvan on 7, 8 and 12 June, and from Budapest on 29 and 30 June and 9 July.
6 Braham, *Politics of Genocide*, 584.
7 Braham, *Politics of Genocide*, 681.
8 See e.g. Braham, *Politics of Genocide*, 592–4.
9 See e.g. Braham, *Politics of Genocide*, 681.
10 Braham, *Politics of Genocide*, 681.
11 Although Endre did make a personal tour of collection camps and ghettos in mid May to see them for himself. See *Szentesi Napló* (13 May 1944), 5.
12 Set up in Kolozsvár, Szamosujvár, Dés, Szilágysomlyo, Szatmárnémeti, Nagybánya, Beszterce, Szászrégen, Marosvásárhely and Sepsiszentgyörgy.
13 At this early stage, it was the confidential order issued by Baky on 7 April 1944 which formed the basis for the concentration of Jews, rather than the later ghettoization order issued at the end of the month. The former stipulated that Jews were to be gathered into collection camps, prior to a partial relocation to urban ghettos. This two-stage process was seen as 'necessary to mitigate against potential homelessness on the part of non-Jews living in the future ghetto area. However, Ferenczy informed the Interior Minister that in Nagyvárad, 'there was no suitable site for the establishment of a collection camp ... and for this reason the Jews were placed in ghettos'.
14 USHMM, RG52.009.04/1, 16.biz.1944, Reports from Ferenczy to Interior Minister (3, 5, 6, 7, 9 and 10 May 1944) (hereafter Ferenczy report).
15 Ferenczy report (3 May 1944).
16 Ferenczy report (5 May 1944) where he gave figures for Kolozsvár (4,930), Marosvásárhely (8,000), Szászrégen (1,500), Nagybánya (2,500), Sepsiszentgyörgy (850) and Dés (5,605), although the run of round numbers suggested that these were estimates.
17 Ferenczy report (6 May 1944) where he reported 9,557 Jews from District IX and 6,587 Jews from District X in collection camps by midday on 5 May, offering specific numbers from a number of camps.

18 Ferenczy report (7 May 1944) where he gave the figures: Kolozsvár (8,000?), Nagyvárad (35,000), Szatmárnémeti (2,852), Beszterce (4,252), Szamosújvár (1,426), Dés (5,502), Nagybánya (5,000), Marosvásárhely (8,000), Szászrégen (1,500) and Sepsiszentgyörgy (850).
19 Ferenczy report (3 May 1944; 5 May 1944).
20 Ferenczy report (6 May 1944).
21 Ferenczy report (7 May 1944; 9 May 1944).
22 Ferenczy report (10 May 1944).
23 Ferenczy report (29 May 1944; 30 June 1944).
24 See e.g. Braham, *Politics of Genocide*, 649
25 Ferenczy report (10 May 1944).
26 Ferenczy report (7 May 1944; 9 May 1944; 10 May 1944).
27 Ferenczy report (10 May 1944).
28 Ferenczy report (7 May 1944; 9 May 1944; 10 May 1944).
29 Ferenczy report (9 May 1944).
30 Ferenczy report (9 May 1944).
31 USHMM RG52.009.04, 34/1944, Mayor of Nagybánya. Minutes of a meeting held at the police station in Munkács (12 May 1944).
32 Ferenczy report (21 May 1944).
33 Ferenczy report (29 May 1944).
34 Ferenczy report (8 June 1944).
35 Ferenczy report (29 May 1944; 7 June 1944).
36 Ferenczy report (29 June 1944).
37 His figures were a little lower than those of Veesenmayer, writing to the German Foreign Office, who gave a total of 437, 402. Braham, *Politics of Genocide*, 673, notes that neither total included 'the Jews removed from the southern parts of Gendarmerie Districts III, IV and V during the special "emergency" measures enacted against them during the week of April 26, 1944'.
38 Ferenczy report (9 July 1944, first report).
39 Ferenczy report (5 May 1944).
40 Ferenczy report (10 May 1944).
41 Ferenczy report (21 May 1944).
42 Ferenczy report (8 June 1944).
43 Ferenczy report (12 June 1944; 29 June 1944).
44 Ferenczy report (5 May 1944).
45 Ferenczy report (6 May 1944).
46 Ferenczy report (6 May 1944).
47 Ferenczy report (6 May 1944).
48 Ferenczy report (12 June 1944).
49 Ferenczy report (29 June 1944).
50 Ferenczy report (29 June 1944).
51 Ferenczy report (3 May 1944).
52 Ferenczy report (7 May 1944).
53 Ferenczy report (5 May 1944; 6 May 1944; 7 May 1944; 9 May 1944).
54 Kádár and Vági, 'Rationality', esp. 38–41.
55 Braham, *Politics of Genocide*, 574.
56 Ferenczy report (5 May 1944).
57 Ferenczy report (6 May 1944; 7 May 1944).
58 Ferenczy report (9 May 1944).
59 Ferenczy report (3 May 1944).
60 Ferenczy report (3 May 1944).
61 Ferenczy report (3 May 1944; 5 May 1944).
62 Ferenczy report (5 May 1944).
63 Ferenczy report (6 May 1944; 7 May 1944; 9 May 1944).
64 Ferenczy report (9 May 1944).
65 Ferenczy report (3 May 1944).
66 Ferenczy report (9 May 1944).

67   Ferenczy report (3 May 1944).
68   Ferenczy report (5 May 1944).
69   Ferenczy report (5 May 1944).
70   Zsolt, B., *Nine Suitcases* (London: Jonathan Cape, 2004) 199.
71   Zsolt, *Nine Suitcases*, 247–8.
72   Uppsala University Library, Raoul Wallenberg Project Archive (hereafter RWPA) FC2, 316, interview with Lajos Bajusz (6 December 1989).
73   Ferenczy report (7 May 1944).
74   Ferenczy report (5 May 1944).
75   Ferenczy report (6 May 1944).
76   Ferenczy report (10 May 1944).
77   Ferenczy report (29 May 1944). He sent a copy of an 'army call up notice' confiscated at Ungvar which came, he reported, from Eichmann.
78   Ferenczy report (12 June 1944).
79   Ferenczy report (12 June 1944).
80   Braham, *Politics of Genocide*, 680, writes that 'Without the wholehearted support of the gendarmeries, the Germans could not possibly have carried out their Final Solution program in Hungary.'
81   Browning, *Ordinary Men*.
82   Ferenczy report (3 May 1944), emphasis mine.
83   Ferenczy report (6 May 1944).
84   Braham, *Politics of Genocide*, 439, 636.
85   Ferenczy report (9 May 1944).
86   Ferenczy report (29 June 1944).
87   Ferenczy report (12 June 1944).
88   Ferenczy report (8 June 1944).
89   Ferenczy report (29 May 1944).
90   Ferenczy report (29 May 1944).
91   Ferenczy report (29 May 1944).
92   Ferenczy report (3 May 1944).
93   Ferenczy report (5 May 1944).
94   Ferenczy report (10 May 1944).
95   Ferenczy report (7 May 1944).
96   Ferenczy report (10 May 1944).
97   Ferenczy report (7 May 1944).
98   Ferenczy report (7 May 1944); Zsolt, *Nine Suitcases*, 246–7, who commented favourably on the corruptability of the police, making them in his eyes 'more humane ...'
99   Ferenczy report (7 June 1944).
100 Ferenczy report (12 June 1944).
101 Ferenczy report (12 June 1944).
102 Ferenczy report (7 June 1944).
103 Kádár and Vági, 'Rationality'; Karsai, 'Last Chapter', 320–2; Dean, *Robbing the Jews*.
104 Ferenczy report (3 May 1944).
105 Ferenczy report (5 May 1944).
106 Ferenczy report (6 May 1944).
107 Ferenczy report (6 May 1944).
108 Ferenczy report (10 May 1944).
109 Ferenczy report (10 May 1944).
110 Ferenczy report (5 May 1944), emphasis mine.
111 See especially Ferenczy report (3 May 1944; 5 May 1944).
112 Cole, *Holocaust City*, 78.
113 Ferenczy report (5 May 1944).
114 Kádár and Vági, *Self-financing Genocide*.
115 Dean, *Robbing the Jews*, 221.
116 Ferenczy report (7 May 1944).

117 Ferenczy report (7 May 1944).
118 Ferenczy report (29 June 1944).
119 Ferenczy report (3 May 1944).
120 Ferenczy report (8 June 1944); Kádár and Vági, 'Rationality', 41–2.
121 Ferenczy reports (29 June 1944, 9 July 1944, first report; 9 July 1944, second report).
122 Ferenczy report (21 May 1944).
123 Ferenczy report (3 May 1944), emphasis mine.
124 Ferenczy report (5 May 1944).
125 Braham, *Politics of Genocide*, 574.
126 Braham, *Politics of Genocide*, 556–60.
127 Ferenczy report (29 May 1944).
128 Ferenczy report (7 June 1944).
129 Zsolt, *Nine Suitcases*, 238.

8 NARRATING CONCENTRATION AND DEPORTATION II: DIARY, MEMOIR AND LETTERS FROM NAGYVÁRAD

1   Zsolt, Ágnes, *Éva lányom. A 13 Éves Éva Harcolt Életéért a Harmadik Birodalom Hóhéraival, de a Német Vadállat Legyőzte Évát* (Budapest: Új Idők Irodalmi Intézet, 1948) (13 February 1944), 7. The diary was translated by Moshe Kohn from Hebrew into English (and hence the translation is far from ideal) and published by Yad Vashem as *The Diary of Éva Heyman* (New York: Shapolsky Publishers, 1988) (hereafter *Diary of Éva Heyman*). I cite from the English translation here (which is generally a fairly decent rendering of the Hungarian original) unless otherwise noted.
2   Hämmerle, C., 'Diaries' in Dobson, M. and Ziemann, B. (eds) *Reading Primary Sources. The Interpretation of Texts from Nineteenth- and Twentieth-Century History* (London: Routledge 2009), 142.
3   *Diary of Éva Heyman* (13 February 1944), 23; (17 February 1944), 35; (21 February 1944), 36.
4   *Diary of Éva Heyman* (17 March 1944), 54–7.
5   *Diary of Éva Heyman* (17 February 1944), 34–5; (14 March 1944), 44.
6   *Diary of Éva Heyman* (26 February 1944), 40.
7   *Diary of Éva Heyman* (14 February 1944), 31; (26 February 1944), 40; (14 March 1944), 45–6; (17 March 1944), 53, 55–6; (5 April 1944), 71; (13 April 1944), 77.
8   *Diary of Éva Heyman* (5 May 1944), 84.
9   *Diary of Éva Heyman* (14 May 1944), 94.
10 Ecséri, L., *Napló, 1944. Egy tizenhat eves kislány naplójának eredeti szövege* (Budapest: T-Twins Kiadó, 1995); Zapruder, A., *Salvaged Pages. Young Writers' Diaries of the Holocaust* (New Haven: Yale University Press, 2002), 445, writes that Éva's diary was 'long considered the only surviving diary written by a young Jewish girl in Hungary'.
11 Letters from Ági Zsolt to Elizabeth Sellers (4 April 1945; 16 May 1945; 22 June 1945). I am very grateful to Kitty Balint-Kurti for giving me copies of these letters to her aunt. Copies are available in the Wiener Library, London, NB 225.
12 Löb, L., 'Translator's Introduction' in Zsolt, *Nine Suitcases*, viii. Éva is surprisingly relatively absent from her stepfather's memoir, a few references aside, e.g. see 231–2.
13 Marton, J., 'Introduction', *Diary of Éva Heyman*, 16–7.
14 Zapruder, *Salvaged Pages*, 445 cf. Vice, S., *Children Writing the Holocaust* (Houndmills: Palgrave Macmillan, 2004), 126.
15 Zapruder, *Salvaged Pages*, 446.
16 Szőke, Gy., '"Én nem akarok meghalni …" Egy Shoa-napló és tanulságai' in Kabdebó, L. and Schmidt, E., *A Holocaust a Művészetekben* (Pécs: Janus Pannonius Egyetemi Kiadó, 1994), 160–4. However, it is striking that there are critical remarks directed at her mother in the published diary. See *Diary of Éva Heyman* (13 February 1944), 23–4; (17 February 1944), 35; (21 February 1944), 36.

17 Young, J., *Writing and Rewriting the Holocaust. Narrative and the Consequences of Interpretation* (Bloomington: Indiana University Press, 1988), 32–3.
18 Young, *Writing and Rewriting*, 32, notes that 'Whatever "fictions" emerge in the survivors' accounts are not deviations from the "truth" but are part of the truth in any particular version.'
19 *Diary of Éva Heyman* (25 March 1944), 62.
20 *Diary of Éva Heyman* (26, 27, 28, 29 March 1944), 63–6.
21 *Diary of Éva Heyman* (16 April 1944), 78.
22 *Diary of Éva Heyman* (1 May 1944), 83.
23 *Diary of Éva Heyman* (29 March 1944), 66.
24 *Diary of Éva Heyman* (22 May 1944), 101.
25 *Diary of Éva Heyman* (27 May 1944), 102.
26 *Diary of Éva Heyman* (20 April 1944), 82; (30 May 1944), 104.
27 See parallels here with Zsolt, *Nine Suitcases*, 215.
28 *Diary of Éva Heyman* (30 March 1944), 67.
29 *Diary of Éva Heyman* (14 May 1944), 94.
30 *Diary of Éva Heyman* (5 April 1944), 70.
31 *Diary of Éva Heyman* (18 April 1944), 79.
32 *Diary of Éva Heyman* (18 May 1944), 97.
33 *Diary of Éva Heyman* (18 May 1944), 99.
34 *Diary of Éva Heyman* (18 May 1944), 97.
35 Vice, *Children Writing*, 127, points to Éva's sexual innocence in the diary.
36 *Diary of Éva Heyman* (16 March 1944), 53.
37 *Diary of Éva Heyman* (18 March 1944), 57.
38 *Diary of Éva Heyman* (5 May 1944), 84.
39 *Diary of Éva Heyman* (10 May 1944), 89.
40 *Diary of Éva Heyman* (13 April 1944), 76.
41 *Diary of Éva Heyman* (30 May 1944), 104.
42 See e.g. *Diary of Éva Heyman* (29 March 1944), 65; (31 March 1944), 68; (5 April 1944), 70; (7 April 1944), 71; (9 April 1944), 73.
43 *Diary of Éva Heyman* (19 March 1944), 57.
44 *Diary of Éva Heyman* (21 March 1944), 61.
45 *Diary of Éva Heyman* (30 March 1944), 66.
46 *Diary of Éva Heyman* (10 May 1944), 91–2.
47 *Diary of Éva Heyman* (17 May 1944), 96.
48 *Diary of Éva Heyman* (29 May 1944), 103.
49 Young, *Writing and Rewriting*, 30.
50 *Diary of Éva Heyman* (30 May 1944), 103.
51 *Diary of Éva Heyman* (9 April 1944), 75.
52 *Diary of Éva Heyman* (10 May 1944), 89.
53 Zsolt, *Éva lányom* (9 April 1944), 51.
54 *Diary of Éva Heyman* (13 February 1944), 24.
55 *Diary of Éva Heyman* (16 March 1944), 47–53; (1 May 1944), 83; (14 May 1944), 96.
56 *Diary of Éva Heyman* (16 March 1944), 48.
57 *Diary of Éva Heyman* (16 March 1944), 50.
58 *Diary of Éva Heyman* (16 March 1944), 48, 52.
59 *Diary of Éva Heyman* (16 March 1944), 51–2.
60 *Diary of Éva Heyman* (16 March 1944), 51.
61 *Diary of Éva Heyman* (17 March 1944), 55.
62 *Diary of Éva Heyman* (16 March 1944), 51.
63 *Diary of Éva Heyman* (16 March 1944), 51.
64 *Diary of Éva Heyman* (13 February 1944), 24.
65 *Diary of Éva Heyman* (14 February 1944), 31–3.
66 *Diary of Éva Heyman* (26 March 1944), 63; (14 May 1944), 96, although cf. (14 May 1944), 95.
67 Zsolt, *Nine Suitcases*, 19.
68 Zsolt, *Nine Suitcases*, 25.

69 Zsolt, *Nine Suitcases*, 99–107.
70 Zsolt, *Nine Suitcases*, 103.
71 Zsolt, *Nine Suitcases*, 49.
72   Zsolt, *Nine Suitcases*, 50.
73 Zsolt, *Nine Suitcases*, 92–3.
74 Zsolt, *Nine Suitcases*, 16.
75 Zsolt, *Nine Suitcases*, 8.
76 *Diary of Éva Heyman* (19 March 1944), 57.
77 See the emphasis on 1944 as continuity in the historiography, and especially in the work of Kádár and Vági, *Self-financing Genocide*.
78 *Diary of Éva Heyman* (13 February 1944), 23–4.
79 *Diary of Éva Heyman* (21 February 1944), 38; (13 February 1944), 26.
80 *Diary of Éva Heyman* (27 March 1944), 64.
81 *Diary of Éva Heyman* (27 March 1944), 64.
82 *Diary of Éva Heyman* (30 March 1944), 67–8.
83 *Diary of Éva Heyman* (13 April 1944), 77.
84 *Diary of Éva Heyman* (19 March 1944), 59–60; (21 March 1944), 61.
85 *Diary of Éva Heyman* (18 April 1944), 78.
86 *Diary of Éva Heyman* (19 April 1944), 79.
87 Zsolt, *Nine Suitcases*, 231–2.
88 Zsolt, *Nine Suitcases*, 233.
89 Zsolt, *Nine Suitcases*, 213.
90 Zsolt, *Nine Suitcases*, 215.
91 Zsolt, *Nine Suitcases*, 214.
92 Zsolt, *Nine Suitcases*, 28, 30.
93 Zsolt, *Nine Suitcases*, 28, 214–5.
94 Zsolt, *Nine Suitcases*, 217.
95 Zsolt, *Nine Suitcases*, 214. Although Zsolt also suggests that there was 'vain and determined posturing behind' his decision to stay. See also 215–16 and his post-facto dismissal of the 'social and moral bonds' binding them together as a family.
96 Zsolt, *Nine Suitcases*, 214.
97 Zsolt, *Nine Suitcases*, 215–16; *Diary of Éva Heyman* (20 April 1944), 82; (30 May 1944), 104.
98 *Diary of Éva Heyman* (29 May 1944), 103, emphasis mine.
99 *Diary of Éva Heyman* (30 May 1944), 104.
100 Zsolt, *Nine Suitcases*, 236.
101 Zsolt, *Nine Suitcases*, 248–9; 257.
102 Letter from Ágnes Zsolt to Elizabeth Sellers (4 April 1945)
103 Roseman, M., 'Surviving Memory: Truth and Inaccuracy in Holocaust Testimony', *The Journal of Holocaust Education* 8, 1 (1999), 1–20.
104 *Diary of Éva Heyman* (14 May 1944), 92.
105 *Diary of Éva Heyman* (14 May 1944), 94.
106 *Diary of Éva Heyman* (14 May 1944), 95.
107 *Diary of Éva Heyman* (22 May 1944), 100.
108 *Diary of Éva Heyman* (14 May 1944), 94; Zsolt, *Éva lányom* (14 May 1944), 67.
109 Zsolt, *Nine Suitcases*, 217–18; 230; 233.
110 Zsolt, *Nine Suitcases*, 243–4.
111 Roseman, 'Surviving Memory', 13; 17.
112 Roseman, 'Surviving Memory', 12.
113 Zsolt, *Nine Suitcases*, 263–324.
114 *Diary of Éva Heyman* (18 April 1944), 78.
115 Braham, *Politics of Genocide*, 1069–1112; Szita, 'Trading in Lives?', esp. 166–71.
116 Zsolt, *Nine Suitcases*, 246.
117 Zsolt, *Nine Suitcases*, 246–7.
118 Letter from Ágnes Zsolt to Elizabeth Sellers (4 April 1945).
119 Letter from Ágnes Zsolt to Elizabeth Sellers (4 April 1945).

120   Zsolt, *Nine Suitcases*, 258, 262.
121   Zsolt, *Nine Suitcases*, 264.
122   Karsai, 'Hungarian Holocaust', 80–1.
123   Zsolt, *Nine Suitcases*, 9.
124   Zsolt, *Nine Suitcases*, 26.
125   Zsolt, *Nine Suitcases*, 31.
126   *Diary of Éva Heyman* (5 May 1944), 87.
127   *Diary of Éva Heyman* (30 May 1944), 104; Zsolt, *Nine Suitcases*, 2–3; 19; 38–9.
128   Zsolt, *Nine Suitcases*, 39.
129   Zsolt, *Nine Suitcases*, 247–8.
130   *Diary of Éva Heyman* (29 March 1944), 65.
131   *Diary of Éva Heyman* (7 April 1944), 72.
132   *Diary of Éva Heyman* (7 April 1944), 72–3.
133   *Diary of Éva Heyman* (20 April 1944), 80.
134   *Diary of Éva Heyman* (20 April 1944), 81–2.
135   *Diary of Éva Heyman* (20 April 1944), 81–2.
136   *Diary of Éva Heyman* (1 May 1944), 83.
137   *Diary of Éva Heyman* (5 May 1944), 84.
138   *Diary of Éva Heyman* (5 May 1944), 84.
139   *Diary of Éva Heyman* (5 May 1944), 85.
140   *Diary of Éva Heyman* (10 May 1944), 90.
141   *Diary of Éva Heyman* (10 May 1944), 90.
142   *Diary of Éva Heyman* (17 May 1944), 96–7.
143   Zsolt, *Nine Suitcases*, 9.
144   Zsolt, *Nine Suitcases*, 9, 16–8, 230, 236, 261.
145   Zsolt, *Nine Suitcases*, 32–3; Löb, 'Translator's Introduction', v–vi, who notes especially *Gerson és neje, A dunaparti nő* and *A kínos ügy.*
146   Zsolt, *Nine Suitcases*, 9–10.
147   Zsolt, *Nine Suitcases*, 56.
148   Zsolt, *Nine Suitcases*, 28, 195–6, 213.
149   Zsolt, *Nine Suitcases*, 37.
150   DEGOB Protocol Number 2623.
151   Zsolt, *Nine Suitcases*, 37.
152   Zsolt, *Nine Suitcases*, 20.
153   Zsolt, *Nine Suitcases*, 20–1.

EPILOGUE

1   I 101, 1330/1944, letter from Vasvár chief constable to deputy prefect (12 May 1944).
2   I 101, 1500/1944, decision of Vasvár chief constable (23 May 1944).
3   Steedman, C., *Dust: The Archive and Cultural History* (New Brunswick: Rutgers University Press, 2002), 45.
4   I 101, Vasvár ghetto name list.
5   *Counted Remnant. Register of the Jewish Survivors in Budapest* (Budapest: Hungarian Section of the World Jewish Congress, American Joint Distribution Committee & Jewish Agency for Palestine Statistical and Search Department, 1946), 755, 1131.
6   His father's absence does not necessarily mean that he did not survive the war. *Counted Remnant* made no claims for being a complete record; indeed, quite the opposite. The editors made explicit the incompleteness of the register and their problems in collecting names. Moreover, János M. may not have been 'Jewish'.
7   Steedman, *Dust*, 54, recounts the story of 'a negro slave', Charlotte Howe, who 'disappears from the records leaving behind fragments of a story made for her by the legal system'.
8   Foucault, M., 'The Life of Infamous Men' in Morris, M. and Patton, P. (eds), *Michel Foucault:*

Power, Truth, Strategy (Sydney: Feral Publications, 1979), 79–80, which is an introduction to an incomplete – and intriguing – project to collect traces of ordinary lives from *letters de cachet* – orders from the king – in seventeenth- and eighteenth-century France.

9   Frojimovics, K. and Molnár, J. (eds), *Gettómagyarország 1944. A Központi Zsidó Tanács iratai. Magyar Zsidó Levéltári Füzetek 5* (Budapest: Magyar Zsidó Levéltár, 2002), 83.

10   Frojimovics and Molnár, *Gettómagyarország*, 112.

11   Karsai, 'Hungarian Holocaust', 83–4.

12   Konrad, Gy., *A Guest in my own Country: A Hungarian Life* (New York: Other Press, 2007), 41–4.

13   Deák, I., 'Fatefulness', *The New Republic* (2 April 2007), 52.

14   RWPA, FC2 527, interview with George Meyer.

15   I draw on an unpublished memoir written by Judit, an oral interview recorded with her in Oxford on 26 November 2009 and personal correspondence between Judit and myself. I am very grateful for Judit's willingness to share her story, documents and photographs with me.

16   On this see Cole, 'Compromising Ghettoization'; Cole, *Holocaust City*.

17   Letter from Judit (Edit) home (to her 'Godfather') (11 July 1944).

18   Letter from Judit (Edit) home (to her 'Godfather') (14 July 1944); Unpublished memoir.

19   Macartney, C., *October Fifteenth. A History of Modern Hungary* (Edinburgh: Edinburgh University Press, 1957) vol. 2, 262.

20   Zsolt, *Nine Suitcases*, 261.

21   RWPA, FC2 539, interview with Margit Jarovitz (16 November 1989).

22   For more on the story of the Holocaust in Budapest, see Cole, *Holocaust City*.

23   RWPA, FC2 544, interview with Ivan Gabor (17 November 1989).

24   Molnár, 'Two Cities'.

25   Ringelheim, J., 'Why Women' in Katz, E. and Ringelheim, J. (eds), *Proceedings of the Conference on Women Surviving the Holocaust* (Occasional Papers from The Institute for Research in History, New York, 1983), 24.

26   See the erection of separate memorials for the labour battalion dead – e.g. the early memorial to the 196 men of labour battalion 161/322 killed in Kiskunhalas in October 1944 erected at the main Jewish cemetery in Budapest, close to the memorial wall for Hungarian Jewish martyrs erected in 1949.

27   Novick, *The Holocaust in American Life*; Cole, T., *Selling the Holocaust* (New York: Routledge, 1999) although the highlighting of the 1960s as a turning point has been more recently criticized. See e.g. Baron, L., 'The Holocaust and American Public Memory', *Holocaust and Genocide Studies* 17, 1 (2003), 62–88, and the subsequent exchange of letters with Novick in 'Letters to the Editor', *Holocaust and Genocide Studies* 18, 2 (2004), 358–75.

28   Jay, M., 'Of Plots, Witnesses, and Judgements' in Friedlander, *Probing the Limits of Representation*, 103.

29   Dwork, D., 'Agents, Contexts, Responsibilities: The Massacre at Budy' in Postone, M. and Santner, E. (eds), *Catastrophe and Meaning. The Holocaust and the Twentieth Century* (Chicago: University of Chicago Press, 2003), 166.

30   Roseman, *Past in Hiding*, 1.

Index